MASTER CLASS
FOR CREATIVE COOKS

Evelyn Rose and Sula Leon

MASTER
CLASS
FOR CREATIVE COOKS

PIATKUS

©1987 by Evelyn Rose and Sula Leon

First published in Great Britain in 1987 by
Judy Piatkus (Publishers) Limited,
5 Windmill Street, London W1P 1HF

Reprinted 1992

British Library Cataloguing in Publication Data

Rose, Evelyn
    Master class for creative cooks
    1. Cookery
    I. Title   II. Leon, Sula
    641.5′028   TX651

    ISBN 0-86188-938-X

Edited by Susan Fleming
Designed and illustrated by Paul Saunders
Photographs taken by Tim Imrie

Phototypeset in Sabon Lasercomp
Printed and bound in Great Britain by
Butler & Tanner Ltd, Frome and London

To all the devotees of Master Class who have encouraged
us to put it into words.

Acknowledgements

From its inception, Master Class has been a team effort and the same spirit has carried on in the preparation of this book. We would like to express our gratitude to all those who have helped us 'get it on the road':

Gill Cormode has been our enormously encouraging and caring editor at Piatkus Books. Di Ward has produced a superbly typed manuscript which Susan Fleming edited with great efficiency and understanding. Iain Donald, executive chef of Stanneylands Hotel, Wilmslow, gave freely of his expertise while we were preparing the food for photography.

Mention must also be made of those who have helped to establish Master Class and without whom this book would not have been conceived:

First our husbands, Myer Rose and Anthony Leon, who have always given us tremendous support, as well as helping us on the financial and management side. Gordon Beech, managing director of Stanneylands Hotel, where we conduct Master Class, has been most co-operative in ensuring the smooth running of the classes. Mollie Edwards, Fay Mesrie and Rose Todd have been an invaluable culinary team. Teisseire of France built the demonstration kitchen to our own design, and Neff UK Limited provided all the appliances.

CONTENTS

INTRODUCING MASTER CLASS

MASTER CLASS lives – quite apart from in the pages of this book. All the recipes we have set before you have been demonstrated at one or other of the cookery sessions we have conducted together there for the past five years. In this book we have simply tried to encapsulate the philosophy of Master Class – using the printed word instead of the spoken word – and to re-create for a wider audience the very special atmosphere that seemed to blossom as people of diverse ages, occupations and backgrounds came together to share one absorbing interest – the love and respect for good food and wine.

When we started Master Classes in Food and Wine in the summer of 1982, we weren't quite sure how they would develop but we were very clear as to what we wanted to do: to pass on our own enthusiasm for food and all that concerns it. For we believe food should be fun, and preparing and presenting it to our families and friends both exciting and rewarding. So we sat down to devise a series of classes that we hoped would be as enjoyable as they would be informative, with beautiful food to admire and to taste, wines to discuss and to drink, and a wide variety of interesting recipes to take home and prepare with new-found confidence.

Our recipes come from the cuisines of many different countries – those of Europe, the Americas and the Middle and Far East. In fact we spend more time searching them out, testing and refining them to meet the criteria we have set for their preparation, flavour and appearance, than we do demonstrating them at our classes.

Although some of the techniques we use are those of the chef rather than of the domestic cook, it has never been our intention to teach the preparation – or the presentation – of restaurant-style dishes. Our kind of cooking is what the French – who always seem to have the right word for it – call *cuisine soignée*, carefully prepared from the choicest ingredients, superbly flavoured and presented with unpretentious elegance – the kind of dishes, in fact, that we ourselves like to serve at home.

The recipes in this book are the 'cream' of this Master Class cuisine – dishes that have not only been greeted with particular enthusiasm when we first demonstrated them but have proved themselves again and again in our own kitchens and on the tables of those who have attended the classes and then reported back to us.

Our Master Class friends tell us that it's the 'asides' – snatches of social history, food science and geography as well as the explanation of specific culinary techniques – that they find as useful as the recipes themselves, as this kind of background gives food a validity beyond the mere satisfaction of the senses. So although at Master Class this kind of information is given informally as we cook side by side, in the book we've set it down separately at the side of the page. It doesn't clutter up the actual cooking instructions, but is there to browse through at leisure.

We hope you will enjoy joining us at Master Class through the pages of this book.

Evelyn Rose and Sula Leon
Manchester, May 1987

Kitchen Favourites

A trio of knives
1. *A cook's knife* (6–7 inches/15–17·5 cm) blade. An all-purpose knife for chopping and slicing.
2. *A serrated edge (tomato) knife.* For slicing all delicate fruits and vegetables.
3. *A 'boning' knife with a 3 inch (7·5 cm)* pointed blade.

Swivel potato peeler
To remove a thin peeling with the greatest ease from root vegetables; for 'ribboning' vegetables (see page 105).
 For making chocolate curls (see page 157).

Rubber spatula, metal handle
Indispensable for removing every trace of mixture from bowls. Our favourite tool for folding together light mixtures such as mousses, creams and meringues. (This type is far more durable and flexible than plastic spatulas.)

Plain rolling pin (without handles) made from a hard wood such as beech
In addition to rolling out pastry, it's useful for crushing small quantities, e.g. crumbs or praline.

Crimper, tweezer or dough pincer
For removing fish bones; decorating biscuits and pastries, e.g. Mamoules (see page 178).

Zester/canelle knife
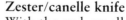
With the end, small quantities of grated zest can be removed from citrus fruit – and there's minimum cleaning required afterwards. With the side, score lemons, cucumbers, courgettes to make decorative edging.

Baller (with two sizes of scoop)
For speedy scooping out of balls of avocado and melon, coring whole fruit such as pears.

Vandyker

V-shaped tool that quickly and efficiently divides tomatoes, melons, oranges and lemons into two decorative halves.

Crêpe pan with rounded contours and first quality non-stick lining
In addition to frying crêpes without tears, useful for dry-frying, e.g. nuts.

Scales which can weigh ingredients in any shape container and can be returned to zero after each addition if necessary
These should be capable of weighing in both metric and imperial amounts by $\frac{1}{2}$ oz and 10 g amounts, up to 5 lb (2·5 kg).

Food processor (3·5 litre bowl capacity)
Totally indispensable, in our opinion, for the complete spectrum of techniques with the exception of: whisking whole or separated eggs and creaming fats and sugar (in both cases it doesn't incorporate enough air); and making breads or sweet yeast doughs that use more than $1\frac{1}{2}$ lb (675g) flour.

Assorted baking trays (different sizes and depths)
For baking biscuits, roulades and vegetables. They should preferably be made from pressed aluminium which does not buckle or distort in the heat of the oven and can be kept shiny-new with soap-filled pads.

Assorted loose-bottomed metal flan tins
These should be interesting rectangular, square or oblong shapes for sweet flans. Round tins for quiches should be 1–$1\frac{1}{2}$ inches (2·5–4 cm) deep so there is a generous ratio of filling to pastry.

Glossary of British and American Terms

We give here the US equivalents of English foods and cooking terms.

UK	US
plain flour	all-purpose flour
special sponge self-raising flour	cake flour plus baking powder
wholemeal flour	wholewheat flour
cornflour	cornstarch
semolina	cream of wheat
caster sugar	superfine sugar
icing sugar	confectioners' sugar
demerara sugar	brown sugar
golden syrup	corn syrup
bicarbonate of soda	baking soda
desiccated coconut	dried and shredded coconut
hazel nuts	filberts
pine kernels	pine nuts
sultanas	white raisins
glacé pineapple	candied pineapple
glacé cherries	candied cherries
jelly	gelatine dessert mix
drinking chocolate	instant chocolate
plain chocolate	semi-sweet chocolate
white fat	shortening

UK	US
vanilla essence	vanilla extract
single cream	light cream
whipping or double cream	heavy cream
aubergines	eggplants
Chinese leaves	Chinese cabbage
courgettes	zucchini
mangetout	snow peas
petit pois	spring peas
spring onions	green onions/scallions
Galia, Ogen or Charentais melons	musk melon or canteloupe
Morello cherries	sour red cherries
butter beans	dried lima beans
chick peas	garbanzo beans
haricot beans	navy beans
sponge fingers	ladyfingers
savoury biscuits	crackers
digestive biscuits	graham crackers
biscuits	cookies
minced meat (beef, veal or lamb)	ground meat (beef, veal or lamb)
to grill	to broil
the grill	the broiler

SOUPS
OF THE DAY

We start our book with seven excellent soups which will set the tone for the most elegant meal. Hot or chilled, garnished with nuts, herbs or croûtons, they are all soups of distinction. To complete the picture we have devised several unusual yeast rolls and one or two 'instant' accompaniments that will give added interest to any soup.

PINE KERNELS

You can only taste the true 'piney' flavour of these delicious nuts when they have been either fried or toasted. Because their oil content is so high they tend to burn easily, so our favourite way of browning them is to dry-fry them in a heavy frying pan. Put the pan over moderate heat, add as many of the nuts as will fit on the bottom and keep on shaking the pan until they're an even golden brown. This fatless method is especially suitable if the nuts are to be used as a soup garnish, as there's no worry they will make the soup greasy.

Curried Cream of Broccoli Soup

Serves 6–8

This soup will freeze for 1 month or keep for 2 days under refrigeration

It's the touch of curry that gives this soup its special distinction – and the brilliant colour that's achieved by the way we cook the broccoli.

1 lb (450 g) very green broccoli
1 oz (25 g/2 tbsp) butter
1 onion, finely chopped
1¼ pints (725 ml/3 cups) vegetable or chicken stock
2 level tbsp cornflour
1 pint (575 ml/2½ cups) semi-skimmed milk
1 teasp salt
10 grinds black pepper
¼ teasp ground nutmeg
½–1 teasp curry powder
5 fl. oz (150 ml/⅔ cup) whipping cream (reserve half for garnish)

FOR THE GARNISH
1 oz (25 g/¼ cup) toasted pine kernels
the reserved cream

1. Cut the broccoli stalks off the flowers, trim the ends and slice ½ inch (1.25 cm) thick. Place them in a soup pan with boiling water to cover, put on the lid and simmer for 5 minutes.
2. Add the florets and boil briskly, uncovered, for a further 4 minutes. Drain and drench with cold water to set the colour.
3. In the same pan, melt the butter and sauté the onion, covered, until soft and golden.
4. Add the broccoli and sauté quickly to absorb the butter then blend or process until puréed, adding a little of the stock.
5. Mix the cornflour and the milk smoothly together in a basin, then turn into the soup pan together with the vegetable purée and stock.
6. Bring slowly to the boil, adding the salt, pepper and spices. Simmer for 3 minutes, then leave for several hours.

TO SERVE

Stir in the cream, and reheat until steaming. Divide the soup between six to eight soup bowls, then ribbon each serving with the reserved cream, pouring it carefully from a small jug. Scatter with a cluster of pine kernels.

PURÉEING SOUPS

For the most velvety texture, use a blender. If you prefer a slightly rougher texture, use a food processor and purée the solids without the liquid. It's all a matter of taste.

Soupe au Cresson

(Chilled cream of watercress soup)

Serves 6–8

The soup will freeze for 1 month (with cream) or keep for 2 days under refrigeration

Chilling soups can deaden the flavour. Not so with this tangy purée – yes, it really needs those four bunches of watercress! It's delicious hot, too.

4 bunches (12 oz/350 g total weight) watercress, 1 bunch reserved for garnish
1½ oz (40 g/3 tbsp) butter
1 medium (5 oz/150 g) onion, finely chopped
white part of a fat leek, finely sliced
1 lb (450 g) potatoes, peeled and thinly sliced
2 pints (1·25 litres/5 cups) vegetable stock
1 bayleaf
1½–2 teasp salt
15 grinds black pepper
10 fl. oz (275 ml/1¼ cups) milk
5 fl. oz (150 ml/⅔ cup) soured cream (or strained Greek-style cow's yoghurt)

FOR THE GARNISH
2 tbsp toasted pine kernels (or flaked almonds)

1. Wash and spin-dry all the watercress, then cut off the leaves from one bunch, re-wrap and refrigerate.
2. Melt the butter in a soup pan, add the onion and leek and sauté, covered, for 5 minutes until soft and golden. Add the potatoes, stock, bayleaf and seasonings, bring to the boil, cover and simmer for 20 minutes until the potatoes are tender.
3. Add the watercress (all the stalks as well as leaves), bring to the boil and simmer, uncovered, for 2 minutes.
4. Purée in a blender or food processor until absolutely smooth. Return the purée to the rinsed pan and bring slowly to simmering point, then stir in the milk, remove from the heat and leave, covered, until cool enough to refrigerate (for at least 12 hours).

TO SERVE
Chop the reserved watercress leaves finely and stir in along with the cream or yoghurt. Taste and add extra salt if necessary. Garnish each serving with a scattering of pine kernels or almonds.

SLIM-LINE SOUPS

If calories count more than flavour or you're cutting down on fat, here are a couple of useful tricks:

- Don't sauté the onions in butter. Instead, omit the fat and use chopped dried onions – they'll reconstitute as they simmer in the soup.

- Use skimmed milk instead of semi-skimmed or whole milk.

- Omit the cream enrichment at the end; swirl in some low-fat natural yoghurt instead. (Don't let the soup come to the boil again or the yoghurt may separate.)

Spinach and Pea Soup with Fresh Mint and Roasted Almonds

Serves 6–8

The soup will keep for 2 days under refrigeration or freeze for 3 months

This is a beautiful green soup with the gentle flavour of the peas sharpened by the tartness of the spinach. The flavour improves as the hours go by.

$1\frac{1}{2}$ oz (40 g/3 tbsp) butter
1 large (8 oz/225 g) onion, peeled and finely chopped
$1\frac{1}{4}$ pints (725 ml/3 cups) vegetable stock
1 lb (450 g) frozen garden peas
1 teasp salt
10 grinds black pepper
1 bunch fresh mint/about 2 cups leaves, loosely packed (or 2 teasp dried mint)
8 oz (225 g) frozen leaf spinach, defrosted
15 fl. oz (425 ml/2 cups) semi-skimmed milk
5 fl. oz (150 ml/$\frac{2}{3}$ cup) single cream (optional)

FOR THE GARNISH
2 oz (50 g/$\frac{1}{2}$ cup) roasted slivered almonds

1. Melt the butter in a soup pan and cook the onion, covered, until soft and golden – about 10 minutes.
2. Add the stock, peas and seasoning, bring to the boil and cook, covered, until the peas are quite tender – about 5 minutes.
3. Add the washed mint leaves and spinach and cook, uncovered, a further 3 minutes.
4. Purée in a blender or food processor.
5. Heat the milk in the soup pan until steaming then add the vegetable purée and bring to simmering point. Taste and re-season. Leave to stand for several hours.

TO SERVE
Reheat and stir in the cream. Scatter each bowlful with roasted almonds.

RIGHT: *Spinach and Pea Soup with Fresh Mint and Roasted Almonds (above), Honey and Walnut Knots (page 21) and Tarragon Spirals (page 22)*

OVERLEAF LEFT: *Lamb and Pine Kernel Purses with Aubergine Pâté (page 41), Piperies Salata (page 132)*

OVERLEAF RIGHT: *Tendrons de Veau à la Gardiane (page 72) and Nouilles au Basilic (page 112)*

LONG-LIFE MUSHROOMS

You may pay a little more for pre-packed cultivated mushrooms but if they're shrink-wrapped, their lifespan in the domestic refrigerator can be extended from 24 hours to five days. It is exposure to the air and a warm atmosphere that makes mushrooms brown and curl up at the edges, so if you do buy them loose, be sure to store them in an airtight container – in the refrigerator.

LEFT: *Cheese and Herb Galette (page 61), Smoked Salmon Crêpes with Sauce Hollandaise (page 30) and Crêpes Soufflés au Fromage (page 31)*

Crème Forestière

(Mushroom and leek soup with wine)

Serves 6–8

The soup will freeze for 3 months or keep for 2 days under refrigeration

The glasses of white wine and sherry combine to give this delicate soup an unexpected depth of flavour. The swirl of cream and fresh herbs make it look deliciously inviting for a summer meal.

2 oz (50 g/¼ cup) butter
1 medium (5 oz/150 g) onion, finely sliced
12 oz (350 g) white part of leek, finely sliced
12 oz (350 g) firm white mushrooms (reserve a quarter), sliced
6 fl. oz (175 ml/¾ cup) dry white wine
2 medium bayleaves
1½ pints (850 ml/3¾ cups) chicken or vegetable stock
1½ teasp salt
15 grinds black pepper
¼ teasp ground nutmeg or mace
1 tbsp cornflour
10 fl. oz (275 ml/1¼ cups) milk
3 tbsp medium dry sherry

FOR THE GARNISH
5 fl. oz (150 ml/⅔ cup) single cream
1 tbsp snipped chives

1. Melt the butter in a soup pan, then sauté the onion, covered, for 5 minutes. Uncover and continue to cook, stirring, for a further 5 minutes until pale and golden.
2. Add the leek and three-quarters of the mushrooms and cook, stirring, for 5 minutes.
3. Pour in the wine and bubble for 3 minutes to intensify the flavour, then add the bayleaves, stock and seasonings. Cover and cook for 15 minutes until the vegetables are tender. Remove the bayleaves.
4. Purée (preferably in a blender), return to the pan and stir in the cornflour and milk which have been mixed to a smooth cream.
5. Add the reserved mushrooms, finely sliced, and bring slowly to the boil. Simmer for 3 minutes, then leave to cool. Refrigerate for at least 8 hours.

TO SERVE
Stir in the sherry and reheat until barely bubbling, re-seasoning if necessary. Put the cream in a small jug, stir in the chives, then spoon a tablespoonful on to each serving.

SOME LIKE IT HOT

We are firmly of the school that prefers its soup to be steaming hot to the last spoonful. To achieve this we cook most of our soups in a pan that is smart enough to go straight from the kitchen stove to the dining-room hot plate – thus avoiding the heat loss that occurs when it is transferred to a soup tureen. Serve the soup in warmed soup bowls.

Our favourite pan – more correctly called a casserole because it has short 'lugs' on either side rather than a utilitarian handle – is made of stainless steel with a heavy aluminium base that ensures an even spread of heat. Enamelled pans may be extremely decorative but they easily develop 'hot spots' which cause thick and creamy soups to catch on the bottom.

Carrot, Orange and Coriander Soup

Serves 6–8

The soup will freeze for 1 month or keep for 2 days under refrigeration

It's the combination of the slightly peppery fresh herb and the spicy powdered one that makes this our favourite version of a soup that has only become popular in recent years. As it's based on a vegetable stock and there's no thickening apart from the puréed vegetables, it's agreeably light to serve before a hearty main course.

1 large (10 oz/275 g) onion, finely sliced
1 oz (25 g/2 tbsp) butter
1 clove garlic, finely chopped
1½ teasp ground coriander
1½ lb (675 g) well flavoured carrots, finely sliced
8 oz (225 g) potatoes, peeled and sliced
2 pints (1·25 litres/5 cups) vegetable stock
10 fl. oz (275 ml/1¼ cups) fresh orange juice
3 strips orange peel
½ teasp salt
¼ teasp white pepper
5 fl. oz (150 ml/⅔ cup) single cream
2 rounded tbsp chopped parsley (or fresh coriander)

FOR THE GARNISH
toasted flaked hazelnuts or brown bread croûtons

1. Sauté the onion in the butter in a covered pan until soft and golden – about 10 minutes. Add the garlic and coriander and cook, stirring, for a further 2 minutes, then add the carrots and potatoes and stir thoroughly to mix them with the onion.
2. Add the stock, orange juice and peel, salt and pepper, then cover and simmer for 20–30 minutes until the vegetables are tender. Remove the orange peel.
3. Purée the soup (preferably in a blender) until absolutely smooth. Leave overnight to mature in flavour.

TO SERVE
Reheat until steaming, add the cream and continue to heat until bubbling. Stir in the fresh herbs. Serve with a scattering of hazelnuts or croûtons.

MEATBALLS NOT CANNON BALLS

A 'binder' of some kind added to meatballs made with fresh mince makes them more tender in texture than when they're made with meat and seasonings alone. Fresh breadcrumbs and soaked and puréed stale bread both work well, but if the meatballs are to be served in a soup, we prefer to use ground rice. This makes them tender but more compact in texture – just nice to bite into with a spoonful of soup.

Herbed Tomato Soup with Miniature Meatballs

Serves 6–8

The soup will freeze for 6 months or keep for 3 days under refrigeration

The combination of the three different kinds of tomato gives this satisfying soup a superb flavour and brilliant colour.

1 oz (25 g/2 tbsp) butter or margarine
1 large onion, thinly sliced
1 clove garlic, chopped
1½ lb (675 g) deep red, ripe tomatoes, quartered, or 28 oz (800 g) canned plum tomatoes
3 teasp brown sugar
1 teasp salt
15 grinds black pepper
10 fl. oz (275 ml/1¼ cups) tomato juice
4 strips orange peel
1 bayleaf and a large sprig of parsley
1 tbsp tomato purée
2 pints (1·25 litres/5 cups) vegetable or chicken stock
1 level tbsp chopped fresh basil (or 1 teasp dried basil)

FOR THE MEATBALLS
12 oz (350 g) fresh minced beef
3–4 tbsp ground rice
1 egg
1 tbsp chopped parsley
½ teasp salt
10 grinds black pepper

1. In a soup pan, melt the butter and sauté the onion and garlic, covered, until golden, about 10 minutes. Add the remaining ingredients (except stock and basil) and simmer, covered, for 30 minutes.
2. Remove the bayleaf and orange peel then purée or blend until smooth. If fresh tomatoes were used, push through a sieve to remove the skin and seeds. Return to the rinsed pan, add the stock and bring to the boil.
3. Meanwhile, mix the ingredients for the meatballs in a large bowl, then leave to firm up for 10 minutes. If too soft to form into balls, add a further tbsp of ground rice. With wetted palms, form into balls the size of a large marble.
4. Drop the meatballs into the boiling soup and simmer very gently for a further 30 minutes. Leave overnight.

TO SERVE
Reheat slowly until bubbling, then stir in the basil.

THE METAMORPHOSIS OF THE ONION

Whenever onion is sautéed in fat – it doesn't matter whether it's butter, margarine or oil – the acid flavour of the raw vegetable is softened and sweetened as the starch in it is changed into sugar. The longer you fry the onion, the sweeter the taste and the richer the colour, until finally the sugar content becomes caramelised and the colour deepens to a mahogany brown, as in steak and onions.

THE DO-IT-YOURSELF CUTTER

Most domestic pastry cutters are not made with a diameter larger than $3\frac{1}{2}$–4 inches (9–10 cm). For larger sized pastry cut-outs use a coffee or tea saucer and a sharp pointed knife.

French Onion Soup under a Pastry Crust

Serves 6–8

The soup will freeze for 3 months or keep for 3 days under refrigeration without the pastry

This is a dramatic starter – you break through the pastry crust to find a bowl of bubbling soup below. The tricky part – fitting the pastry 'cap' to the soup bowl – can be done in advance, and the complete dish can be baked fresh just 15 minutes before serving.

1 oz (25 g/2 tbsp) butter or margarine
2 teasp oil
1 lb (450 g) onions, finely sliced
1 level teasp brown sugar
1 teasp salt
15 grinds black pepper
1 oz (25 g/$\frac{1}{4}$ cup) flour
3 pints (1·75 litres/7$\frac{1}{2}$ cups) hot well-flavoured beef stock or consommé
4 fl. oz (125 ml/$\frac{1}{2}$ cup) dry white wine or vermouth
1$\frac{1}{2}$ lb (675 g) puff pastry
1 egg, separated

1. Melt the butter or margarine with the oil and as soon as it stops foaming add the onion and turn to coat in the fat. Cover and cook gently for 15 minutes.
2. Add the sugar, salt and pepper and continue to cook for another 20 minutes, uncovered, until the onions are a rich golden brown.
3. Sprinkle in the flour and cook for a further 3 minutes, then add the hot stock and alcohol. Simmer, half covered, for 1 hour, then leave to go cold. Divide between six to eight heatproof deep soup bowls or individual soufflé dishes.
4. Roll out the pastry $\frac{1}{4}$ inch (6 mm) thick and cut into rounds 2 inches (5 cm) wider in diameter than the chosen bowls.
5. Whisk the egg white until frothy and then use it to paint a 1 inch (2·5 cm) deep band all the way round the top of each bowl. Take each circle of pastry in turn and place it, without stretching it, across the top of each bowl, then crimp with a fork to seal it all the way round.
6. Thin the egg yolk with a teaspoon of water and brush it evenly over the pastry. Arrange the bowls on a baking sheet and chill for at least 30 minutes to allow the pastry to relax.

TO SERVE
Shortly before dinner, preheat the oven to Gas 7 (425°F, 220°C) and bake for 15 minutes or until the pastry is a rich brown. Serve at once.

EASY-BLEND YEAST

In a perfect world, we'd always use fresh yeast – there's a kind of primitive pleasure in watching it become transformed from a piece of 'putty' to a bubbling, frothy mass – but it's just when we decide to bake bread or rolls that we haven't got any in the home.

So that's why we're so enthusiastic about the 'easy-blend' yeast – a dried yeast that's twice as active as the regular dried variety, so that half as much will work twice as fast. What's more, it doesn't need to be 'brought back to life' or 'proved' as with regular dried yeast. Instead, you just treat it like baking powder – it's almost as fine – and mix it with the dry ingredients, so baking becomes as easy as cake.

And as this easy-blend yeast has a shelf life of 6 months, you can decide to have a bread bake-in whenever you please.

Honey and Walnut Knots

Makes 20 knots

The rolls freeze for 4 months

The malted wheat and rye grains in granary flour give it a particularly nutty flavour. And when you enrich the brown dough itself with an oil that's actually pressed from walnuts, you get quite delectable rolls that go especially well with any smoked salmon or avocado starter. They're also good with soup.

$1\frac{1}{4}$ *lb (575 g/5 cups) granary flour*
4 oz (125 g/1 cup) white bread flour
1 sachet easy-blend yeast
3 level teasp salt
1 rounded tbsp thin honey
3 tbsp huile de noix (walnut oil)
*5 fl. oz (150 ml/$\frac{2}{3}$ cup) boiling water made up to 15 fl. oz
(425 ml/2 cups) with cold water – or 14 fl. oz (400 ml/$1\frac{3}{4}$
cups) if mixed in a food processor*
*$3\frac{1}{2}$ oz (100 g/bare 1 cup) walnuts, finely chopped (reserve
2 tbsp for garnish)*

FOR THE GLAZE
*1 teasp salt dissolved in 1 tbsp boiling water
reserved nuts*

1. In the bowl of the food mixer (or a large food processor) mix all the dry ingredients.
2. Add the honey, oil and water, then process to a dough, using either the dough hook for 4 minutes or the metal blade of the food processor for 1 minute, until a soft but non-sticky dough is formed that leaves the sides of the bowl clean.
3. Turn on to a lightly floured board, work in the nuts and knead by hand for 30 seconds.
4. Turn the dough into a large, lightly oiled bowl, turn over to coat with the oil, cover with clingfilm and leave to rise until doubled in bulk.
5. To shape the knots, divide the risen dough into twenty pieces – each will weigh 2 oz (50 g) – then roll each piece into a little ball, then into a 7 inch (17·5 cm) long rope. Tie into a knot.
6. Arrange the knots 2 inches (5 cm) apart on trays lined with silicone paper and brush with the glaze.
7. Slip each tray into a large plastic bag and leave until spongy again – about 25 minutes.
8. Sprinkle evenly with the reserved nuts, and bake at Gas 8 (450°F, 230°C) for 15–18 minutes until a rich brown.

RISING DOUGH IN THE MICROWAVE

Although it's true that a slow rise promotes the finest texture, a little help from the microwave can cut rising time by half. This is what to do:

1. Make sure the bowl containing the kneaded dough is tightly covered with clingfilm.
2. Microwave on 100% power for 40 seconds for dough made with 1 lb (450 g) flour or over – or for 20 seconds for dough made with less than 1 lb (450 g) flour.
3. Leave in the machine for 10 minutes, then repeat. The dough should now feel pleasantly warm.
4. In exceptionally cold conditions, repeat the process after a further 10 minutes.
5. Allow the dough to rise at normal kitchen temperature until double in bulk and spongy to the touch.

DOUGH – THE RISING TIMES

- In an airing cupboard:
  45–60 minutes
- In a pleasantly warm kitchen:
  1½–2 hours
- In a cold larder:
  8–12 hours
- In the refrigerator:
  12–24 hours

Tarragon Spirals

Makes 24 spirals

Cooked spirals freeze for 2 months, or raw for 1 month

We serve these rolypoly rolls warm and piled high in a bread basket with any soup or starter that goes well with their fresh tarragon filling.

FOR THE DOUGH
9 oz (250 g/2¼ cups) each wholemeal and white bread flour
1 oz (25 g/2 tbsp) granulated sugar
1 packet easy-blend yeast
2 level teasp salt
3 oz (75 g/⅓ cup) soft butter or margarine (or 5 tbsp oil)
1 egg, beaten (reserve 2 tbsp for glazing)
8 fl. oz (225 ml/1 cup) hand-hot water

FOR THE HERB BUTTER
6 oz (175 g/¾ cup) butter or margarine, softened
2 rounded tbsp chopped parsley
2 tbsp chopped fresh tarragon
1 teasp dried Herbes de Provence
15 grinds black pepper
½ teasp sea salt
1 tsp grated lemon rind

1. Put all the dough ingredients, in the order given, into the bowl of the mixer or food processor and beat until the mixture leaves the bowl almost clean – 1 minute in the food processor, 4 minutes in the mixer. It should be a soft scone-like dough. If too wet, add a further tablespoon or two of flour until the mixture can be gathered into a soft ball.
2. Grease the inside of a mixing bowl with oil, put in the dough, then turn it over so that it is coated on all sides. Cover with clingfilm and leave to rise until double in bulk.
3. While the dough is rising, make the herb butter by beating together all the ingredients.
4. To shape the rolls, divide the risen dough in half and work on one portion at a time.
5. Roll the dough into a rectangle 12 × 8 inches (30 × 20 cm), spread with half the herb butter, and roll up like a Swiss roll.
6. Cut into twelve 1 inch (2·5 cm) wide slices, and arrange in bun tins, cut side up.
7. Repeat with remaining dough and herb butter and brush with the reserved egg. Slip the bun tins into large plastic bags, and leave for 45–60 minutes or until puffy.
8. Bake at Gas 7 (425°F, 220°C) for 15 minutes until a rich brown. (To reheat, place rolls in a foil parcel in a hot oven and reheat for 10 minutes. Or reheat in the microwave.)

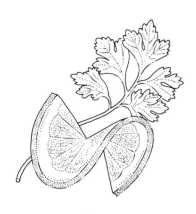

Crispy Seed Fingers

Serves 6–8

Ready-to-bake fingers will freeze for up to 1 month, or refrigerate overnight

Fingers of bread, dipped in plain or herb butter and baked till crisp make a pleasant change from croûtons to serve with soup or salads. Both the sesame and the poppy seed fingers have their aficionados – we like to make both kinds – and the contrasting seeds make a pretty display in a wicker basket.

FOR THE SESAME FINGERS
6 large slices brown or white bread (toast thick)
3 oz (75 g/⅓ cup) butter or margarine, melted
3 oz (75 g/¾ cup) sesame seeds (white if possible)
sea salt

FOR THE POPPY SEED AND HERB FINGERS
6 large slices brown or white bread (toast thick)
3 oz (75 g/⅓ cup) butter or margarine, melted
2 oz (50 g/½ cup) poppy seeds
2 level tbsp mixed chopped fresh herbs – parsley, chives, basil
1 teasp dried Herbes de Provence
10 grinds black pepper
pinch paprika pepper
sea salt

1. Remove the crusts from the bread, and cut each piece into four to six fingers.
2. Put the melted fat, seeds and other ingredients (except the salt) in two shallow containers.
3. Quickly dip the bread fingers in and out of both the fat and seeds, coating both sides.
4. Arrange on a rack or cooling tray, sprinkle lightly with sea salt and bake in a slow oven, Gas 2 (300°F, 150°C) until crisp – about 15 minutes.

PITTA

This Middle Eastern bread is really a kind of pancake which is baked in an oven heated to such a high temperature that it causes the dough to balloon up, forming a pouch inside.

It can be made at home, as below, or bought from most bakers' or grocery shops.

1 lb (450 g) bread flour
1 teasp each sugar and salt
1 sachet easy-blend yeast
10 fl. oz (275 ml/1¼ cups) hand-hot water

Mix the dry ingredients thoroughly, make a well in the centre and pour in the water, then draw in the surrounding flour, mixing to a firm dough. Knead until smooth and stretchy, then divide into twenty pieces and roll each one into a round thin 'pancake'. Allow to rise for 30 minutes, then roll out again and leave for a further 30 minutes. Preheat the oven thoroughly to the maximum temperature then bake the breads on trays for 6 or 7 minutes or until puffed and slightly browned.

Pitta Toasts

Serves 6–8

Pitta – the bread that's eaten all over the former Ottoman Empire, which includes Greece, Turkey and the Middle East – is usually quickly reheated then used as a 'scoop' for dips like hummus and taramasalata. We've treated it another way – spreading it with a savoury butter then crisping it in a quick oven. This way it makes a delicious accompaniment for a soup or a starter.

2–3 large brown or white pitta breads

FOR THE HERB BUTTER
4 oz (125 g/½ cup) butter or margarine, softened
2 tbsp mixed chopped fresh herbs – parsley, chives, dill, basil (or 2 tbsp chopped parsley)
1½ teasp dried Herbes de Provence
15 grinds black pepper

FOR THE TOPPING
2 tbsp sesame seeds (or 4 tbsp grated Parmesan cheese)

1. To make the herb butter, cream the butter or margarine until like mayonnaise, then beat in the herbs and pepper.
2. Separate each pitta into its two halves, then cut each half into four (eight pieces per pitta).
3. Spread the herb butter on to the pitta pieces, sprinkle with the sesame seeds or cheese, and bake on a baking sheet in a quick oven, Gas 6 (400°F, 200°C), for 5–6 minutes until golden. Serve warm.

Mushroom Croissants

Makes 6

The croissants will freeze for 1 month

Not your actual flaky buttery croissant, but one made with a fluffy yeast dough which makes a perfect 'envelope' to hold the savoury cheese and mushroom filling. These go well with soup for a substantial light meal.

FOR THE DOUGH
8 oz (225 g/2 cups) strong white bread flour
1 teasp sugar
salt
1 sachet (7 g) easy-blend yeast
butter
3 fl. oz (75 ml/⅓ cup) hand-hot milk
1 large egg

Dot the rectangle of dough with the extra $\frac{1}{2}$ oz (15g/1 tbsp) butter

Fold into three.

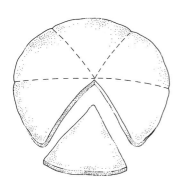

Divide circle of dough into six triangles.

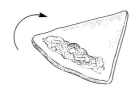

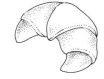

Roll up from wide end to form crescent shape.

FOR THE FILLING
8 oz (225 g) very fresh mushrooms, coarsely chopped
4 oz (125 g/1 cup) mature Cheddar cheese, grated
$\frac{1}{2}$ teasp Dijon mustard
2 tbsp fresh chopped parsley
pinch ground nutmeg

FOR THE GLAZE
1 egg, beaten
1 tbsp sesame seeds

1. To make the dough in the food processor, blend the flour, sugar, 1 teasp salt and the yeast for 2 seconds. Drop in 1 oz (25 g/2 tbsp) butter and process for 5 seconds then add the milk and egg and process until a soft scone-like dough is formed. If very sticky add a further tbsp flour. Process for 1 minute to knead the dough, then turn out on a floured board and knead by hand for 30 seconds.

2. To mix the dough by hand, stir the dry ingredients together in a large bowl, rub in the butter, then mix to a soft but non-sticky dough with the milk and egg, adding a little extra flour if necessary. Turn out on to a floured board and knead by hand until smooth and springy.

3. Lightly oil a large mixing bowl, put in the ball of dough and turn it over so that it is coated with the fat – this prevents it drying out. Cover with clingfilm and leave until doubled in size – about 40 minutes. (Hasten this process with a microwave as follows. Microwave the bowl of dough on full power for 20 seconds. Leave for 5 minutes then repeat. The dough should feel comfortably warm. Leave until double in bulk.)

4. Roll the dough into a rectangle 12 × 6 inches (30 × 15 cm). Dot two-thirds of the dough with $\frac{1}{2}$ oz (15 g/1 tbsp) butter (as for flaky pastry). Fold in three and seal the ends. Leave for 10 minutes to relax.

5. Prepare the filling while the dough is rising. Gently sauté the mushrooms in a nut of butter for 5 minutes then allow to bubble until the liquid that has exuded from them evaporates.

6. Cool a little, then mix with the cheese, mustard, parsley, nutmeg and $\frac{1}{2}$ teasp salt.

7. To make the croissants, on a lightly floured board roll the dough into a 14 inch (35 cm) circle. Brush with a little beaten egg.

8. Cut into six equal triangles, then divide the filling between them, placing the mixture at the wider end. Roll up tightly, curl into a crescent shape and place on a greased baking sheet. Brush with the remaining egg and scatter with sesame seeds.

9. Slip into a large plastic bag and leave to rise until double in size and puffy to the touch – about 20 minutes.

10. Bake at Gas 6 (400°F, 200°C) for 15 minutes or until golden brown. Serve warm or cold. May be reheated.

SUPERB STARTERS

Take your pick from our unusual avocado starters. Sample a trio of delicious savoury crêpes. Or, for a fresh approach to pâté, forget the classic fat-rich French recipes and try our innovative pâté recipes which use traditional ingredients such as chicken livers, smoked fish and exotic vegetables in a lighter, more modern manner.

For something completely different, we have raided the repertoires of several different cuisines for 'first impressions' that have special visual appeal and a variety of exotic flavours.

THE DUD AVOCADO

That's the one that never ripens and whose flesh remains as tough as a turnip whatever you try. It's probably been frosted at some time in its life, so cut your losses and throw it away. Or you could take it back and complain – it wasn't fit for sale in the first place.

Unless you're sure of a supply already labelled 'ready for eating' the best policy is to buy avocados several days in advance then leave them to ripen in the fruit bowl. (For express ripening, put them in a plastic bag with a banana – which gives off ethylene gas to help speed up the process – and leave in the airing cupboard for about 36 hours.) Dark spots on the skin – rather like those on a banana – are a sure sign of ripening for most varieties. They should also 'give' to gentle pressure when cradled in your hand. With the 'Haas' variety, however, the skin colour is the clue – it turns from muddy green to black. Once ripened, avocados can be kept in 'suspended animation' in the refrigerator for at least 5 days before they begin to look soggy and sad.

Avocado Halves stuffed with a Piquant Fish Salad

Serves 8

Fish salad keeps 24 hours under refrigeration

Count this pretty-as-a-picture starter as part of the table decorations – especially if the serving plates are lined with seasonal green leaves.

4 medium avocados
1 tbsp lemon juice

FOR THE FISH AND POACHING LIQUID
1 lb (450 g) filleted and skinned halibut or haddock
1 teasp sugar
pinch white pepper
1 teasp salt

FOR THE DRESSING
small handful fresh parsley, chopped
1 medium clove garlic, crushed
2 tbsp each sunflower oil and huile de noix (walnut oil)
1 tbsp lemon juice
2 tbsp raspberry vinegar
½ teasp mild chilli powder or a pinch cayenne
pinch salt
8 grinds black pepper
2 rounded tbsp mayonnaise
5 fl. oz (150 ml/⅔ cup) fromage frais (or thick soured cream)
2 oz (50 g/½ cup) walnuts, coarsely chopped

FOR THE GARNISH
cocktail gherkins or stuffed olives
paprika pepper

1. Poach the fish in water to barely cover, with the sugar, white pepper and salt, for 20 minutes, covered, on top of the stove, or for 6 minutes on full power in the microwave. Cool for 5 minutes, then lift the cooked fish out with a slotted spoon. Place in a mixing bowl, and flake roughly with a fork.
2. In a large bowl whisk together all the dressing ingredients (except the cream and walnuts) until a thick emulsion is formed. Fold in the cream and walnuts, and spoon on top of the flaked fish. Toss gently together, then chill.

TO ASSEMBLE
An hour before serving, cut the avocados in half and twist to separate. Remove the stones and brush the cut flesh with lemon juice. Arrange on individual plates, fill with the salad, mounding it up well, and garnish with gherkin fans or 4 oz (125 g/1 cup) olives and a pinch of paprika.

A MELON MYSTERY SOLVED

How could 500 melon halves have been zigzagged round their edges in time for lunch, we wondered at a recent charity function. Then one of us discovered the ingenious 'vandyker'. It gets its name from those amazing cut-out collars in the portraits by the famous Dutch painter of the same name. It's V-shaped and with one thrust it can cut two 'zigzags' at a time – from tomatoes, oranges and lemons as well as melons. Halves of small fruits decorated in this way make charming containers for sauces; larger ones such as the melon are ideal for sweet or savoury salads. (See page 10.)

Brandy balloons make dramatic containers for savoury starters, like this avocado cocktail. The miniature glasses are just the right scale for sorbets.

Avocado, Melon and Smoked Salmon Cocktail

Serves 6–8

Melon and avocado keep (separately) for up to 12 hours under refrigeration

It's the juxtaposition of shapes and colours, just as much as the flavours, that makes this such a ravishing starter. Melon balls give off so much juice on standing that we prefer to mix them with the dressed avocado balls only an hour or so before serving.

3 large or 4 medium, ripe but fairly firm avocados
2 medium fully-ripe Ogen or Galia melons
4 oz (125 g) sliced good quality smoked salmon or gravlax

FOR THE DRESSING
1 rounded tbsp lemony mayonnaise
2 tbsp each sunflower oil and huile de noix (walnut oil)
1 tbsp lemon juice
2 tbsp raspberry or white wine vinegar
good pinch salt
8 grinds black pepper
1 tbsp fresh chopped mint (or 1 teasp dried)

FOR THE GARNISH
sprigs fresh dill

1. To make the dressing, put the mayonnaise into a bowl, then whisk in all the other ingredients. (If you cannot get a raspberry vinegar, you will need to add a teasp caster sugar to balance the acidity of the ordinary wine vinegar.)
2. Cut each avocado in half, remove the stones, then scoop out small balls of the flesh with the small scoop of a melon baller. Submerge the avocado balls in the dressing, cover and refrigerate for several hours.
3. Use the large baller to scoop out the flesh from the halved and seeded melons, then place the balls in a sieve over a basin and refrigerate as well.
4. Roll up each slice of smoked salmon in a long roll. Refrigerate.

TO SERVE
An hour before dinner, mix the melon balls gently with the avocado balls. Cut each long roll of smoked salmon into several $\frac{3}{4}$ inch (2 cm) wide little rolls. Half an hour before dinner, arrange the melon and avocado balls with their dressing in tall glass flutes, adding two or three salmon rolls to each glass. Garnish with a sprig of fresh dill, and chill until required.

Avocado Mousse

Serves 6–8

The mousse will freeze for 1 month, or keep for 24 hours under refrigeration

Because the avocado flesh has such a creamy texture – it used to be called 'Midshipman's Butter' in the days of sailing ships – it makes a particularly delectable mousse with only small amounts of yoghurt and mayonnaise. Although individual mousses look the most effective for a lunch or dinner, the mixture can be turned out of a long loaf tin to decorate a buffet table. There may be a slight discoloration (because of the oxidation of the avocado flesh) after 24 hours, but this will be concealed when the mousses are unmoulded.

small handful parsley
1 tbsp snipped chives
3 medium, fully-ripe avocados
1 teasp salt
$\frac{1}{4}$ teasp white pepper
$1\frac{1}{2}$ tbsp lemon juice
4 rounded tbsp mayonnaise
$\frac{1}{2}$ oz (15 g/1 sachet) gelatine
3 tbsp hot water
5 fl. oz (150 ml/$\frac{2}{3}$ cup) soured cream (or strained Greek-style cow's yoghurt)
4 oz (125 g) smoked salmon, cut in tiny cubes

FOR THE GARNISH
8 oz (225 g) fresh or frozen asparagus, cooked until barely tender
2 lemons, cut in wedges

1. Put the parsley and chives in the food processor and process until chopped.
2. Peel and stone the avocados, cut in chunks then add to the herbs in the processor with salt, pepper, lemon juice and mayonnaise. Process until smooth.
3. Sprinkle the gelatine on to the water then stir over gentle heat until clear (or microwave on 100% power for 40 seconds). Pulse into the first mixture, then turn into a mixing bowl and fold in the cream or yoghurt.
4. Lightly oil eight 4 oz (125 g) timbale moulds or soufflé dishes, and divide the smoked salmon cubes between them, patting into an even layer. Spoon the mousse on top and smooth level. Cover tightly with clingfilm and refrigerate for at least 3 hours.

TO SERVE
Run a knife round the edge of each mould and turn out on to individual serving plates. Garnish with the asparagus tips and lemon wedges.

AVOCADO HOLLANDAISE

This pale green variation on the classic theme is particularly delicious with cold poached salmon or with a fish in pastry such as the Sole Lautrec (see page 64).

1 small, very ripe avocado
9 oz (250 g/1 cup + 2 tbsp)
* unsalted butter, cut into 1 inch*
* (2·5 cm) chunks*
2 tbsp lime juice
1½ tbsp white wine vinegar
4 egg yolks
1½ teasp caster sugar
pinch salt

1. Peel the avocado and remove the stone. Purée the flesh in the food processor or blender, then remove. There is no need to wash the bowl.
2. Bring the butter to the boil in one pan, the lime juice and vinegar in another.
3. Put the yolks, sugar and salt in the food processor or blender for 2 seconds, then add the boiling vinegar mixture, trickling in slowly whilst processing. Do the same with the foaming butter, trickling it in until you have a thickish smooth sauce.
4. Finally, pulse or blend in the avocado purée.

Smoked Salmon Crêpes, Sauce Hollandaise

Serves 6–8 (makes 12 crêpes)

Filled crêpes keep 2 days under refrigeration

Stage by stage, you build up this elegant dish – the crêpes, the filling and the Hollandaise sauce can all be made well in advance. Then it just needs a quick reheating job to set the crêpes, savoury and bubbling, before your guests.

FOR THE CRÊPE BATTER
4 oz (125 g/1 cup) plain flour
2 eggs
1 oz (25 g/2 tbsp) butter or margarine, melted (or 2 tbsp sunflower oil)
½ teasp salt
8 fl. oz (225 ml/1 cup) milk (or water)

FOR THE FILLING
6 oz (175 g) smoked salmon
3 hard-boiled eggs
2 oz (50 g/¼ cup) soft butter or margarine
1 tbsp fresh chopped dill (or 1 teasp dried)
1 teasp grated lemon rind
10 grinds black pepper

FOR THE HOLLANDAISE
1 tbsp lemon juice
3 teasp wine vinegar
4½ oz (140 g/½ cup + 1 tbsp) butter or margarine, cut into 1 inch (2·5 cm) chunks
2 egg yolks
1 teasp caster sugar
pinch salt

1. To make the crêpes, process all the ingredients in a blender or food processor until smooth and covered with tiny bubbles – about 30 seconds. Pour into a jug and leave to settle for 10 minutes.
2. To cook the crêpes, heat a 6 inch (15 cm) crêpe or omelette pan with a teaspoon of oil until you can feel the heat on your hand held 2 inches (5 cm) above the pan, then wipe out the pan with kitchen paper. Spoon approximately one-third of a ladle of batter into the pan and swirl it round to cover the bottom in a thin, even layer.
3. Cook over moderate heat until golden brown underneath, turn and cook the second side until golden. Turn on to a board covered with silicone or greaseproof paper. Repeat with the remaining batter, regreasing as necessary.
4. To make the filling, process all the ingredients until puréed. (They may be put through a fine mincer and bound with

the butter.) Have ready a 12–14 inch (30–35 cm) gratin dish, greased with a little butter or oil.

5. Divide the filling between the crêpes, spreading it in a narrow strip an inch (2.5 cm) away from the bottom edge.

6. Roll up and place side by side (seam side down) in the gratin dish and brush lightly with a little extra sunflower oil. (The dish may be refrigerated at this point.)

7. To make the Hollandaise, put the lemon juice and vinegar in one small pan and the fat chunks in another. Put the yolks and seasonings into a blender or food processor.

8. Simultaneously heat the vinegar mixture until bubbling, the fat chunks until foaming, and process the egg yolks for 2 seconds.

9. Trickle the vinegar mixture on to the yolks, processing all the time, followed by the hot fat, processing until it becomes a smooth thick sauce like mayonnaise.

TO SERVE

Preheat oven to Gas 4 (350°F, 180°C). Put in the crêpes and bake for 10 minutes to heat through, then coat with the Hollandaise and return to the oven for a further 5 minutes until golden brown and bubbly. Serve at once.

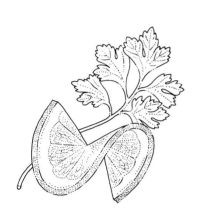

Crêpes Soufflés au Fromage

(Crêpes filled with a cheese soufflé)

Serves 6–8

Freeze uncooked filled crêpes for 1 month

These are pure magic. They go straight from the freezer to the oven and emerge with each crêpe folded round a light-as-air cheese soufflé.

1 recipe crêpe batter (see page 30)

FOR THE SOUFFLÉ MIXTURE
1½ oz (40 g/3 tbsp) butter
1½ oz (40 g/6 tbsp) flour
6 fl. oz (175 ml/¾ cup) milk
½ teasp salt
pinch white pepper
¼ teasp ground nutmeg
3 eggs, separated
6 oz (175 g/1½ cups) mature Cheddar cheese, grated

FOR THE TOPPING
1 oz (25 g/2 tbsp) butter, melted
4 tbsp grated Parmesan cheese
2 tbsp each dried breadcrumbs and ground hazelnuts (or almonds)

A CULINARY MYTH EXPLODED

Soufflés have been with us for a comparatively short time, for it was less than 200 years ago when Count Rumford invented the 'damper', giving the cook proper control over the oven temperature.

To produce a mile-high soufflé does not demand any special skills, nor is it necessary to rush it into the oven the minute it's been mixed – we frequently keep oven-ready soufflés (protected from draughts by a large bowl) for up to an hour without any ill effect. But it *is* vital to whisk the egg whites until they hold stiff glossy peaks, to stir a quarter of this meringue into the basic sauce foundation to lighten it (to equalise the textures) and then to *fold* the two mixtures together, preferably with a rubber spatula. And because a constant temperature is vital, it's prudent to set the oven a little higher to allow for the loss of heat when the soufflé is put in and only then turn it down to the baking temperature recommended.

1. Make the crêpes and cook as on page 30.
2. To make the soufflé mixture, put the butter, flour, milk and seasonings into saucepan, and bring slowly to the boil, whisking until smooth and thickened. Bubble for 2 minutes.
3. Remove from the heat and stir in the egg yolks and cheese. Cool for 10 minutes.
4. Whisk the whites until they hold soft glossy peaks, then *stir* a quarter of this mixture into the sauce to lighten it. Slowly pour the sauce down the side of the bowl of whites, folding the two mixtures together with a rubber spatula.
5. To assemble the crêpes, arrange them side by side on a board and divide the soufflé mixture evenly between them. Fold each crêpe first into half and then into quarters, to enclose the soufflé mixture, then arrange on a greased baking sheet.
6. Brush each crêpe with the melted butter and scatter with the mixed cheese, breadcrumbs and ground nuts. Open freeze until solid then cover tightly with foil.

TO BAKE

Preheat the oven to Gas 6 (400°F, 200°C) and bake the frozen crêpes for 20–25 minutes. They will stay puffed for 15 minutes in a very low oven.

Crespelle alla Romana

(Crêpes filled with spinach and anchovies)

Serves 6–8

Complete dish keeps 2 days under refrigeration and freezes for 1 week

The anchovies add piquancy to the typical Italian filling of spinach and cheese in these delicate crêpes. This is an ideal dish for a late supper – perhaps after the theatre – as it's not too rich, and can be reheated in the time it takes to down a drink. It takes only 4–5 minutes in the microwave, but then will need a quick flash under the grill to brown it.

1 recipe crêpe batter (see page 30)

FOR THE SAUCE
15 fl. oz (425 ml/2 cups) milk
6 peppercorns
1 bayleaf
1 sprig parsley
2 oz (50 g/¼ cup) butter
1½ oz (40 g/6 tbsp) flour
½ teasp salt
speck white pepper
5 fl. oz (150 ml/⅔ cup) single cream

KEEPING CRÊPES

Crêpes – which are really upmarket pancakes, with added eggs and fat – can be most successfully stored at all their different stages both in the refrigerator and the freezer.

1. Batter can be refrigerated for up to 24 hours then given a good stir to combine the solids and liquids (which tend to separate on standing).
2. The cooked crêpes can be refrigerated *unfilled* for 24 hours and frozen for up to 3 months.
3. Filled crêpes can be refrigerated for up to 24 hours and frozen for up to 1 month.
4. Filled crêpes coated with sauce can be refrigerated for up to 24 hours and frozen for up to a week.

To pack cooked crêpes, allow them to stop steaming then pile up on top of each other – there is no need to interleave them with film. Overwrap with film and foil or a plastic bag. Allow to come back to room temperature before separating.

FOR THE FILLING
1 small onion, finely chopped
1 oz (25 g/2 tbsp) butter
10 oz (275 g) frozen leaf spinach, well drained
1 can anchovies, drained and finely chopped
$\frac{1}{4}$ teasp ground nutmeg
8 grinds black pepper
3 tbsp grated Parmesan cheese
2 oz (50 g/$\frac{1}{2}$ cup) Cheddar cheese, finely grated

FOR THE TOPPING
2 tbsp grated Parmesan cheese
2 oz (50 g/$\frac{1}{2}$ cup) Cheddar cheese, grated

1. Make the crêpes as on page 30, but only fry them on the second side briefly, until a pale gold.
2. To make the sauce, heat milk, peppercorns, bayleaf and parsley until steaming, then leave to infuse, covered, for 10 minutes.
3. Melt the butter in a saucepan, stir in the flour and cook for 1 minute until the roux lightens in colour, then whisk in the strained milk and seasonings and bubble, stirring, for 3 minutes. Stir in the cream.
4. To make the filling, sauté the onion in the butter until soft and golden, then add the drained spinach and chopped anchovies and cook for 2–3 minutes, stirring constantly, until all the butter has been absorbed. Turn into a mixing bowl and stir in the nutmeg, pepper, cheeses, and 5 tbsp of the sauce.
5. Lightly smear the bottom of a 12–14 inch (30–35 cm) gratin dish with extra butter. Spread each crêpe with a bare tbsp of filling and roll up into a cylinder. Arrange side by side in the buttered dish and mask with the remaining sauce. Top evenly with the mixed cheeses. (The dish may be refrigerated at this point, but should be left at room temperture for 1 hour before reheating.)

TO SERVE
Reheat in a very hot oven, Gas 8 (450°F, 230°C), for 10 minutes or, if more convenient, grill gently for the same time until the dish is golden brown and bubbly.

EIGHT OF A KIND

For an individual presentation, line 8 small soufflé dishes with smoked salmon, making sure that each slice is long enough to extend above the rim of the dish. (You will need 6 oz (175 g) altogether.) Layer with the three pâtés, then lay the overhanging slices gently on the top layer. Chill overnight, then turn out on to individual glass plates and garnish with a small salad of decorative leaves such as quattro stagione, oak leaf or frisée lightly dressed with a vinaigrette containing a little houile de noix. (See page 135.)

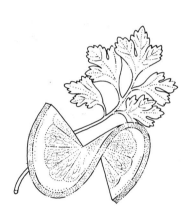

Gleneagles Pâté

Serves 8–10

The pâté will freeze for 2 months or keep for 1 week under refrigeration

Our friend and fellow food-writer Mary Berry introduced us to this stunning presentation when she was our guest cook. We've taken a few Master Class liberties with her recipe but the basic presentation – of a rainbow terrine of smoked fish pâtés – remains the same.

4 oz (125 g) smoked salmon in long slices
salt and freshly ground black pepper

FOR THE TROUT PÂTÉ
2 medium smoked trout, approx. 6 oz (175 g) when skinned and boned
2 oz (50 g/$\frac{1}{4}$ cup) soft butter
3 oz (75 g/$\frac{1}{3}$ cup) cream cheese
juice and grated rind of $\frac{1}{2}$ lemon

FOR THE SMOKED SALMON PÂTÉ
4 oz (125 g) smoked salmon pieces
2 oz (50 g/$\frac{1}{4}$ cup) soft butter
2 oz (50 g/$\frac{1}{4}$ cup) cream cheese
juice of $\frac{1}{2}$ lemon
2 teasp tomato purée
3 teasp chopped fresh dill (or $\frac{1}{2}$ teasp dried)

FOR THE MACKEREL PÂTÉ
6 oz (175 g) smoked mackerel fillets, skinned and boned
2 oz (50 g/$\frac{1}{4}$ cup) soft butter
3 oz (75 g/$\frac{1}{3}$ cup) cream cheese
1 teasp creamed horseradish
juice of $\frac{1}{2}$ lemon

FOR THE GARNISH
several sprigs fresh dill

1. Rinse out a 2 pint (1·25 litre/5 cup) terrine or loaf tin with cold water then line with clingfilm, extending it above the top of the terrine.
2. Cover the base and sides with the slices of smoked salmon.
3. Purée all the ingredients for the trout pâté in a food processor, seasoning wih $\frac{1}{2}$ teasp salt and some pepper. Turn into the prepared container and smooth level.
4. Make the smoked salmon pâté in the same way, adding pepper and some salt if necessary. There is no need to wash the bowl in between. Carefully spread this mixture on top of the trout.
5. Repeat this process with the mackerel pâté, seasoning to taste, and spread on top of the salmon pâté.
6. Wrap any surplus clingfilm up and over the top of the pâté

and chill in the refrigerator for several hours or preferably overnight before serving.

TO SERVE

Turn the terrine out on to a long narrow platter, or slice and arrange on individual plates, and garnish with sprigs of dill.

A VERY SPECIAL LOW-FAT PÂTÉ

'Chopped liver', the delicious pâté which figures in every Jewish dream of home, owes its light yet unctuous texture to the hard-boiled eggs used to replace much of the fat content that normally acts as a 'binder' in the majority of classic recipes. In the Jewish recipe, however, every 6 oz (175 g) of fat is replaced by two minced or puréed hard-boiled eggs and only 2 oz (50 g) of fat. Try it for a change.

A Pâté of Chicken Livers and Walnuts

Serves 8

The pâté will freeze for 2 months or keep 3 days under refrigeration

This is our favourite 'all purpose' pâté, with or without the walnuts. It's smooth and satisfying on the tongue and the flavour actually improves as the days go by.

1 large (8 oz/225 g) onion, finely chopped
1 medium clove garlic, crushed
2 oz (50 g/$\frac{1}{4}$ cup) soft margarine (or 3 tbsp rendered chicken fat)
5–10 grinds (1 teasp) sea salt
1 lb (450 g) chicken livers, grilled
20 grinds black pepper
good pinch ground nutmeg
4 hard-boiled eggs, shelled and halved
4 oz (125 g/1 cup) walnuts, coarsely chopped

1. Fry the onion and the garlic gently in the fat until a rich brown. As the onion cooks, sprinkle it with the sea salt. Lift out on to a plate.
2. In the same fat, toss the livers for 1 minute. Season with pepper and nutmeg.
3. Put the onion and the garlic with their juices into the blender or food processor and process until smooth, then add the livers and eggs and process again.
4. Taste and add more seasonings if necessary. Pulse in the walnuts.

SERVING SUGGESTIONS

Turn into a terrine or eight individual cocottes and chill for at least 3 hours; pipe into drained artichoke bases; pipe into tiny tartlet cases; use as a spread for toast fingers; use to fill tiny tortillas.

Two-Nut Pâté en Croûte

Serves 8–10

The pâté will keep for 2 days under refrigeration

We found the inspiration for this truly inspired pâté in Rose Elliot's *Gourmet Vegetarian Cooking* (Fontana Collins). It seems universally popular.

1 lb (450 g) wholemeal puff pastry
1 egg yolk mixed with 1 teasp water

FOR THE FILLING
4 oz (125 g/1 cup) walnuts
12 oz (350 g/3 cups) cashew nuts
1 oz (25 g/2 tbsp) butter
1 large (8 oz/225 g) onion, finely chopped
1 stick celery, finely chopped
1 large clove garlic, crushed
2 oz (50 g/$\frac{1}{2}$ cup) pistachios, skinned and coarsely chopped
8 oz (225 g) natural chestnut purée, mashed
4 oz (125 g/1 cup) Cheddar cheese, grated
2 eggs
2 tbsp brandy
$\frac{1}{2}$ teasp each paprika pepper and ground coriander
1 teasp sea salt
15 grinds black pepper
1 tbsp vegetable pâté ('Tartex' or similar)

FOR THE SAUCE
5 fl. oz (150 ml/$\frac{2}{3}$ cup) each soured cream and natural yoghurt
2 tbsp chopped fresh herbs (parsley, chives, tarragon)
$\frac{1}{2}$ teasp salt
8 grinds black pepper

1. To make the filling, grind or process the walnuts and cashews until like coarse sand.
2. Melt the butter and sauté the onion, celery and garlic until softened and golden – about 10 minutes.
3. Turn into a bowl and add all the remaining ingredients (except the vegetable pâté), mixing thoroughly.
4. To shape the crust, roll out the pastry into a rectangle 12 × 16 inches (30 × 40 cm).
5. Spread thinly all over with the vegetable pâté, leaving 1 inch (2.5 cm) of pastry clear all round.
6. Put the filling in the centre, shaping it with a knife or spreader, into an oblong approx 12 × 3 × 3 inches (30 × 7·5 × 7·5 cm). Brush the edges of the pastry with a little of the egg yolk glaze, then fold over to encase the filling (not too tightly, to allow for expansion), cutting away any excess pastry. This can be used for decoration.
7. Arrange the pastry 'parcel', seam side down, on a dampened baking sheet. Make several decorative cuts across the

top to allow steam to escape, then brush with the glaze. Freeze for half an hour.

8. Bake at Gas 7 (425°F, 220°C) for 30 minutes then turn down to Gas 5 (375°F, 190°C) for a further 30 minutes.

9. Meanwhile make the sauce by stirring together all the ingredients, then chill.

TO SERVE

Allow the pâté to cool for 15 minutes then serve with vegetables, or serve at room temperature with a salad such as Garden Salad with Summer Herbs (see page 123). The cold sauce can be served with either hot or cold pâté.

A RELAXED SUNDAY LUNCH

Begin with steaming bowls of a soup such as Crème Forestière or Curried Cream of Broccoli Soup, accompanied by warm Tarragon Spirals. Add a cheese board that combines the creamy, the farmhouse and the blue. Finally, select some of the more interesting Middle-Eastern 'mezzes' – tasty little dishes such as a home-made aubergine or courgette pâté, stuffed vine leaves and hummus from the deli – and you have the new formula for a relaxed Sunday lunch between friends, the kind that finds you still talking over the coffee at teatime.

But this kind of meal can only be counted as a success if it has been put together with the minimum amount of cooking – at least on the Sunday morning.

Caved Katsus Tsimchoni

(Vegetarian 'liver' pâté)

Serves 8

Do not freeze. The pâté will keep for 3 days under refrigeration

This does indeed resemble a pâté of chicken livers, and vegetarians could persuade themselves it had a very similar taste. But it's a delicious dish in its own right.

*1½ lb (675 g) aubergines, peeled and cut in 1 inch
(2·5 cm) cubes
salt
2 medium (5 oz/150 g) onions, coarsely chopped
5 tbsp sunflower oil
1 oz (25 g/2 tbsp) butter or margarine
1 clove garlic, finely chopped
5 hard-boiled eggs, shelled and halved
10 grinds black pepper*

1. Put the aubergine cubes into a salad spinner, sprinkling each layer with salt (1 tbsp altogether). Leave for 30 minutes then rinse and spin dry.

2. Cook the onions, covered, in the oil and butter over moderate heat until softened – about 8 minutes – then uncover and cook steadily until a deep golden brown.

3. Add the aubergines and garlic, stir well then cover and cook for 15 minutes or until the aubergine is absolutely tender.

4. Tip the contents of the pan into the food processor, add the halved eggs, black pepper and ½ teasp salt, and pulse until finely chopped – like a coarse liver pâté.

TO SERVE

Turn into a terrine or oval dish and chill thoroughly until required.

SAVOUR THE FLAVOUR

Any savoury mousse or pâté, whether made from vegetables, fish, meat or fowl, improves in flavour with every passing hour so that we sometimes feel that it's the final portion – the one that has to be scraped from the edges of the dish – that tastes the best! We try to prepare this kind of mixture at least 24 hours in advance, but if this is not possible, make it early in the morning for consumption at night.

Courgette Pâté

Serves 6–8

The pâté will keep for 3 days under refrigeration

Lighter in texture and taste, but equally as delicious as the aubergine pâté; it also makes an excellent dip to serve with pre-dinner drinks.

1 oz (25 g/2 tbsp) butter or margarine
1 medium onion, thinly sliced
1½ lb (675 g) courgettes, topped, tailed and thinly sliced
½ teasp sea salt
10 grinds black pepper
pinch cayenne (or chilli powder)
1 medium sprig parsley
3 hard-boiled eggs, shelled and quartered

1. Melt the fat and sauté the onion over moderate heat until it has turned a rich gold, then add the courgettes and seasonings and toss well.
2. When the courgettes begin to colour, cover and steam them over low heat, shaking the pan occasionally, until they feel tender when pierced with a sharp knife – 5–6 minutes.
3. Chop the parsley in the food processor then add the hard-boiled egg quarters with the vegetables and juices and process until the mixture becomes a smooth pâté.

TO SERVE

Turn the pâté into a terrine or pottery bowl, cover and chill for several hours, then leave at room temperature for half an hour before serving.

Petites Tartes aux Fines Herbes

(Individual savoury tarts with a delicate herb cheese filling)

Serves 8

Filled raw tartes may be frozen for 1 month

This is the Master Class version of the famous 'Quiche au Fromage Blanc' which we first tasted in its birthplace on the 'Route du Vin' in Alsace. Although the texture was superb, we did find the flavour a little bland, so we've used a herb-flavoured cream cheese and set the filling in tarts made from a particularly crisp and tasty brown pastry. The individual presentation also looks more elegant for a starter. We've added a touch of luxury with the smoked salmon garnish, but that's a little 'window dressing' which is only optional –

PASTRYMAKING BY MACHINE

The finest pâtissier we know – Swiss-born Jean Durig – makes all his pastry with machines so sophisticated that he can programme them to replicate exactly the hand-craft skills it took him an intensive seven-year apprenticeship to acquire.

The most indispensable machine in our kitchen – the domestic food processor – is not in our view so successful, at least when it comes to making the kind of pastry – flaky as well as short – that we prefer for the shells of savoury tartes and quiches. For as it mixes the fat, flour and liquid to a dough with the steel knife, it *over*-mixes the fat, producing a shortbread rather than a pastry. Our solution is to rub the fat in by machine until each particle is the size of a hazelnut, then to pulse in the liquid for 2 seconds only, and finally to tip the damp mixture into a bowl and gather it into a dough by hand.

Perhaps the next generation of domestic machines will be as human-identical as Jean's commercial model!

but nice. The tarts are best served warm but never straight from the oven. They can be reheated.

FOR THE PASTRY

5 oz (150 g/$\frac{2}{3}$ cup) butter or firm margarine, cut in 1 inch (2·5 cm) cubes
4 oz (125 g/1 cup) each fine-milled wholemeal flour and white self-raising flour
$\frac{1}{2}$ teasp salt
2 teasp soft brown sugar
1 teasp dry mustard
2 teasp dried Herbes de Provence
1 egg, beaten with 1 teasp wine vinegar and 1 tbsp cold water

FOR THE FILLING

5 oz (150 g/$\frac{2}{3}$ cup) herb cheese
3$\frac{1}{2}$ oz (100 g/$\frac{1}{3}$ cup) full fat cream cheese
2 oz (50 g/$\frac{1}{2}$ cup) Gruyère cheese, grated
3 egg yolks
1 whole egg
8 fl. oz (225 ml/1 cup) single cream
1 tbsp snipped fresh chives
1 teasp finely grated lemon rind
15 grinds black pepper
$\frac{1}{2}$ teasp sea salt

FOR THE GARNISH

frisée or oak-leaf lettuce
2–3 tbsp Master Class vinaigrette (see page 122)
4 oz (125 g) smoked salmon rolls

1. To make the pastry cases, preheat the oven to Gas 6 (400°F, 200°C) and have ready eight 4 inch (10 cm) loose-bottomed tart cases, 1 inch (2.5 cm) in depth, arranged on a baking tray.
2. By hand or machine, cut the fat into the mixed flours and seasonings until each particle is about the size of a small pea.
3. Sprinkle with the beaten egg mixture, then gather into a dough – it should be malleable but not sticky.
4. Roll out $\frac{1}{8}$ inch (3 mm) thick on a floured board, and using a 6 inch (15 cm) saucer as a guide, cut into eight circles.
5. Gently ease the circles into the cases and trim level with a sharp knife. Prick all over with a fork then line with a square of foil, pressing it into the shape of the case.
6. Bake for 15 minutes, remove foil and dry off in the oven for a further 2 minutes. Remove from the oven and turn it down to Gas 5 (375°F, 190°C).
7. To make the filling, put the cheeses into a bowl and gradually stir in the beaten egg yolks followed by the remaining ingredients.
8. Pour into a jug and divide between the pastry cases.
9. Return the filled pastry cases to the oven and bake for a further 25 minutes until puffed and firm to a gentle touch.

(May be frozen at this point, or the filling and the part-baked cases can be refrigerated, then assembled and baked when required.)

TO SERVE

Carefully remove from the metal sides and base and place each tart on an individual plate. Garnish with a little salad tossed with vinaigrette and two smoked salmon rolls. Serve warm – about 15 minutes after baking.

THE ELECTRIC DEEP-FRYER

This is a good investment if you enjoy deep-fried foods such as fish, chicken, fritters and chips, as the thermostatic controls take away all the guesswork from what can otherwise be a hit-and-miss technique with an ordinary pan. It also prevents most (but not all) of the oily fumes permeating the kitchen – not to mention your hair and clothing. But it does need an initial large investment in oil – 3 litres (about $5\frac{1}{4}$ pints) for a family-sized model – and the fryer itself needs regular cleaning as well as straining of the oil after every use to remove any debris from coating crumbs or batter.

Deep-Fried Camembert with a Port and Redcurrant Sauce

Serves 6–8

When you cut into each crispy triangle, you release the delicious aroma of half-melted cheese. Don't attempt to keep them hot, however, as they may collapse; reserve this recipe for a dinner with close friends who don't mind you disappearing into the kitchen just before the meal. The sauce can be made well in advance, however, as it doesn't need to be hot – and the frying operation only takes 2 minutes.

12 oz (350 g) jar redcurrant jelly or other red jelly
2 tbsp each port and lemon juice
6–8 individual triangles of Camembert
1 egg, beaten
6 oz (175 g/2 cups) medium oatmeal (or porridge oats put in food processor until as fine as dry crumbs)
oil for deep-fat frying

FOR THE GARNISH
Several sprigs coriander

1. Heat the jelly, port and lemon juice together, stirring until smooth. Divide between six to eight small plates.
2. Dip each wedge of cheese first into the beaten egg and then into the oatmeal. Repeat the process again, patting the oatmeal on firmly. Chill for at least 30 minutes to set the coating.
3. When ready to serve, heat the oil to 375°F (190°C) in a heavy pan or deep-fryer. Gently lower the Camembert portions into the fat and cook for 2 minutes.
4. Lift out and drain on crumpled kitchen paper, then arrange on the sauce. Serve immediately, garnished with tiny sprigs of coriander.

HIGH TECH IN THE MEDITERRANEAN KITCHEN

The food processor is now 'endemic' in the Middle East and is widely used to make the traditional creamy pâtés such as hummus and taramasalata. However, for vegetable mixtures such as this Aubergine Pâté – 'Patlican Salata' in Turkey, 'Chatzilim' in Israel and 'Baba Ghanoush' in all the Arab lands – many culinary purists still favour the old-fashioned wooden-handled chopper or even a large cook's knife, as chopping produces a mixture that still has some 'texture' in it. They first chop the aubergine flesh roughly, then add the remaining ingredients little by little, chopping all the time, until the mixture lightens and thickens as the oil and the tahina paste are absorbed. You can take your choice.

Lamb and Pine Kernel Purses with Aubergine Pâté

Serves 6–8   Makes 20 purses

Raw pastries may be frozen for 3 months. Raw and cooked pastries will keep 3 days under refrigeration

For this dish we've devised a more sophisticated presentation than the typical Middle Eastern meat pie from which it is derived. Because fillo pastry is very malleable when fresh, we gather it into little purse shapes filled with a minted meat mixture. We then pipe a sesame-flavoured aubergine purée into little pots to serve as an accompaniment – the purses hot from the oven, but the sauce thoroughly chilled.

10 sheets fillo pastry, a good 8 oz (225 g) approx.
4 oz (125 g/½ cup) butter or margarine, melted

FOR THE AUBERGINE PÂTÉ
1½ lb (675 g) fine aubergines
large sprig parsley (2 tbsp when chopped)
2 cloves garlic, peeled and halved
3 rounded tbsp canned or bottled tahina
3 tbsp lemon juice
½ teasp each salt and ground cumin
10 grinds black pepper
pinch cayenne pepper

FOR THE FILLING
2 tbsp oil
1 oz (25 g/¼ cup) pine kernels
1 large onion, finely chopped
1 clove garlic, crushed
1 lb (450 g) lean minced lamb
½–1 teasp salt
10 grinds black pepper
2 teasp tomato purée
4 tbsp water
2 rounded tbsp fresh chopped parsley
2 tbsp fresh chopped mint (or 2 teasp dried)
1 teasp ground cumin
4 tbsp long-grain rice, cooked in 5 fl. oz (150 ml/⅔ cup) boiling water or stock

FOR THE GARNISH
black olives

1. Make the aubergine pâté first. Preheat the oven to Gas 8 (450°F, 230°C) or preheat the grill. Prick the aubergines all over with a fork and bake or grill for 25–30 minutes or until they begin to collapse and feel absolutely tender when pierced with a skewer.
2. Leave until cool enough to handle, then cut in half. Scrape

the flesh out of the skin, and put in the food processor or blender with the parsley and garlic. Process until puréed – about 5 seconds.

3. Add the tahina and 2 tbsp of the lemon juice alternately, processing all the time. Add the seasonings. Taste, adding extra lemon juice if necessary. (It should have a taste of lemon, but not be sour.) Cover and chill for several hours.

4. To make the filling, heat the oil and fry the pine kernels until golden. Drain on crumpled kitchen paper.

5. In the same fat sauté the onion and garlic until just beginning to colour, then add the meat and continue to cook until it loses its redness, stirring all the time. Add all the remaining ingredients plus the cooked rice, and simmer for 5 minutes. Remove to a bowl and leave to go cold.

6. To assemble the purses, lightly grease a baking sheet with some of the melted fat and put one sheet of the pastry on a board. Brush lightly with melted fat and cover with a second layer. Brush that lightly too, then cut into four squares.

7. Put a rounded tablespoon of the meat filling in the centre of each square, and gather up into a purse, twisting the top to seal it.

8. Repeat with the remaining pastry and meat, to make twenty purses, and arrange on the greased baking sheet. Brush each purse lightly with the remaining fat. (The purses may be refrigerated or frozen at this point.)

9. To bake the purses, preheat the oven to Gas 6 (400°F, 200°C), and bake for 25–30 minutes, or until a rich golden brown.

TO SERVE
Arrange two to three purses on individual plates, and garnish with black olives and a pot of chilled aubergine pâté.

CHOPPING, SLICING AND DICING SMALL AMOUNTS OF ONION

Use a very sharp cook's knife with a 6–7 inch (15–17·5 cm) blade. We prefer a chopping board made of dense translucent plastic approximately ½ inch (1·25 cm) thick – any thicker and the board becomes very heavy to move around.

This kind of board is particularly hygienic because although the knife will make cuts on the surface, these do not penetrate below it. It is also kind to the blade of the knife – unlike a laminated board which will blunt the blade in no time.

Meat and Pine Kernel Pasteles

Makes 24 small pies

The raw pasteles will freeze for 2 months

Miniature meat pies with a decorative 'piecrust' edging that can really only be taught by example. But they're just as delicious if you make them in the same way as mince pies. Serve with Aubergine Pâté (see page 41).

FOR THE PASTRY
12 oz (350 g/3 cups) plain flour
1 teasp salt
6 oz (175 g/¾ cup) butter or firm margarine, cut in 1 inch (2·5 cm) chunks
2 tbsp oil
5 tbsp (approx.) warm water

Boards made of this plastic can be washed in the dishwasher or swabbed down with diluted bleach.

1. Peel the onion then cut it in half through the root end. Hold it firmly with one hand and slice down vertically with the other, but do not go through the root end.

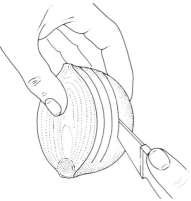

2. Grip the onion firmly by spreading the fingers across the top, make three to four lengthways cuts, keeping the root end intact.

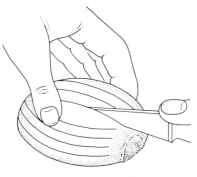

3. Gripping the onion firmly to keep the slices together, slice down crossways – producing tiny 'dice' of chopped onion.

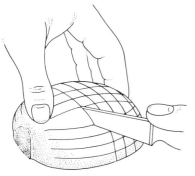

FOR THE MEAT FILLING
1 oz (25 g/¼ cup) pine kernels
2 tbsp oil
1 medium onion, finely chopped
1 lb (450 g) raw minced beef (or lamb)
½ teasp each ground cinnamon and allspice
1 teasp salt
10 grinds black pepper

FOR THE GLAZE
1 egg, beaten
sesame seeds

1. To make the meat filling, fry the pine kernels gently in the oil until brown then drain on crumpled kitchen paper.
2. In the same oil, sauté the onion gently until golden brown, then add the meat and continue to cook until it is a uniform brown all over.
3. Add 5 tbsp cold water and seasonings, and simmer uncovered until the moisture has almost evaporated and the meat looks juicy. Stir in the pine kernels, turn into a basin and allow to go cold.
4. To make the pastry, put the flour, salt and fat into a large bowl and sprinkle with the oil. Rub in the fat as for shortcrust pastry, then sprinkle with enough of the water to make a firm but non-sticky dough.
5. Roll out ⅛ inch (3 mm) thick on a lightly floured board and, using plain metal cutters, cut the dough into equal quantities of 3½ inch (8·75 cm) and 2 inch (5 cm) rounds. There should be about twenty-four of each.
6. To shape the cases in the traditional way, use your fingers to make pleats round the larger circles to form cups ¾ inch (2 cm) deep. Fill with the cooled meat, then put a 2 inch (5 cm) circle on top and twist together into a 'piecrust' edging. (The cases can also be shaped in patty tins, filled and sealed like mince pies.) Arrange on ungreased baking sheets about 1 inch (2·5 cm) apart.
7. Paint the pies with the beaten egg, scatter with the sesame seeds, and bake in a quick oven, Gas 6 (400°F, 200°C), for 25 minutes until a rich brown.

TO SERVE
Arrange two pasteles on each plate and serve with Aubergine Pâte (see page 41), either spooned in a small cocotte or sitting at the side.

GIVING BASIL SOME
TENDER LOVING CARE

Fresh basil bruises easily, the leaves
discolour and darken and some of
the precious flavouring juice may
escape. So handle it lightly without
crushing until you are ready to
pound it into pesto.

Gnocchi Verdi al Pesto

Serves 6–8

The gnocchi will keep for 1 day under refrigeration

If you don't grow your own basil, it may be a wiser policy
to buy the pesto sauce – it's the generous quantity of the fresh
herb that gives this pasta dish its special distinction. Use
double quantities of Parmesan cheese if you can't buy Pecorino for the pesto.

1 oz (25 g/2 tbsp) butter
1 tbsp finely chopped onion
*8 oz (225 g) frozen chopped spinach, defrosted and well
drained in a sieve*
8 oz (225 g/1 cup) Ricotta cheese
3 oz (75 g/¾ cup) plain flour
½ teasp ground coriander (or nutmeg)
salt
2 egg yolks
4 tbsp grated Parmesan cheese
3 oz (75 g/¾ cup) Cheddar cheese, grated

FOR THE PESTO
3½ oz (100 g/1 cup, loosely packed) fresh basil leaves
5 tbsp virgin olive oil
1 clove garlic, chopped
pinch sea salt
2 tbsp pine kernels
*1 oz (25 g/¼ cup) each Parmesan and Pecorino cheeses, finely
grated*
1 oz (25 g/2 tbsp) soft butter

1. To make the gnocchi, melt the butter and sauté the onion
   until a pale gold, then add the spinach and cook, stirring,
   for 5 minutes until the butter is absorbed.
2. Transfer to a mixing bowl and stir in the Ricotta, flour,
   coriander and 1 teasp salt, mixing thoroughly. Add the egg
   yolks and the grated cheeses, and stir to blend. Transfer
   to a shallow container and put in the freezer to firm up
   for 10 minutes.
3. Have ready a large pan with 3 pints (1·75 litres/7½ cups)
   boiling water and 1 tbsp salt. Meanwhile make small
   pellets of 1½ × ¾ inches (3·75 × 2 cm) from the mixture,
   dipping hands in flour if mixture sticks.
4. When the water is boiling, drop in six of the pellets at a
   time and cook at a steady boil for 2–3 minutes. Lift out
   with a slotted spoon and arrange in a large buttered gratin
   dish. Repeat until all the gnocchi are cooked. (They may
   be refrigerated for up to 24 hours at this point, but leave
   at room temperature for 1 hour before serving.)
5. To make the pesto, put the basil leaves, oil, garlic, salt

and pine kernels into the food processor and process until smoothly puréed, scraping down the sides once or twice. Turn into a bowl and beat in first the cheeses and then the butter. Set to one side.

TO SERVE
About 10 minutes before serving, grill the gnocchi in the dish gently until piping hot. Meanwhile, thin the pesto with a tablespoon of boiling water, spoon over the gnocchi and serve with a bowl of extra grated Parmesan cheese.

A HOME-MADE HERB CHEESE

This allows you to choose the fat content of the cheese from low-fat cottage, quark and fromage blanc to the richer curd and full fat varieties (the fat content is on the label).

Beat together 8 oz (225 g/1 cup) soft cheese, $\frac{1}{2}$ teasp sea salt, 10 grinds black pepper, pinch each cayenne pepper and garlic salt, 2 teasp each chopped parsley, chives and lemon thyme, $\frac{1}{4}$ teasp dried fines herbes or Herbes de Provence. Leave to mature in the refrigerator overnight.

Two-Fish Roulades, Horseradish Cream Sauce

Serves 6–8
Makes 16 roulades – 8 trout, 8 smoked salmon

Do not freeze. Ready-to-bake roulades keep 2 days under refrigeration

Layers of flaky fillo pastry are wrapped round two exquisite fish fillings – smoked salmon and smoked trout. The result may be described as first cousin to a Russian blini, but it is crisper and lighter to eat.

8 sheets fillo pastry, 8 oz/225 g approx.
3 oz (75 g/$\frac{1}{3}$ cup) butter, melted
coarsely ground hazelnuts or almonds

FOR THE SMOKED TROUT FILLING
2 smoked trout, 6 oz (175 g) flesh in total
5 oz (150 g/$\frac{2}{3}$ cup) herb cream cheese
2 teasp lemon juice

FOR THE SMOKED SALMON FILLING
4 oz (125 g) smoked salmon
5 oz (150 g/$\frac{2}{3}$ cup) pepper cream cheese (au poivre)
$\frac{1}{2}$ teasp grated lemon rind

FOR THE SAUCE
10 fl. oz (275 ml/$1\frac{1}{4}$ cups) strained Greek-style cow's yoghurt
(or soured cream)
2 teasp creamed horseradish (from a jar)
1 tbsp fresh chopped dill (or 1 teasp dried)
pinch salt
speck white pepper

FOR THE GARNISH
sprigs dill

1. To prepare either filling, process all the ingredients in a food processor until smooth and creamy.

2. To assemble the roulades, have ready a baking sheet, lightly greased with some of the melted butter.

3. Lay one sheet of fillo on a board and brush evenly with melted butter. Lay a second sheet on top and brush again. Cut through the pastry vertically to make four strips, each approximately $4\frac{1}{2}$ inches (11·25 cm) wide.

4. Using half the quantity of trout filling, divide it evenly between the four pieces of pastry, laying it in a narrow strip at the bottom edge. Turn in the sides to enclose the filling, then roll up firmly.

5. Repeat with two more sheets of pastry and the remaining trout filling.

6. Brush all over with melted butter than dip the top of each roulade lightly into the nuts. Arrange 1 inch (2·5 cm) apart on the greased baking sheet.

7. Make a further eight roulades, this time with the smoked salmon filling. Brush with butter and arrange on the same baking sheet, but do not dip in the nuts. (The roulades may be refrigerated, covered with foil, at this point.)

8. To make the sauce, any time up to 48 hours in advance, stir all the ingredients together, cover and chill.

9. To cook the roulades, preheat the oven to Gas 6 (400°F, 200°C), and bake for 15–18 minutes or until a rich golden brown.

TO SERVE

Arrange one trout and one smoked salmon roulade on a small plate with a pot of sauce at the side. Garnish with a sprig of fresh dill.

A FOOD WRITERS' SYMPOSIUM

After the learned papers had been delivered, and we were all a little wiser on such esoteric culinary matters as the cooking oils of the Aztec Indians and miscellaneous medieval thickeners, you can probably guess what the 130 assorted cookery writers, academics, social anthropologists and amateur 'foodies' gathered from all over the world at a recent Oxford Food Symposium did next. You've got it . . . we exchanged recipes.

We were particularly fascinated by some of the more exotic vegetarian dishes which we had enjoyed at the 'bring your own speciality dish' luncheon – in particular, those originating in Indonesia and the Middle East. We

Kulku Bademja

(Baked aubergine omelette)

Serves 4–5

These interesting Middle Eastern baked omelettes are usually served as a light main course. However, as they travel well, they also make excellent picnic fare. Squares of omelette (at room temperature) speared on cocktail sticks also serve as delicious cocktail party titbits.

2 medium aubergines (8–10 oz/225–275 g each)
salt
2 strands saffron (optional)
3 tbsp olive oil
1 large beef tomato, finely sliced
1 small onion, finely chopped
1 medium clove garlic, finely chopped
2 tbsp finely chopped dill (or parsley)
10 grinds black pepper
6 large eggs, beaten

persuaded Rosamond Man, the author of the delightful *Complete Mezze Table* (Ebury Press) to give us her recipe for this baked aubergine omelette.

This kind of 'egg cake' – often called an 'eggah' – can be variously flavoured with sautéed vegetables such as mushrooms, spinach, courgettes, leeks, aubergines or asparagus, which are generally folded into a savoury egg custard, thickened with grated cheese. Rosamond's recipe is unusual in that it substitutes extra eggs for the milk, but it is given a very special depth of flavour by the sautéed aubergines.

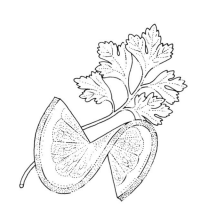

1. Cut the aubergines into roughly 1 inch (2·5 cm) chunks, put on a large plate or salad spinner and sprinkle liberally with salt. After 30 minutes rinse well with cold water and drain thoroughly.
2. While the aubergine is standing, grill the saffron strands until crisp, then crush and cover with a tablespoon of boiling water.
3. Heat the oil in a large frying pan, add the well dried aubergine chunks, the tomato, onion and garlic, and sauté gently for 5 minutes. Stir in the dill, saffron, black pepper and 1 teasp salt.
4. Preheat the oven to Gas 4 (350°F, 180°C) and oil a gratin baking dish approx. 10 inches (25 cm) in diameter.
5. Stir the vegetable mixture into the eggs, turn into the baking dish and cook, covered, for 20 minutes. Uncover for a further 25 minutes or until firm to a gentle touch.

TO SERVE

Leave to cool before cutting.

Three-Cheese Eggah with Tuna Fish

Serves 4–5

A very simple variation using Lancashire, Parmesan and Cheddar cheeses.

3 large eggs
1 fat spring onion, finely chopped
1 × 7 oz (200 g) can tuna fish, drained and flaked
2 tbsp milk (or single cream)
4 oz (125 g/1 cup) crumbled Lancashire cheese
2 tbsp grated Parmesan cheese
½ teasp salt
10 grinds black pepper
knob soft butter
½ teasp dried Herbes de Provence
4 tbsp grated Cheddar cheese

1. Whisk the eggs to blend then stir in all the other ingredients except the Cheddar cheese.
2. Turn into a greased gratin dish approx 10 inches (25 cm) in diameter, and sprinkle with the grated Cheddar cheese.
3. Bake at Gas 4 (350°F, 180°C) for 30 minutes or until firm to the touch and a rich brown on top.

A PRETTY KETTLE OF FISH

We're hooked on fresh salmon and trout because of their light texture and subtle flavours. The first few recipes in this chapter use the whole fish, and we give detailed instructions on how to skin and bone a cooked salmon. Then follow dishes which are ready-portioned to avoid any last minute stress. Finally we have what we call 'fish à la carte'. Choose from a variety of dishes that include fish soufflés, fish gratiné, fish wrapped in pastry, layered in pancakes or jellied in a wine sauce.

GREEN GODDESS SAUCE

This is a good alternative sauce for salmon, served warm or cold. It will keep for 1 week under refrigeration.

4 tbsp snipped dill (or a mixture of chopped parsley, chives and tarragon)
1 egg
½ teasp salt
pinch white pepper
1 teasp each dry mustard and caster sugar
2 teasp lemon juice
2 teasp anchovy purée (or 6 canned anchovy fillets, finely chopped)
8 fl. oz (225ml/1 cup) sunflower oil
1 teasp wine vinegar
5 fl. oz (150 ml/⅔ cup) soured cream (or fromage frais or strained Greek-style cow's yoghurt)

1. Put the herbs, egg, salt, pepper, mustard and sugar into a blender or food processor and process until the herbs are chopped – about 30 seconds.
2. Add the lemon juice and anchovy and process briefly to blend.
3. Put the oil into a jug and, with the motor running, pour in a thin but steady stream on to the egg mixture – it will lighten in colour and become thick and creamy.
4. Pulse in the vinegar and the cream until the colour is even.
5. Turn into a serving dish, cover tightly and refrigerate for at least 8 hours to allow the flavours to develop.

Oven-Baked Salmon with a Cucumber Sauce

Serves 6–8

This is our standard way of cooking a whole salmon, plain and simple. And it never fails to produce a moist, tender fish. It's also the quickest way to cook several salmon for a party – you can fit four fish at once into most domestic ovens.

Serve warm with the cucumber sauce, cold with mayonnaise or Green Goddess sauce.

1 × 3–4 lb (1·5–1·75 kg) salmon
salt
white pepper
2–3 lemon slices

FOR THE SAUCE
1 cucumber
5 fl. oz (150 ml/⅔ cup) soured cream (or strained Greek-style cow's yoghurt)
5 fl. oz (150 ml/⅔ cup) single cream
1 tbsp fresh chopped dill (or chives)
2 level teasp caster sugar

1. Season the body cavity of the fish with salt and pepper.
2. Lay a piece of lightly oiled foil (large enough to enfold the fish) in a baking dish. Lay the fish on top, add the slices of lemon, then tightly seal the foil.
3. Bake for 15 minutes to the pound (450 g) in an oven preheated to Gas 2 (300°F/150°C). Leave at room temperature for 15 minutes, then skin.
4. Meanwhile, to make the sauce, peel then coarsely grate the cucumber and leave in a colander, lightly sprinkled with salt, for 10 minutes.
5. Dab dry with kitchen paper then place in a small pan with the remaining sauce ingredients, including some salt and pepper, and set aside.

TO SERVE
Just before serving, gently heat the sauce ingredients, stirring well until the liquid is barely bubbling. Pour into a sauceboat and serve with the warm fish.

BEURRE MANIÉ

To thicken a sauce based on hot cooking liquid – as in the recipe opposite – the professional chef makes a paste from equal quantities of butter and flour and adds it to the pan a little at a time until the sauce is sufficiently thickened. This paste – known as 'beurre manié' (worked butter) – is really an uncooked roux. If you attempted to thicken the sauce with dry flour the starch granules would 'clump' as they hit the hot liquid, setting into hard little granules without any thickening power. But the fat in the 'buerre manié' keeps the starch grains separate so that as they burst in the hot liquid they produce a smooth and creamy sauce.

Whole Salmon with a Delicate Wine and Cream Sauce

Serves 6–8

The salmon is filleted and skinned before cooking which makes it very easy to serve.

1 × 3–4 lb (1·5–1·75 kg) salmon or salmon trout, filleted and skinned
1 oz (25 g/2 tbsp) butter
sea salt and white pepper
1 tbsp flavourless oil (sunflower)
2 shallots (or large spring onion bulbs), finely sliced
10 fl. oz (275 ml/1¼ cups) medium dry white wine

FOR THE SAUCE
poaching liquid from the fish
1½ oz (40 g/3 tbsp) butter
1 oz (25 g/¼ cup) flour
5 fl. oz (150 ml/⅔ cup) each double cream and soured cream
3 teasp fresh chopped fennel

FOR THE GARNISH
several sprigs fennel

1. Preheat the oven to Gas 5 (375°F, 190°C), and butter a double piece of foil large enough to parcel the salmon. Lay the foil in a baking tin, and place one fillet on top. Season with 1½ teasp salt and ¼ teasp white pepper and sprinkle with the oil. Lay the second fillet on top of the first, reforming the fish.
2. Heat the shallots and wine in a saucepan until steaming then pour over the fish and seal it in a parcel. Mould it into the shape of a whole *unboned* fish – that is, plump and rounded.
3. Bake for 30 minutes, then open the foil and carefully pour the liquid (now containing the juices from the fish) into the saucepan. Turn the oven down to its lowest temperature, close the parcel again and return to the oven. It can now be kept warm for up to 1 hour.
4. To make the sauce, remove the shallots from the saucepan with a slotted spoon. Cream together the butter and flour (beurre manié) and add to the liquid in the saucepan a teaspoon at a time, whisking with a small balloon whisk after each addition.
5. Slowly stir in the creams with a wooden spoon and bubble gently until the sauce will coat the back of a spoon. Taste and add extra salt and pepper if necessary then stir in the chopped fennel.

TO SERVE
Put a platter (long enough to hold the fish) to warm in the oven. Open the parcel of fish then invert the warm platter on

SKINNING AND BONING COOKED SALMON

The skin will lift off easily when the fish is cooked to the correct degree. But where do you start? This is our way to skin and bone a cooked salmon, warm or cold:

1. Using a long fairly slim knife, cut horizontally along the top of the back, then across the tail and round the head (if still attached).
2. Gently peel off the skin and pull off the fins.
3. Using the back of the knife, scrape away the thin layer of brown flesh along the backbone and down the middle of the fish.
4. Carefully roll the fish over and repeat on the second side. Arrange on the serving dish.
5. Turn the knife flat then work it along the back of the fish so that it lies on the backbone. Ease the fillet gently from the bone and lift off. (If the fish is very large you may have to cut the fillet in half and lift it off in two sections.) Carefully lay the filleted section to one side.
6. To remove the bone, cut through the flesh at the head and tail with scissors, then peel the bone away, lifting it with the fingers of one hand whilst you use the knife held below the bone to press down any flesh that might stick to it.
7. Replace the upper fillet.
8. To serve cold, simply cover the entire surface of the fish with overlapping half slices of cucumber. To prepare the cucumber, groove a whole cucumber with a cannelle knife, cut it in half lengthwise then slice it paper thin (on a food processor or mandoline). Soak the half slices in salted water for 30 minutes, rinse and dry on paper towels.

top and turn them over together so that the fish is in position on the dish. Discard the foil. Reheat the sauce until bubbly then spoon over and around the fish. Garnish with fennel sprigs and asparagus spears and serve at once.

Salmon in Champagne

Serves 10–12

We acquired this recipe from a friend who always cooks it when the family come home. We cook it with any *methode champenoise* sparkling wine – those bubbles do seem to add a very special flavour! It is excellent served with Strawberry and Cucumber Salad (page 133).

3 shallots, thinly sliced
1 large carrot, thinly sliced
2 stalks of celery, thinly sliced
1 × 4½–5 lb (2·25–2·5 kg) salmon, cleaned and with head removed
1 tbsp virgin olive oil
1 teasp salt
¼ teasp white pepper
8 fl. oz (225 ml/1 cup) champagne or other sparkling white wine (can be leftover)

FOR THE GARNISH
8 oz (225 g) even-sized strawberries, thickly sliced
½ cucumber, thinly sliced
sprigs of fresh dill or mint

1. Preheat the oven to its highest temperature.
2. Lay the sliced vegetables in the stomach cavity of the fish, then sprinkle with the olive oil and seasonings.
3. Line a baking tin with foil and lay a second piece (large enough to enclose the fish) on top. Transfer the fish to the foil, pour over the champagne, then seal into a parcel.
4. Place in the oven, then immediately turn it down to Gas 4 (350°F, 180°C) and bake for 20 minutes. Then turn off the oven, but leave the fish in it for 3 hours to complete cooking.
5. Open the 'parcel', remove and discard the vegetables and pour the cooking liquid into a small container (it can be frozen for later use). The fish will now skin easily and can be placed on a serving dish, then covered with film or foil until required.

TO SERVE
Leave the salmon at room temperature for at least an hour, then decorate with slices of cucumber and strawberries and the sprigs of herbs. Serve with the salad.

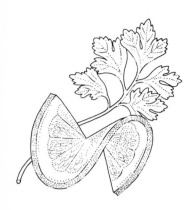

Souffléd Trout baked in Tarragon Butter

Serves 6

The whole trout have their backbones removed before they are stuffed with a delicate mousseline of sole and then cooked in tarragon-flavoured butter. Just before serving, the delicious cooking juices are mixed with soured cream and raisins – to make an 'instant' sauce.

6 × 8–10 oz (225–275 g) rainbow trout
salt and white pepper
3 oz (75 g/⅓ cup) butter, melted
3 teasp chopped fresh tarragon (or 1 teasp dried)

FOR THE MOUSSELINE OF SOLE
11 oz (300 g) lemon sole fillets (skinned weight)
3 egg whites
10 fl. oz (275 ml/1¼ cups) double cream
10 grinds black pepper
⅛ teasp ground nutmeg

FOR THE SAUCE
5 fl. oz (150 ml/⅔ cup) soured cream
3 rounded tbsp seedless raisins, soaked in hot water to cover
½ teasp grated lemon rind

1. Ask the fishmonger to cut off the head and remove the central bone of each trout by cutting along its back leaving the stomach intact. At home, remove any small bones with tweezers and sprinkle with salt and white pepper.
2. To make the mousseline, cut the lemon sole into 1 inch (2·5 cm) chunks and process on the food processor until finely puréed. Add the remaining ingredients, including 1½ teasp salt, slowly through the feed tube, processing continuously until the mixture is smooth and fluffy. Freeze for 15 minutes.
3. To stuff the trout, lightly salt the insides of the fish then divide the mousseline evenly between them and gently press them closed.
4. Arrange the trout side by side in an ovenproof dish and spoon over the melted butter mixed with the chopped tarragon. Cover with a piece of buttered silicone or grease-proof paper. (The fish can now be refrigerated for up to 6 hours and then left at room temperature for 30 minutes before cooking.)
5. To cook the trout, preheat the oven to Gas 4 (350°F, 180°C), and bake for 25 minutes. This can be done 1 hour before serving and the trout kept hot for up to 30 minutes in a low oven, Gas ½ (250°F, 120°C).
6. Remove the fish from the oven, peel the top skin off each, then arrange them on a long, warm serving plate. Cover loosely and keep warm in the turned-down oven.

7. To make the sauce (which can be reheated), add the soured cream, drained raisins and lemon rind to the juices still in the dish, stir well, then heat slowly on top of the stove until bubbly. Add salt and white pepper if necessary.

TO SERVE

Spoon the sauce over the fish and grill for 3–4 minutes or until steaming. Serve at once.

ALSATIAN RIESLING

The crisp dry Riesling wine produced in Alsace marries to perfection with the freshwater fish such as pike, carp and trout that grow plump and sweet in its rivers and streams.

Sometimes the fish is poached 'au bleu' in the wine which is then used as the foundation for a sauce; or it may be fried in butter which is then used to flavour the sauce. The skin of poached fish is best removed before serving as the texture is most unappealing in the mouth, but fish fried under a crisp coating of seasoned flour can be left unskinned – and becomes rather like the Spanish 'escabèche' (fried and marinated fish) when it's coated with an aromatic and creamy wine sauce.

Truite à l'Alsacienne

Serves 6–8

The trout are first fried à la meunière – in a simple coating of seasoned flour. Then a sauce is made with the buttery juices thickened with a liaison of egg yolks rather than flour. The frying of the fish can be out of the way before guests arrive and then the sauce is quickly put together just before serving. The fish can be kept hot in a low oven, Gas 2 (300°F, 150°C) for up to 30 minutes, though the fresher it is eaten after frying, the better.

6–8 rainbow trout, weighing 8–10 oz (225 g–275 g) each, cleaned through the gills, heads intact
salt
4 oz (125 g/1 cup) flour
white pepper
4 oz (125 g/½ cup) butter
1 tbsp oil

FOR THE SAUCE

5 fl. oz (150 ml/⅔ cup) Alsatian Riesling or similar medium dry white wine
10 fl. oz (275 ml/1¼ cups) whipping cream
pinch nutmeg
2 egg yolks
2 teasp each fresh chopped tarragon and parsley

1. Wash and salt the fish, and allow to drain in a colander for 10 minutes.
2. Put the flour, 2 teasp salt and a speck of pepper on to a square of greaseproof paper or a shallow dish as long as the fish. Lift the fish by the tail and, one at a time, roll them quickly in the flour, making sure each fish is coated thinly but completely. This gives a light but crisp coating.
3. Cook the fish in two batches. Heat the empty frying pan for 2 minutes then put in the butter and oil. The minute the butter starts to foam, lower in the fish side by side, making sure the underside of each fish is lying flat in the bubbling fat.

4. Cook steadily at a gentle bubble for 5 minutes, by which time the underside should be a rich crisp brown. Carefully turn each fish over, using two spoons so that you do not pierce the flesh. Fry the second side for a further 5 minutes, then lift out and put the fish side by side in a shallow entrée dish and keep hot (see above).

5. Make the sauce. If the butter is badly discoloured, pour it off and add another 2 oz (50 g/¼ cup) butter to the pan. Add the wine and cream and bubble until reduced by about one-third. Taste – the flavour should be creamy with winey overtones. Season with salt, pepper and nutmeg. Beat the egg yolks in a small basin, then gradually add about a third of the hot liquid, stirring well.

TO SERVE

Return the sauce to the pan, whisking until steaming (don't let it boil). Add herbs and pour over and around the fish.

POTS ... AND POTS

Any cold sauce for eating with grilled fish seems to taste better from an individual pot set on each plate. Our favourites include glazed brown ones (sold as butter dishes), glass ones (sold as vinaigrette containers) and white ovenproof porcelain ones (usually known as 'petit pots'). Everyone's idea of 'little' is different, but as a rough guide the liquid capacity for sauce pots should be approximately 6–8 teasp (30–40 ml).

Salmon and Sea Bass Kebabs with a Greek Dill Sauce

Serves 8

If you are a true fish aficionado, you'll warm to this method – pioneered by both the Greeks and the Turks – of grilling chunks of prime fish under a light coating of sesame seeds and buttered crumbs. We usually serve the kebabs hot off the grill, inside or out, but providing they're eaten within an hour of cooling they're also splendid for a lunch-time cocktail party.

12 oz (350 g) each sea bass and salmon, 1 inch (2·5 cm) thick, filleted
salt and black pepper
3 oz (75 g/⅓ cup) butter, melted
2 tbsp sesame oil
10 level tbsp fresh breadcrumbs
2 teasp grated lemon rind
6 tbsp white sesame seeds
32 small mushrooms, stalks cut level with the caps
8 wooden skewers about 9–10 inches (23–25 cm) long

FOR THE DILL SAUCE
8 fl. oz (225 ml/1 cup) strained Greek-style cow's yoghurt (or soured cream)
4 tbsp fresh chopped dill
1 tbsp mild liquid honey

1. Cut the washed fish into 1 inch (2·5 cm) cubes and sprinkle with 1½ teasp salt and 15 grinds pepper.

THE BIG FREEZE

The delicate structure of salmon flesh is easily damaged when it is frozen either in a raw or a cooked state. Once upon a time we accepted that the texture of the fish would be less than perfect if we served it out of season. Now, however, the technique of fish farming has improved to such an extent that not only is salmon available for almost 12 months of the year but the texture of the larger farmed fish is almost impossible to differentiate from the wild. So freezing salmon becomes quite unnecessary.

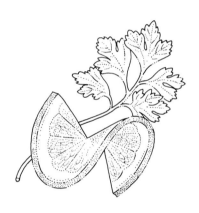

2. Put the melted butter in a bowl and stir in the sesame oil. In another bowl mix the breadcrumbs, lemon rind and sesame seeds.
3. Put the fish into the fat, turn to coat, then roll in the breadcrumb mixture and lay on a board. Paint the mushrooms all over with the melted fat as well.
4. Thread the salmon, bass and mushrooms alternately on the skewers, leaving room in between so that the fish can cook evenly. Brush all over with any remaining fat.
5. Grill for 15–20 minutes, turning once or twice. In a fan-assisted oven, air-grill for 15 minutes according to directions.
6. To make the sauce, stir all the ingredients together until smooth, seasoning with $\frac{1}{2}$ teasp salt and 8 grinds black pepper.

TO SERVE

Serve the kebabs hot off the grill or within 10 minutes if to be served warm, or within an hour if to be served cold. Accompany with the sauce.

Darne de Saumon a l'Oseille
(Salmon steaks in a sorrel sauce)

Serves 6–8

Fifty years ago, one of our grandmothers used to pick sorrel in "the rough" of a golf course in suburban Manchester. She made it into a borscht from her native Latvia – sorrel as an ingredient was barely known in Britain at that time. Now it is newly fashionable and very easy to grow – we do just that in our own back garden. The shredded leaves add a delicate but piquant flavour to an exquisite cold sauce which is made solely from the reduced court bouillon (cooking liquid) and a mixture of soured and double cream.

The salmon may be cooked in a large frying pan on top of the stove or in a baking dish in the oven.

2 shallots (or 4 spring onion bulbs) finely chopped
butter for greasing the cooking dish
6–8 × 6 oz (175 g) middle cut salmon steaks ($\frac{3}{4}$ inch/2 cm thick)
1$\frac{1}{2}$ teasp salt
good pinch white pepper
8 fl. oz (225 ml/1 cup) dry white wine (such as Chablis)
4 fl. oz (125 ml/$\frac{1}{2}$ cup) water or fish stock

SAUCE AU CITRON VERT

If sorrel is unavailable, here's a superb alternative sauce, using watercress instead.

juice and grated rind of 1 lime
3 fl. oz (75 ml/6 tbsp) reduced
cooking liquid
5 fl. oz (150 ml/⅔ cup) soured cream
5 fl. oz (150 ml/⅔ cup) double cream
leaves from 2 bunches of very fresh
watercress (total weight
approx. 6 oz/175 g)
3 teasp whole-grain mustard (eg
Moutarde de Meaux)
½ teasp salt
10 grinds black pepper

Make in exactly the same way as for the sorrel sauce opposite, reserving a few sprigs of watercress for garnishing the salmon.

FOR THE SAUCE
8 sorrel leaves
5 fl. oz (150 ml/⅔ cup) sour cream
5 fl. oz (150 ml/⅔ cup) double cream
juice and grated rind of 1 lemon
½ teasp salt
10 grinds black pepper
good pinch cayenne pepper

FOR THE GARNISH
1 lemon
1 lime

1. Sprinkle the shallots on the base of the buttered dish or pan. Lay the steaks on top and sprinkle with the seasonings.
2. Add the wine and water, bring up to the simmer on top of the stove. Poach, covered, for 5 minutes, or put in a quick moderate oven, Gas 5 (375°F 190°C) for 10 minutes or until it flakes when tested with a fork.
3. Allow the fish to cool in the cooking liquid and then transfer to a board, using a slotted fish slice. Remove the skin and centre bone. Cover loosely to prevent drying out.
4. Strain the poaching liquid into a small pan and bubble vigorously until there is about 3 fl. oz (75 ml/⅓ cup) liquid left. Leave to cool completely.
5. Put the sorrel leaves into the food processor and add the poaching liquid, creams, lemon juice and rind and seasonings, and process until thickened to coating consistency. (*By hand:* whisk all ingredients together well, until of coating consistency, having first finely chopped the sorrel leaves.) Pour into a jug.

TO SERVE
Shortly before serving, spread ¾ of the sauce on a large fish platter or individual plates. Lay the salmon steaks on top and drizzle the remaining sauce over them. Garnish with lemon and lime twists.

Poached Steaks of Halibut or Turbot with a Pistachio Butter Sauce

Serves 6–8

The cooked dish may be refrigerated for up to 24 hours

This is a delightful presentation for a summer buffet lunch. As with most cold fish dishes, it is best made the day it is to be served when the texture of the fish is still light and creamy – it tends to firm up when refrigerated. The sauce can be

THE FISH FUMET PAR EXCELLENCE

We didn't fully appreciate the virtues inherent in making fish stock at home until we were given a gift of a carton by a friend who had lovingly reduced 3 lb (1·5 kg) bones and 2 pints (1·25 litres) water to a cupful of concentrated 'fumet'. The resulting Sole Veronique boasted the finest sauce we've ever tasted. If the stock is used only for poaching the fish and not as part of a sauce, it can be strained then frozen for later use – it gets richer and more concentrated every time.

To make it, put 3 lb (1·5 kg) sole or plaice bones in a large pan together with a bayleaf, a sprig parsley, a few peppercorns and 2 pints (1·25 litres/5 cups) cold water. Bring slowly to the boil then simmer, covered, for 30 minutes then strain and simmer gently until you have 10 fl. oz (275 ml/1¼ cups) left. Use or freeze as required.

The recipe above is however a counsel of perfection.

made the day before, however, then spooned over the freshly poached fish.

6–8 × 6 oz (175 g) portions of steaked halibut or turbot fish, cut ¾ inch (2 cm) thick
salt
10 fl. oz (275 ml/1¼ cups) fish stock (sufficient to barely cover the fish)
sprig parsley
6 peppercorns
narrow strip lemon peel

FOR THE PISTACHIO BUTTER SAUCE

3 oz (75 g/¾ cup) pistachios, blanched and skinned (see page 145) (reserve 2 tbsp for garnish)
2 teasp sunflower oil
4 oz (125 g/½ cup) unsalted butter, softened
2 rounded tbsp lemony mayonnaise
5 fl. oz (150 ml/⅔ cup) soured cream (or strained Greek-style cow's yoghurt)

1. Sprinkle the washed fish lightly with salt, arrange in a large lidded frying pan, barely cover with the stock and add the parsley, peppercorns and lemon peel. Bring slowly to simmering point, then cook with only the occasional bubble breaking the surface, until the fish is firm to gentle touch and has lost its glassy appearance – about 6 minutes.
2. Use a fish slice to transfer the fish to kitchen paper to remove excess moisture, then lay them side by side on a long fish platter. (Freeze the strained cooking liquid for future use.)
3. To make the sauce, put the pistachios and oil into the food processor and process until pasty – about 2 minutes.
4. Add to the butter which has been creamed in a basin, then add the mayonnaise and soured cream (or yoghurt) and fold together using a balloon whisk.
5. Taste and add salt and pepper if necessary. Spoon over the fish, coating it completely.

TO SERVE

Serve at room temperature, sprinkled with the reserved nuts, chopped.

Individual Trout Soufflés with Smoked Salmon and Coriander Sauce

Serves 6–8

The ready-to-bake soufflés will stand quite happily for several hours. When they're baked they can be kept warm for up to 15 minutes out of the oven but still in the bain-marie.

2 lb (1 kg) fresh trout (weight when whole), filleted and skinned
1 medium clove garlic, crushed
½ teasp onion salt
1 teasp salt
good pinch white pepper
2 eggs
2 tbsp fresh chopped coriander
10 fl. oz (275 ml/1¼ cups) double cream
6–8 × 3–3½ oz (75–100 g) 'block' fillets of plaice, skinned

FOR THE SAUCE
4 oz (125 g/½ cup) unsalted butter
2 × 4 oz (125 g) courgettes, cut in matchsticks
2 oz (50 g) smoked salmon, cut in matchsticks
2 tbsp fresh chopped coriander
10 grinds black pepper

FOR THE GARNISH
6–8 rounds of bread, the same diameter as the soufflé dishes

1. To prepare the soufflé, cut the trout into 1 inch (2·5 cm) chunks and purée in the food processor. Add the garlic, seasonings, eggs, coriander and cream and process until really smooth and creamy. Chill.
2. Grease six to eight 6 fl. oz (175 ml) soufflé dishes with extra butter, and lay a fillet of plaice on to the base and up the sides of each dish. Fill with the trout mixture, then fold the ends of the plaice over the top. Cover each dish with well-buttered foil. (The uncooked soufflés may now be refrigerated for up to 6 hours.)
3. To cook the soufflés, preheat the oven to Gas 3 (325°F, 160°C), and put in a roasting tin half filled with very hot water.
4. Arrange the filled soufflé dishes in the roasting tin and bake for 15–20 minutes or until firm to a gentle touch. At the same time, 'toast' the rounds of bread – they will take about 20 minutes in the oven.
5. To make the sauce, melt the butter then stir in the other ingredients and simmer together for 3 minutes.

TO SERVE
Lay a round of toast on each individual plate. Run a knife round each mousse and turn out on to the toast. Spoon over some of the sauce.

REVIVING CHOUX PASTRY

Baked choux pastry, whether for sweet or savoury use, is kept in suspended animation in the freezer, then springs to life when briefly reheated. If the choux buns are to be served without filling (as with cheesy gougères), simply reheat them for 4 minutes in a hot oven, Gas 7 (425°F, 210°C), which will thaw and re-crisp them at the same time. If they are to be filled, allow them to cool, then fill as required. Either way they will have the same texture as if freshly baked that day.

Petits Choux à la Russe

Makes 48 petits choux   Each filling sufficient for 24

Serves 10–12

The empty choux will freeze for 3 months. The fillings will keep for 2 days under refrigeration

Smoked salmon and caviar blinis with a chaser of vodka were the favoured foods of Imperial St Petersburg – and with good reason. For the oil in the salmon insulates the stomach against the effect of the alcohol and the salty caviare keeps a good thirst going. We applaud the Russians for their good sense – and taste – but prefer our own version of smoked salmon and caviar (well, lumpfish roe) mixed with cream cheese and piped into tender little choux buns. And make ours champagne!

FOR THE CHOUX PASTE
4½ fl. oz (140 ml/½ cup + 2 tbsp) each water and milk
3½ oz (100 g/⅓ cup) butter
½ teasp each salt and sugar
5 oz (150 g/1¼ cups) flour
4 eggs

FOR THE CAVIAR AND SMOKED SALMON FILLING
8 oz (225 g/1 cup) curd cheese
4 fl. oz (125 g/½ cup) soured cream (or strained Greek-style cow's yoghurt)
2 oz (50 g) lumpfish roe
2 oz (50 g) smoked salmon, cut in julienne
8 grinds black pepper
2 teasp fresh snipped dill (if available)

FOR THE AVOCADO AND GREEN PEPPER FILLING
2 medium (or 1 large) fully ripe avocados, peeled, stoned and cut in 1 inch (2·5 cm) chunks
1 large sprig parsley
1 teasp snipped chives
2 spring onions with 4 inches (10 cm) of the trimmed green, cut in 1 inch (2·5 cm) sections
1 small green pepper, halved, seeded and cut in 1 inch (2·5 cm) chunks
8 oz (225 g/1 cup) curd (medium fat) cream cheese
1 teasp salt and 15 grinds black pepper
2 tbsp lemon juice

1. To make the choux pastry, put the water, milk, butter, salt and sugar in a heavy-based pan, bring to the boil and cook for 1 minute, stirring.
2. Remove from the heat and stir in the flour vigorously until the mixture is smooth.
3. Return to the heat for a further minute, or until the dough can be rolled round the pan. Tip into a bowl or (preferably) a food processor.

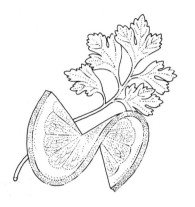

4. Now add the unbeaten eggs, one at a time, beating or processing vigorously after each addition. When all the eggs are incorporated, the mixture should be smooth and shiny.
5. Using a ½ inch (1·25 cm) nozzle and a piping bag (or the tip of a teaspoon) make little 'bulbs' of dough, about 1½ inches (3·75 cm) across, leaving 2 inches (5 cm) between each bulb.
6. Bake in a preheated oven at Gas 7 (425°F, 220°C) for 15 minutes or until crisp and golden brown. Take out of the oven, quickly make a slit in the side of each to let out the steam, then return to the turned-off oven for 5 minutes to dry.
7. To make the fillings, combine all the ingredients for the caviar and smoked salmon filling until the texture is like thick butter cream. Use a food processor to mix the ingredients for the avocado and green pepper filling to a smooth creamy purée. Chill both for several hours before using to stuff the choux.
8. To assemble, up to 2 hours before serving, slice each bun in half and fill with the different fillings – twenty-four of each. Replace the tops and chill until required.

Fresh Salmon Galette

Serves 6–8

The cooked crêpes will freeze for 1 month. The assembled but unbaked dish will keep for 1 day under refrigeration

Layers of tender crêpes are sandwiched with a fresh salmon pâté then served under a crown of soured cream.

1 recipe crêpe batter (see page 30)

FOR THE SALMON FILLING
1 lb (450 g) salmon, filleted
8 oz (225 g/1 cup) curd (medium fat) cheese
1 can anchovies, drained (or 2 teasp anchovy essence)
1 tbsp fresh snipped dill (or 1 teasp dried dill)
1 tbsp lemon juice
½ teasp grated lemon rind
1 egg
½ teasp salt
3 shakes white pepper

FOR THE TOPPING
1 oz (25 g/2 tbsp) butter, partly melted
2 tbsp finely grated Parmesan cheese

CHEESE AND HERB GALETTE

Make exactly as for the Fresh Salmon Galette, but substitute the cheese filling for the salmon filling.

Serves 6–8

12 oz (350 g/1½ cups) curd (medium fat) cheese
6 oz (175 g/1½ cups) mature Cheddar cheese, grated
1 egg plus 1 egg yolk
3 tbsp mixed chopped fresh herbs (parsley, chives, tarragon)
1 teasp salt
15 grinds black pepper

To make the filling, put the cheeses into a bowl, then gradually beat in the egg and egg yolk, followed by all the remaining ingredients. The mixture will be thick but spreadable.

TO SERVE WITH THE GALETTE
10 fl. oz (275 ml/1¼ cups) soured cream
good pinch paprika pepper

1. To make the crêpes, prepare the batter and fry as described on page 30.
2. To make the filling, cook the salmon first. Wrap in foil, cover with cold water, bring slowly to the boil, and simmer for 6 minutes. Cool for 10 minutes then unwrap.

   To cook in a microwave, lay on a plate covered with film then cover the fish with pierced film. Microwave for 5 minutes on 100% power then leave to stand for a further 5 minutes.

   Remove the skin from the salmon and pick out any fine bones with tweezers.
3. Put all the filling ingredients into the food processor and process until smooth and creamy.
4. To assemble and bake the galette, preheat the oven to Gas 5 (375°F, 190°C). Butter the inside of a 7 inch (17·5 cm) cake tin.
5. Lay a pancake on the base of the tin, spoon a heaped tbsp filling on top and use the back of the spoon to spread it evenly. Repeat with the remaining crêpes and filling, finishing with a crêpe.
6. Spread the soft butter evenly on the top crêpe, then scatter with Parmesan, cover with foil and bake for 35 minutes.
7. Uncover, turn oven up to Gas 7 (425°F, 220°C) and cook to brown the top for a further 5 minutes.
8. Take out and allow to cool for 5 minutes, then loosen from the sides with a knife and stand the tin on a canister of smaller diameter. Pull down the sides, and place the galette on a serving dish.

TO SERVE
Serve in wedges accompanied by soured cream topped with a sprinkle of paprika.

TOMATO PURÉE ON TAP

The can in which concentrated tomato purée is packed has a special coating which prevents it from being corroded by the acid in the tomato. This acidity does however lengthen the refrigerator life of leftover purée and it will remain in perfect condition for up to 10 days. After that time, though, mould may start to grow on the surface.

It's safer therefore to keep the opened container in the freezer and simply 'feed' from it – many dishes only need a spoonful or so of the purée for colour or flavour. Usually one can dig out the frozen purée with a spoon, but if it has frozen solid, leave it to soften at room temperature for 15–20 minutes. Any remaining purée can then be safely refrozen.

Individual Fresh Salmon Soufflés

Serves 6–8

You'd never believe – when your fork goes through these light and tender little soufflés – that they had just enjoyed their second bake of the day!

2 oz (50 g/½ cup) flour
butter or margarine
10 fl. oz (275 ml/1¼ cups) milk
salt
¼ teasp white pepper
2 teasp tomato purée
1 teasp dried tarragon
2 oz (50 g/½ cup) Gruyère cheese, grated
4 eggs, separated
7 oz (200 g) cooked salmon, skinned and flaked
(10 oz (275 g) raw fillet)

FOR THE SAUCE
10–15 fl. oz (275–425 ml/1¼–2 cups) whipping cream
salt and 10 grinds black pepper
1 tbsp fresh snipped dill (or 1 teasp dried dill)
2 oz (50 g/½ cup) Gruyère cheese, grated

1. Preheat the oven to Gas 5 (375°F, 190°C), put a roasting tin half filled with hot water in the oven, and butter six to eight teacups.
2. To make the soufflés, put the flour, 2 oz (50 g/¼ cup) butter and the milk into a heavy-based pan and whisk together over medium heat until thickened. Bubble for 3 minutes then stir in 1 teasp salt, the pepper, tomato purée and tarragon. Take off the heat and add the cheese.
3. Drop the egg yolks into the hot sauce, whisking well after each addition then, finally, stir in the salmon.
4. Whisk the egg whites in a large bowl with a pinch of salt until they hold soft, glossy peaks and *stir* a quarter into the sauce to lighten it, then *fold* in the rest, using a rubber spatula. Divide the mixture between the prepared cups then arrange in the roasting tin and cook for 20 minutes.
5. Remove from the oven and the roasting tin, cool for 5 minutes, then carefully turn out into individual gratin dishes or one large one. (The soufflés can now be left at room temperature for up to 2 hours. They *will* collapse, but will rise again on second cooking.)

TO SERVE
When ready to cook, preheat the oven to Gas 8 (450°F, 230°C). Mix the cream, ½ teasp salt, the pepper and dill together then pour over and around the soufflés. Scatter with the cheese, and bake for 15 minutes until well-risen and bubbling. Serve at once with the sauce.

GRATING CHEESE IN THE FOOD PROCESSOR

We were grating cheese for Master Class one day when the works became completely gummed up with melted cheese. After a short conference we decided that the heat of friction which is generated when you use a food processor had indeed melted the fat content of the Cheddar cheese. The solution – which goes for any hard-pressed cheese – was to cut it into pieces the right size for the feed tube, and then to *freeze* them for 30 minutes before processing. Problem solved!

Gratin de Sole aux Champignons
Serves 6–8

Do not freeze

Nothing could be simpler than this dish of fish and potatoes cooked in a 'sauce' of seasoned cream, yet we have found it to be one of our most popular dishes. Maybe it's something to do with the fact that the whole dish can be ready in its casserole hours in advance, and then put in the oven as the first guests arrive. Or it could be something to do with the superb if uncomplicated flavour.

2 lb (1 kg) new potatoes, scrubbed
salt
6–8 × 6 oz (175 g) fillets of lemon sole (or 12–16 smaller ones), washed and skinned
10 fl. oz (275 ml/1¼ cups) whipping cream
¼ tsp white pepper
1 medium onion, finely chopped
butter
8 oz (225 g) button mushrooms, thinly sliced
6 tbsp grated Cheddar or Gruyère cheese

1. Cook the potatoes in their skins until barely tender; skin when cool, then slice ⅜ inch (1 cm) thick.
2. Lightly salt the fish, and season the cream with 1½ teasp salt and the pepper.
3. Gently sauté the chopped onion in 2 oz (50 g/¼ cup) butter until soft and golden. Add the mushrooms, stir and continue to sauté until any liquid has evaporated – about 5 minutes.
4. Take a dish about 1½ inches (3·75 cm) deep and wide enough to hold the folded fillets in one layer, and butter it well. Arrange the sliced potatoes evenly over the bottom. Lay the folded fillets side by side on top and scatter with the sautéed onions and mushrooms.
5. Finally, spoon over the seasoned cream and scatter evenly with the grated cheese.
6. Place a sheet of buttered paper lightly on top. The dish can now be refrigerated for up to 12 hours. Leave at room temperature for 1 hour before baking.
7. Bake in a slow moderate oven, Gas 3 (325°F, 160°C), for 30 minutes until the sauce is bubbling very slightly and the fish has lost its glassy appearance. Take off the paper and grill gently for 3–4 minutes until a rich golden brown, then serve at once.

TAKING THE RELAXED VIEW

Rolling out dough inevitably stretches it beyond its normal elasticity and if baked immediately it will shrink in the heat of the oven. It's good policy, therefore, to allow it to 'relax' after shaping – for at least 15 minutes – so that it will keep a good shape.

In the case of puff pastry, this relaxing period also allows the layers of fat in the dough to re-solidify after handling. This gives the water in the pastry an opportunity to expand the layers of dough (kept apart by the fat) before the fat has melted and been absorbed by the flour.

To make a lime or lemon basket

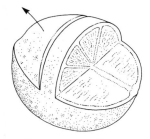

Cut and remove wedges.

Scoop out flesh under handle and from basket base.

RIGHT: *Whole Salmon with a Delicate Wine Sauce* (*page 50*) *with a Strawberry and Cucumber Salad* (*page 133*)

Sole Lautrec

Serves 8

In each individual puff pastry case there is a rolled fish fillet 'lined' with a slice of smoked salmon. The avocado-flavoured Hollandaise provides the perfect foil.

8 × 4 oz (125 g) lemon sole fillets, skinned
fish seasoning salt
8 slices smoked salmon, $\frac{3}{4}$ oz (20 g) each
3 tbsp fresh chopped parsley
3 tbsp fresh snipped dill
2 teasp finely grated lemon rind
2 × 1 lb (450 g) packs puff pastry
1 egg yolk mixed with 1 tbsp cream or top of milk
1 recipe Avocado Hollandaise (see page 30)

1. Wash and dry the fish, arrange on a board skin side down, and sprinkle lightly with the fish seasoning salt.
2. Lay a slice of smoked salmon on each fillet, and roll up from the wider end.
3. Mix the herbs and lemon rind together and divide into two portions.
4. Roll out each pack of pastry $\frac{1}{4}$ inch (6 mm) thick, and trim into a 12 inch (30 cm) square. Sprinkle each with one portion of herbs. Press the herbs into the pastry using a rolling pin. Divide each pastry square into 4 × 6 inch (15 cm) squares.
5. Lay a rolled fillet of fish diagonally, seam side down, on each square, moisten edges of pastry with water, bring the four corners together and pinch the edges together to seal.
6. Arrange on a dampened baking sheet, and chill for 15 minutes to allow the pastry to relax. Glaze with the yolk and cream mixture. (The pastries can now be refrigerated for up to 8 hours.)
7. Bake in a hot oven – Gas 7 (425°F, 220°C) – for 20–25 minutes or until a rich brown. They may be kept hot for 20 minutes in a slow oven, Gas $\frac{1}{4}$ (225°F, 100°C).
8. For the sauce, see page 30. This can be prepared 1 hour before serving and left at room temperature.

TO SERVE

Serve the fish envelopes with a spoonful of the Avocado Hollandaise – which looks particularly effective served in lime baskets.

ON NOT SPOILING BY BOILING

Experience proves the undoubted truth of the old adage that the stew that boils is the one that spoils. This is an even more important principle when it comes to fish, the tender protein of which can become dry and tough at simmering, let alone boiling, point. So the relevant term for cooking fish in liquid is 'poaching' – when the temperature of the water is between 180–189°F (82–87°C) compared to a simmering temperature of 205–209°F (96–98°C) and a boiling point of 212°F (100°C).

As you can't be taking the temperature of the water every 5 minutes, it's more practical to rely on the *visual* signs. At poaching temperature the water will barely 'tremble' with only an occasional bubble breaking the surface.

LEFT: *Individual Trout Soufflé with Smoked Salmon and Coriander Sauce* (*page 58*) *with a Country Garden Salad with a Blue Cheese Dressing* (*page 125*)

Truite au Vin Blanc

Serves 6–8

The cooked dish keeps for up to 4 days under refrigeration

We hope the purists won't object, but we have substituted the more delicate rainbow trout for the coarser fleshed mackerel in the classic recipe.

4 × 8 oz (225 g) pink-fleshed trout, filleted, then cut lengthwise in two (reserve bones and head)

FOR THE COURT-BOUILLON
½ bottle dry white wine, preferably Muscadet
5 fl. oz (150 ml/⅔ cup) water
1 medium onion, thinly sliced
1 medium carrot, thinly sliced
1 unpeeled lemon, thinly sliced
1 clove garlic, crushed
1 teasp mixed pickling spice including a dried chilli pepper
½ teasp salt
1 teasp sugar
sprig each fennel and parsley

FOR THE GARNISH
sprigs fennel
narrow segments cut from 2 navel oranges

1. To make the court-bouillon, put the fish bones and all the remaining ingredients into an 8 inch (20 cm) pan, bring to the boil, then simmer uncovered for 30 minutes to extract and concentrate the flavours. Leave to cool.
2. Arrange the fish fillets side by side in a wide pan or flameproof casserole. Strain the court-bouillon over them, bring slowly to the boil, then allow the liquid to bubble gently for just 3 minutes. Take off the heat, cover the pan and leave until the stock is cold.
3. Lift the fillets out of the liquid, carefully remove the skin, then arrange side by side in a gratin dish.
4. Bring the liquid to the boil and boil hard until it has a good strong flavour – after 3–5 minutes. If it is very acid, add another teasp of sugar. Pour a few spoonfuls over the fish to coat it lightly (any leftover stock can be frozen for later use). Chill the dish overnight but preferably for 24 hours.

TO SERVE
Arrange the fillets on individual glass plates, and decorate with the orange segments and fennel sprigs.

MEAT TO SUIT THE OCCASION

First we suggest a variety of roasts – beef, veal and lamb. They are all splendid dinner party pieces, and much of the work can be done in advance.

Our meat thoughts from abroad, which follow, take you on a culinary journey through the meat courses of Greece, Spain, Turkey, Provence and Italy. And for the buffet table, here are some inspired dishes for both indoor and alfresco dining – simple to prepare, and even simpler to serve.

JUS LIÉ

Serves 8

*15 fl. oz (425 ml/2 cups) strong
    beef stock*
1 carrot, chopped
½ onion, chopped
1 fat stalk celery, chopped
*10 fl. oz (275 ml/1¼ cups) medium
    dry fruity red wine*
1 large sprig parsley
1 small bayleaf
*1 teasp each tomoto purée and
    brown sugar*
2 teasp cornflour

1. Put all the ingredients except
the cornflour into a pan, bring to
the boil, partially cover, and
simmer for 30 minutes to
concentrate the flavour.
2. Lift out the bayleaf and sprig of
parsley, then purée the liquid and
vegetables in a blender or food
processor. If not absolutely
smooth, push through a sieve. It
may be frozen or refrigerated at
this point.
3. Put the cornflour into a bowl
and mix to a cream with 2 tbsp
water. Add to the sauce, bring to
the boil and simmer for 2 minutes
until smooth and glossy. The sauce
can now be reheated when
required.

Carré d'Agneau aux Beaux Champs

(Boned rack of lamb with spinach and mushrooms wrapped
in puff pastry and served with a rich gravy)

Serves 8

The prepared raw dish will freeze for 1 month

A superb presentation for a dinner party. Juicy noisettes of
young lamb are enfolded in spinach and mushrooms, then
baked in a crisp golden pastry case. This recipe lends itself
particularly well to individual presentation *à la nouvelle
cuisine*. The lamb can be wrapped in pastry and frozen; the
gravy or sauce – Jus Lié, see opposite – can be prepared in
advance.

4 tbsp olive oil
*2 teasp each finely chopped fresh rosemary and fresh thyme
(or ½ teasp each of the dried herbs)*
*2 racks lamb, each with 6–8 lamb cutlets, all bones and fat
removed*
salt
black pepper
1 lb (450 g) puff pastry
1 egg yolk mixed with 1 teasp water

FOR THE SPINACH MIXTURE
*8 oz (225 g) frozen spinach, chopped
grated nutmeg*

FOR THE DUXELLES (MUSHROOM PÂTÉ)
*8 oz (225 g) mushrooms, finely chopped
2 tbsp shallots or spring onions, finely chopped
2 tbsp unsalted butter or margarine
4 tbsp dry white wine*

1. Combine the oil and herbs in a flattish dish and turn the
   lamb in the mixture to coat them. Cover and leave to
   marinate in the refrigerator for up to 12 hours, turning
   once or twice.
2. Remove the lamb from the oil, allowing excess to drip
   off, and sprinkle with 2 teasp salt and 20 grinds black
   pepper.
3. Heat a non-stick frying pan for 3 minutes over moderate
   heat and in it sear the meat for 30 seconds on each side,
   or until it is well browned. Transfer to a plate and allow
   to cool.
4. To make the spinach mixture, defrost the spinach and
   squeeze very well in a sieve to remove moisture. Mix with
   grated nutmeg, a pinch of salt and 5 grinds black pepper,
   and put on one side.
5. To make the duxelles, sweat the mushrooms and shallots
   in the fat over a moderate heat for about 5 minutes or

FREEZE NOW, BAKE LATER

Puff pastry, whether commercial or home-made, does not respond well to reheating once it has been baked. So it is better to freeze the complete pastry dish raw, then defrost it and bake it just before serving. All meat fillings freeze well, and though mixtures that contain beaten egg do not freeze well when cooked, there are no problems when they are frozen raw. This applies to both savoury and sweet custards, and mixtures containing egg and cheese.

The pastries should be glazed as directed (this prevents the surface drying out) then open-frozen until solid, before wrapping in foil or freezer bags.

For a richer colour, re-glaze just before baking.

PICTURES ON A PLATE

One of the more practical and charming legacies of the late and generally unlamented nouvelle cuisine is the practice of arranging food in a decorative way on each individual plate, and then serving it straight from the kitchen. These individual 'set pieces' not only allow for more artistic presentation than when food is served from a large platter, but, perhaps more importantly, ensure that it reaches each guest at the optimum temperature. In the restaurant kitchen the food plates are set on a hot surface and arranged under a strong light which helps the different 'elements' of the dish to keep hot. In the domestic kitchen it's more a matter of hot plates plus a simpler and speedier arrangement.

until the shallots are softened. Add the wine and cook over a moderately high heat, stirring until all the liquid has evaporated. Season with $\frac{1}{2}$ teasp salt and 8 grinds black pepper, and transfer to a bowl to cool.

6. To assemble the dish, work with half of the other ingredients, and prepare one rack of lamb at a time. Divide the pastry in two. Roll one piece into a rectangle four times the width of the rack and 4 inches (10 cm) longer than its length.

7. Spread the spinach purée down the centre of the pastry (same size as the rack), spread the mushroom mixture on top and finally place the meat on top of that.

8. Brush the edges of the pastry with the egg yolk glaze and then enclose the lamb completely in the pastry, trimming off any excess.

9. Repeat with the second rack and the remaining ingredients.

10. Arrange the pastry parcels seam side down on a slightly wetted baking sheet and brush all over with the glaze. Make a small hole at one end to allow excess steam to escape. (The dish may be refrigerated for no longer than 3 hours at this point, or frozen. Allow to defrost for 4 hours before baking.)

11. About 35 minutes before you wish to serve the lamb, bake in a very hot oven, Gas 8 (450°F, 230°C), for 25–30 minutes.

12. Meanwhile make the Jus Lié – although it can be made in advance and then refrigerated for up to 2 days or frozen for up to 1 month.

TO SERVE

Cool the lamb for 5 minutes, then slice each rack into six to eight slices, discarding the end pieces. Pour a little hot sauce on to each heated plate and arrange two slices of lamb on top (do this in the kitchen).

Serve with a bouquet of fresh vegetables arranged on a side plate, or with Courgettes en Barque (see page 107).

HANGING MEAT

The eating quality of beef – in particular those cuts that are to be dry-roasted or grilled – depends more on the length of time it has been hung or 'aged' than on any other single factor – and that includes the breed, age and condition of the animal.

It is thought that during the hanging period the enzymes present in the meat muscle initiate the tenderising process, whilst the breakdown of the different proteins into their individual (and incidentally highly flavoured) amino acids accounts for the improvement in the taste.

It's wise, therefore, either to forewarn your butcher or to enquire as to the 'history' of any beef roasting joint or grills before you buy them.

The meat should have been aged for ten to fourteen days by hanging it uncovered in the butcher's cold store at a temperature of between 32° and 34°F (0°–1°C). It's not really practical to do this with individual joints or cuts in a domestic refrigerator as the ambient temperature is generally much higher and in any case the meat would dry out before it had been sufficiently aged.

ROASTING MEAT

To take the guesswork out of roasting, a meat thermometer is invaluable. Be sure to follow the manufacturer's instructions, and in particular do not allow the thermometer to touch any bone as this may distort the temperature reading.

Filet de Boeuf Dijonnaise

(Roast beef with a savoury mustard coating)

Serves 8

Freeze cooked for 3 months. Keeps under refrigeration for 3 days

This recipe is unusual on two counts: the beef is painted all over with a thick paste of savoury mustard so that it requires no basting; and the cooking time is split in two so that even with tardy guests it can be served exactly 'à point'. The first stage of roasting is completed early in the day after the meat has been standing for 2 hours (see Step 3), and then the meat is quickly roasted again in the evening.

3 lb (1.5 kg) fillet (or eye of first cut wing rib of beef), seasoned with 20 grinds black pepper
salt

FOR THE COATING
3 level tbsp Dijon mustard
1 tbsp dark soy sauce
1 clove garlic, crushed
1 teasp dried Herbes de Provence
1 teasp beef seasoning salt
2 teasp grated fresh ginger
1 teasp olive oil

1. About 2 hours before you intend to start roasting the meat, put all the coating ingredients (except the oil) into a small bowl and stir to blend, then gradually beat in the oil.
2. Paint this mixture all over the beef with a pastry brush, making sure you cover the underside as well.
3. Place the meat on a rack in a roasting tin and leave at room temperature for 2 hours.
4. Preheat the oven to Gas 6 (400°F, 200°C), and calculate the cooking times: allow a *total* cooking time of 12 minutes per lb (450 g) for the fillet, plus 12 minutes over. For the eye of rib allow a *total* cooking time of 18 minutes per lb (450 g) and 18 minutes over.
5. Cook the fillet for 32 minutes. For the eye of rib, cook for 45 minutes. Allow to go cold.
6. To complete the cooking, cook the fillet for a further 16 minutes at the same temperature. For the eye of rib, cook for a further 27 minutes.
7. Salt the meat lightly, which can now be kept hot for up to 20 minutes, while the first course is being eaten, in a warming oven, Gas $\frac{1}{2}$ (250°F, 120°C).

TO SERVE
Garnish with vegetable purées (see page 106).

ORANGE ZEST

It is in the zest – the peel without the pith – that the flavouring oils are to be found and, incidentally, most of the Vitamin C. The actual orange flesh contains only a quarter of the total amount of the vitamin to be found in the whole fruit.

If the dish contains liquid – like a soup or a casserole – the orange flavour can be added by simmering a few thinly pared strips of the zest in the pan for at least 30 minutes. For cakes or icings, add the finely grated zest to the butter or margarine instead (the fat acts as a flavour catalyst and intensifies the orangey taste). The same goes for lemons and limes.

Veau Poêle au Vermouth

(Stuffed shoulder of veal braised in vermouth)

Serves 8

The veal will freeze for 2 months and leftovers will keep for 3 days under refrigeration

As with all meat from immature animals, veal is very tender in texture but lacks fat and flavour. It therefore responds best to braising on a bed of aromatic vegetables – a mirepoix – with vaporised wine helping to keep it moist and flavourful. A thorough browning of the joint before the dish is covered also helps to caramelise the surface juices and so give a richer taste.

1 × 4 lb (1·75 kg) shoulder of veal, boned and pocketed
2 tbsp oil
1 medium onion, finely chopped
2 large carrots, finely chopped
5 fl. oz (150 ml/⅔ cup) dry white vermouth
salt
black pepper
2 bayleaves

FOR THE STUFFING
2 oz (50 g/¼ cup) butter or margarine
4 oz (125 g) shallots or large bunch spring onion bulbs, finely chopped
2 cloves garlic, finely chopped
6 oz (175 g/3 cups) fresh breadcrumbs
grated rind 1 lime
grated rind of ½ orange
1 tbsp each lime juice and orange juice
2 oz (50 g/½ cup) pistachios, blanched and chopped
2 oz (50 g/½ cup) pine kernels, toasted
2 tbsp chopped mixed herbs – parsley, lemon grass, coriander, tarragon (or 2 tbsp parsley and 1 teasp dried Herbes de Provence)
1 large egg, beaten

FOR THE SAUCE
8 fl. oz (225 ml/1 cup) meat stock
1 teasp cornflour mixed with 2 tbsp vermouth

1. To make the stuffing, melt the fat and sauté the shallots and garlic until golden – about 5 minutes.
2. Mix all the other ingredients (except the egg) in a basin, and season with 1 teasp salt and 10 grinds black pepper.
3. Pour the shallots and garlic on to the breadcrumb mixture and stir in enough beaten egg to make a moist mixture that just clings together.

FLOUR-FREE GRAVY

The 'mirepoix' of finely cut root vegetables that is used to flavour the liquid for a braised joint or bird can provide a natural thickening for the sauce to serve with it.

To prepare this sauce, lift out the cooked meat and keep it warm then turn the liquid and all the flavouring vegetables into a blender or food processor. Purée until absolutely smooth – you may need to thin it down with a little wine or stock.

Reheat the sauce, reseason, and voila! – a superbly flavoured starch-free sauce for the weight watcher.

4. To stuff the veal, lay it on a board and stuff the pocket loosely. (If there is no pocket, lay the meat flat and spread evenly with the stuffing, then roll up into a neat shape.) Sew or skewer closed.

5. Dab the surface dry with paper towels. The meat can be refrigerated overnight at this point, then left at room temperature for 1 hour before cooking.

6. To cook the veal, preheat the oven to Gas 4 (350°F, 180°C), and heat the oil in a heavy casserole. Brown the meat thoroughly on all sides – this may take 15 minutes.

7. Remove the meat to a plate and sauté the vegetables in the same fat until soft and golden. Add the vermouth and bubble until it has almost evaporated.

8. Lay the meat on top of the vegetables, season with 1 teasp salt and 15 grinds black pepper, and tuck the bayleaves down the side. Cover and cook in the preheated oven for 2 hours. The veal is ready when it feels soft to the touch and is a mahogany brown in colour.

9. Lift the meat on to a serving plate and cover loosely. It may now be kept hot for up to 30 minutes at Gas $\frac{1}{4}$ (225°F, 110°C).

10. To make the sauce, skim off as much fat as possible from the casserole liquids, then pour in the stock and the cornflour liquid. Stir well, then simmer until thickened.

11. Purée the contents of the casserole in a blender or food processor, then leave in a small pan ready to reheat just before serving.

TO SERVE

The meat may be carved in the dining room, or sliced thickly then arranged on a heated platter and coated with the sauce in the kitchen.

Tendrons de Veau à la Gardiane

(Braised strips of veal in a Provençal sauce)

Serves 4–6

The veal may be frozen for 3 months or will keep for 3 days under refrigeration

This is a very old Provençal dish – we have found a recipe for it in a Victorian cookbook published in 1884. Its origins probably go back very much further, however, to the traditional cuisine of the 'guardian' who look after the wild horses and cattle of the Camargue, hence the use of local foods such as olives and olive oil, garlic and wild thyme.

4 tbsp olive oil
2–2½ lb (1–1·25 kg) boneless breast or shoulder of veal, cut into approx. 5 oz (150 g) slices
1 lb (450 g) shallots or pickling onions
1 tbsp tomato purée
3 garlic cloves, finely chopped
1 sprig thyme (or 1 teasp dried thyme)
8 oz (225 g) button mushrooms
8 fl. oz (225 ml/1 cup) white wine
1½ teasp salt
20 grinds black pepper
12 black olives
12 green olives

1. Heat the olive oil in a 8–9 inch (20–22·5 cm) heavy-based casserole, then put in the veal slices and cook them on both sides until well browned. Put to one side.
2. Using the same oil, sauté the whole onions until golden, then add the purée and a few moments later, return the meat to the casserole together with the garlic, thyme and mushrooms.
3. Pour over the white wine and season with salt and pepper. Increase the heat.
4. As soon as the liquid begins to boil, cover the casserole, reduce the heat, and allow to simmer for 1½ hours on top of the stove or 2 hours in the oven, at Gas 3 (325°F, 160°C), stirring from time to time to prevent sticking.
5. Add the olives 15 minutes before the end of the cooking time.

TO SERVE
Serve with rice or with scrubbed but unpeeled new potatoes boiled till tender, dried off in the empty pan then dusted with sea salt.

SHALLOT SKINS

Peeling a shallot (let alone a pound of them) can try the patience of even the most dedicated cook. Here's a trick from Burgundy that works like a dream. Cover the unpeeled shallots with hot water, bring to the boil, simmer for 5 minutes then drain and drench in cold water – the skins will then slip off easily.

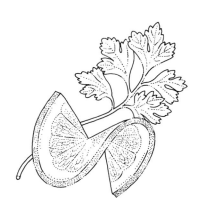

Cacerola de Carne con vino y Naranjas

(Beef cooked in orange juice and red wine)

Serves 6

This casserole will freeze for 3 months or keep 3 days under refrigeration

This is an uncomplicated stew in the Spanish manner, given an especially refreshing flavour by the combination of citrus oils and red wine.

2 tbsp oil
$2\frac{1}{2}$ lb (1·25 kg) topside or top rib of beef, cut in 2 inch (5 cm) chunks
1 oz (25 g/2 tbsp) butter or margarine
1 large (8 oz/225 g) onion, finely chopped
2 cloves garlic, finely chopped
juice from 2 large oranges, approx. 6 fl. oz (175 ml/$\frac{3}{4}$ cup)
10 fl. oz (275 ml/1$\frac{1}{4}$ cups) fruity red wine
4 strips orange peel
3 strips lemon peel
1 cinnamon stick
1 bayleaf
4 cloves
2 teasp salt
15 grinds black pepper
4 oz (125 g) fat black or green olives
2 teasp cornflour mixed to a cream with 2 tbsp cold water

FOR THE GARNISH
2 oranges, segmented

1. In a flameproof casserole, heat the oil and sauté the chunks of beef until a rich brown on all sides.
2. Add the butter or margarine and sauté the onion and garlic more gently until golden.
3. Pour in the orange juice and enough wine barely to cover the meat.
4. Add the fruit peels, the spices, salt and pepper.
5. Cover and simmer gently on top of the stove for 2 hours, or for 2$\frac{1}{2}$ hours in a slow oven, Gas 2 (300°F, 150°C), until the meat is tender.
6. About 15 minutes before the end of the cooking time, stir in the olives and the cornflour liquid.

TO SERVE
Serve straight from the casserole, garnished with the orange segments and accompanied by Rösti Forestière (see page 115).

HOW TO SEGMENT ANY CITRUS FRUIT

1. Use a small, razor-sharp, serrated knife to remove both the orange zest and the thick white pith, revealing the flesh.
2. Cut between the sections, releasing the fleshy segments.
3. Squeeze the remaining 'skeleton' of the fruit in the hand and use the juice that is extracted as required.

Pizza par Excellence

Makes 2 × 10–11 inch (25–27·5 cm) pizzas

*The unbaked dough will keep for up to 2 days under refriger-
ation, punching down occasionally, or will freeze for up to 1
month*

Sephardic Jews, who have lived for centuries around the
Mediterranean, have been making this very special version of
pizza for generations. It is made without cheese and is topped
instead with cumin-scented minced meat. It is often made in
miniature – when it is known in Arabic as *Lahma bi Ajeen*,
bread and meat – as finger food for parties, but we find it
equally sensational cooked in normal pizza-style rounds, each
serving three to four good appetites.

FOR THE DOUGH
1 sachet easy-blend yeast (or ½ oz/15 g/1 cake fresh yeast)
11 oz (300 g/2¾ cups) plain flour
1½ teasp each salt and sugar
2 tbsp olive oil
1 egg
5 fl. oz (150 ml/⅔ cup) hand-hot water

FOR THE TOPPING
2 medium onions, finely chopped
2 tbsp oil
1 lb (450 g) lean minced beef (or lamb)
1 tbsp tomato purée
1 teasp each brown sugar and salt
15 grinds black pepper
1 teasp ground allspice (piment)
1½ teasp ground cumin
good pinch cayenne pepper
3 tbsp chopped fresh parsley
1 tbsp lemon juice

FOR THE GARNISH
4 oz (125 g) salami

1. To make the dough, mix easy-blend yeast with the flour,
   salt and sugar; if fresh yeast is used dissolve it in the water.
   Mix all the dough ingredients together to form a soft
   but non-sticky ball of dough. Add a little extra flour if
   necessary.
2. Knead by hand or machine until smooth, then place the
   dough in an oiled mixing bowl. Turn it over to coat
   thoroughly with oil, then cover with clingfilm and leave
   in the kitchen until double in bulk – about 1 hour.
3. To make the topping, sauté the onions in the oil until
   softened and golden, then mix in a bowl with the remaining topping ingredients, using the hands to make sure the
   mixture is evenly blended together.

4. To assemble and bake the pizzas, preheat the oven to Gas 8 (450°F, 230°C), and grease two baking sheets or 10–11 inch (25–27·5 cm) pizza pans.
5. Divide the risen dough in half and knead each portion for a minute or two to distribute the gas bubbles evenly.
6. Roll out or press into two 10–11 inch (25–27·5 cm) rounds and place on the baking sheets or pizza pans. Spread each round with an even layer of the topping, making sure the dough is covered right to the edges, then decorate with the sliced salami.
7. Leave for 15 minutes then bake for 15–20 minutes until the meat is a rich brown and the salami has curled. Serve immediately.

WINE EN CASSEROLE

In addition to its role as a flavouring, wine – like other culinary acids such as lemon juice and vinegar – helps to tenderise the meat which is cooked in it. *Any drinkable dry or medium dry wine will serve admirably as a cooking medium.* To draw out the maximum flavour it's more important to concentrate the wine by simmering it rather than by using an expensive bottle. After all, the alcohol content is completely vaporised during the cooking process; one is simply trying to capture the flavour which has developed during the process of vinification.

The heavier, more fruity red wines are particularly suitable for beef stews and braises. White vermouth – prepared from a blend of white wines variously flavoured (according to brand) with secret combinations of herbs, spices, barks and flowers – adds a special piquancy to casseroles made with lamb and veal.

Arni me Fasolia Fresca

(Greek lamb casserole with vermouth and whole green beans)

Serves 6–8

This casserole will freeze for 2 months or keep for 2 days under refrigeration

Little beef is raised in Greece and so sheep must provide the main source of meat – and that means using every part from head to tail. This recipe makes use of the cheap but sweet neck chops which, though too tough to grill, respond well to a gentle braising in white wine – or, as we prefer because of its more sophisticated flavour, white vermouth. You can tell it's of peasant origin because a single pot is used to cook both the stew and the accompanying green beans.

6–8 lamb neck steaks, approx. 6 oz/175 g each
2 oz (50 g/½ cup) flour
1½ teasp salt
20 grinds black pepper
2 tbsp dried mint
2 tbsp olive or sunflower oil
1 large (10 oz/275 g) onion, finely chopped
2 garlic cloves, finely chopped
8 fl. oz (225 ml/1 cup) dry white vermouth (or dry white wine)
2 teasp sugar
8 oz (225 g) tiny button mushrooms
8 oz (225 g) whole green beans (haricots verts or bobo beans)

1. Season the flour with the salt, pepper and half the dried mint, and coat the lamb with this.
2. Heat the oil and sauté the onion and garlic until a pale gold. Add the meat and sauté until a rich brown.

3. Add the vermouth or wine and bubble for 3 minutes to concentrate the flavour, then add all the remaining ingredients (except the beans). Simmer for 1 hour on top of the stove or $1\frac{1}{2}$ hours in a slow moderate oven, Gas 3 (325°F, 160°C).

4. About 20 minutes before the end of the cooking time add the raw beans, stir well, and continue to cook until beans and meat are tender.

TO SERVE

Serve with new potatoes or fresh pasta.

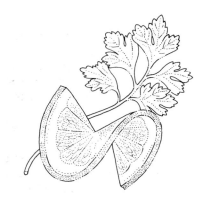

Patlican Dolmasi

(Stuffed aubergines, Izmir style)

Serves 6–8

The cooked dish will freeze for 2 months or keep for 2 days under refrigeration

From the ancient port of Smyrna (known as 'Izmir' since the days of Kemal Ataturk), merchants have for centuries shipped the famous dried fruits of Turkey all over the western world. Try and find the genuine Turkish dried apricots for this dish – they are darker in colour and less attractive to the eye than the Californian variety, as well as being a little too acid for sweet dishes such as the Khoshab on page 154. But they do give a superb flavour to savoury dishes such as this. In Turkish homes 'dolmasi' – stuffed vegetables – are simmered for hours at the back of the stove with barely a bubble breaking the surface, and they come to no harm. So if it's more convenient to leave the dish in the oven for a longer time span, simply reduce the temperature.

3–4 oval aubergines, 8 oz/225 g each
3 tbsp oil

FOR THE MEAT MIXTURE
1 thick slice bread, roughly torn
1 medium onion, roughly chopped
1 egg, beaten
1 teasp salt
10 grinds black pepper
1 teasp cinnamon
$1\frac{1}{2}$ lb (675 g) minced fresh lamb (or beef)
2 tbsp currants
2 tbsp pine kernels, toasted (see page 14)

THE PULSE ACTION OF THE FOOD PROCESSOR

A 'pulse' control that allows you to operate the metal blade of the food processor in short controlled bursts rather than in a continuous action, ensures that foods are not overprocessed and can be chopped rather than puréed if required.

Except where the food needs to be reduced to a smooth purée (as in the egg and onion foundation for a minced meat mixture), we use this pulse action almost exclusively as we find that the action is much more akin to hand chopping.

If your machine does not incorporate an automatic pulse switch, you can duplicate the action by operating the machine in short bursts of 2 or 3 seconds duration rather than by operating it continuously for 8 or 9 seconds at a time.

FOR THE SAUCE

8 oz (225 g/1½ cups) dried apricots, soaked in hot water to cover for 10 minutes
4 tbsp brown sugar
1 tbsp lemon juice

1. To prepare the meat mixture, purée the bread, onion, egg and seasonings in a food processor or blender.
2. Put in a bowl with the meat, currants and pine kernels, and put to one side.
3. To prepare the aubergines, cut each aubergine in half lengthwise then use a grapefruit knife (or spoon) to scoop out the flesh leaving ½ inch (1·25 cm) edging of flesh. This keeps the aubergines in shape when baked.
4. Put the flesh into the food processor and pulse until in roughly ½ inch (1·25 cm) chunks. This can also be done by hand.
5. Heat the oil in a heavy frying pan over moderate heat then add the chopped flesh and cook until absolutely tender, stirring occasionally.
6. Add to the meat mixture, then use a fork to stir all the ingredients together.
7. To stuff the aubergines, divide the meat mixture between the aubergine halves, mounding it slightly.
8. In the oil remaining in the pan (add an extra tbsp if necessary) fry the stuffed aubergines, meat side down, for 5 minutes or until they can be detached easily from the pan and a rich brown crust has formed.
9. Arrange in an ovenproof casserole large enough to hold the aubergines side by side (or use a roasting tin).
10. Surround with the soaked apricots and their soaking liquid, sprinkle with 1 tbsp of the brown sugar, cover and cook in a slow moderate oven – Gas 3 (325°F, 160°C) – for 1 hour, then uncover and sprinkle with the remaining brown sugar and the lemon juice. Cover and continue to cook for a further hour.
11. Baste well, then continue to cook for a further 30 minutes to allow the sauce to thicken to a syrupy consistency.

TO SERVE

Serve from the casserole or arrange in a shallow dish surrounded by the sauce.

A BEEF CONSOMMÉ WITH A HEART

Put a smear of oil in the bottom of a shallow roasting tin, add 2 lb (1 kg) well dried shin of beef and 4 lb (2 kg) beef bones, cut in 3–4 inch (7·5–10 cm) lengths, together with 2 peeled and halved onions and 2 fat carrots, scrubbed and quartered. Brown for 40 minutes in a hot oven, Gas 7 (425°F, 220°C), turning occasionally.

Take the tin from the oven and pour off any fat, then transfer the meat and vegetables to a large soup pan. Deglaze the roasting tin with 10 fl. oz (275 ml/1¼ cups) warm water, stirring well, and heating gently to loosen any congealed juices.

Add this liquid to the soup pan together with enough cold water to cover the ingredients by at least 1 inch (2·5 cm). Add 2 level teasp salt, 2 stalks celery, 1 unpeeled garlic clove, a sprig parsley, bayleaf and 1 teasp powdered bouquet garni. Bring to the simmer then remove any scum using a wet metal spoon. Partially cover the pan and simmer for 4–5 hours. (If possible, do this in the oven, as you will get an even better flavour and colour.) Do not let the liquid boil at any time as it will then become cloudy instead of clear.

Strain the consommé and remove the meat (reserve for another use). Discard the bones and vegetables. When cold, refrigerate overnight. Next day remove any surface fat, divide into cartons and freeze.

Albondigas

(Meatballs in a wine sauce)

Serves 6

The cooked dish will freeze for 2 months or keep for 2 days under refrigeration

Delicious Latin-American meatballs made with wine, raisins and chilli pepper.

1 medium (5 oz/150 g) onion, roughly chopped
2 eggs
2 large slices brown or white bread, torn up
2 teasp tomato purée
salt and black pepper
1 teasp chilli powder
1½ lb (675 g) lean minced beef
2 oz (50 g/6 tbsp) raisins
4 tbsp chopped parsley
2 oz (50 g/½ cup) flour seasoned with 1 teasp salt and 15 grinds black pepper
2 tbsp sunflower oil

FOR THE SAUCE
1 medium (5 oz/150 g) onion, finely chopped
2 tbsp olive or sunflower oil
1 tbsp flour
½ bottle dry red wine
10 fl. oz (275 ml/1¼ cup) beef consommé or good beef stock
1 teasp ground cumin
2 teasp brown sugar
1 bayleaf

1. To make the sauce cook the onion in the oil until soft and golden, then add the flour and cook for 3 minutes until it begins to colour. Add the wine and bubble for 3 minutes then add the stock, cumin, sugar, bayleaf, ½ teasp salt and 10 grinds black pepper. Whisk until boiling, then simmer uncovered for 10 minutes.
2. To make the meatballs, in a food processor, purée the onion, eggs and bread with the tomato purée, 1 teasp salt and 10 grinds black pepper. Turn into a bowl with the chilli, beef, raisins and parsley, and work together until evenly but lightly mixed. To make the mixture easier to handle, leave to rest for 15 minutes.
3. Form the mixture into 2 inch (5 cm) balls, roll in the seasoned flour, and brown in the hot oil in a frying pan.
4. As they are cooked, add them to the simmering sauce, then cover and simmer gently on top of the stove for 30 minutes, or 45 minutes in a moderate oven, Gas 4 (350°F, 180°C). Towards the end remove the lid and bubble the sauce to a rich coating consistency.

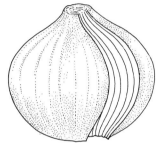

Cut the onion to the centre.

Onion, showing open cut after boiling.

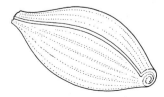

Layer of onion ready to stuff.

Onion Mahshi, Baghdad Style

(Stuffed and rolled onions in a sweet and sour sauce)

Serves 6–8

The cooked dish will freeze for 1 month or keep for 2 days under refrigeration

The assembly of this dish really needs to be seen to be believed. However, we hope the drawing makes quite clear the way in which each successive layer of onion becomes a neat little oval container for the rice and meat stuffing. Like all stuffed vegetable dishes, this takes very kindly to reheating, so it's great to make one day and serve for a buffet meal on the next.

*3 large onions, each 10 oz (275 g), peeled
vegetable oil
Approx. 10 fl. oz (275 ml/1¼ cups) meat stock
2 tbsp wine vinegar
1 rounded tbsp brown sugar*

FOR THE FILLING
*4 level tbsp Basmati or other long-grain rice
4 fl. oz (125 ml/½ cup) chicken stock
12 oz (350 g) fresh minced meat (beef or lean lamb)
2 tbsp chopped parsley
½ teasp each ground allspice (or cinnamon) and salt
10 grinds black pepper*

1. For the filling, heat 1 tbsp oil and cook the rice in it for 2 minutes, stirring, until the fat is absorbed. Add the stock, cover and cook until the liquid is absorbed – 5 minutes.
2. Put the meat into a bowl with the parsley and seasonings, then stir in the rice.
3. To prepare the onions, make a cut with a sharp knife from top to bottom on one side of each onion, through to the centre.
4. Put into a pan of boiling water and cook until the onions are soft and start to open – 10–15 minutes. Drain well, then separate each layer carefully.
5. Put a tablespoon of the filling into each hollow onion layer and roll up tightly, squeezing to close it.
6. Heat 4 tbsp oil in a heavy frying pan and sauté the onion parcels gently, turning until evenly browned.
7. Pack in one layer in a shallow casserole and barely cover with meat stock. Sprinkle with the wine vinegar and brown sugar. Cover and cook in a moderate oven, Gas 3 (325°F, 160°C), for 2 hours, removing the lid for the last half hour to caramelise the onions and concentrate the sauce.

Stuffed onion ready for the pot.

A CRAB APPLE AND MINT JELLY

This is far superior in flavour to any commercial jelly and well worth every ounce of effort required to make it. Most crab apple trees produce a larger crop than their owners can use, so it is not difficult to acquire a couple of pounds. Otherwise use well-flavoured cooking apples.

Put 2 lb (1 kg) de-stalked and washed crab apples in a preserving pan and cover with 1 pint (575 ml/2½ cups) cold water. Simmer gently, uncovered, stirring and crushing the fruit occasionally until it is absolutely tender – about an hour.

Leave to drip overnight through a scalded jelly bag. Next day, measure the juice and make up if necessary to 1 pint (575 ml/2½ cups) with water.

Put back in the preserving pan with 1 lb (450 g/2 cups) preserving or granulated sugar, the juice and grated rind of ½ lemon and 2 tbsp white wine vinegar. Stir until the sugar has dissolved then boil until it has reached setting point – about 8–10 minutes. Stir in 4 tbsp finely chopped mint. Leave in the pan for 15 minutes, stir well then pour into four small jars (heated for 10 minutes in a low oven) and cover with wax discs. When quite cold, cover with lids or cellophane.

Noisettes à la Menthe

(Lamb cutlets in mint aspic)

Serves 6–8

The noisettes will keep for 2 days under refrigeration

This is a very pretty – and tasty – dish to set before guests at a summer meal. Make a point of buying the very finest quality cutlets – the meat will then be very fine in texture and tender, qualities that are especially necessary when it is to be served cold.

12–16 first-cut lamb cutlets, trimmed of all fat and with the bone shortened to 2 inches (5 cm)
black pepper
sea salt

FOR THE MINT ASPIC
10 fl. oz (275 ml/1¼ cups) each dry white wine and strong chicken stock (completely free of fat)
8 oz (225 g) mint jelly, preferably home-made
½ oz (15 g/1 tbsp) gelatine
4 tbsp finely chopped fresh mint
1–2 tbsp fresh lemon juice

FOR THE GARNISH
small sprigs fresh mint
2 lemons

1. Sprinkle both sides of each cutlet with black pepper, then dry-fry in a very hot frying pan until each side is a rich brown – 4 minutes on each side. Drain well on paper towels, and sprinkle lightly on both sides with salt.
2. To make the mint aspic, put the wine and stock into a pan and bubble gently until reduced to 15 fl. oz (425 ml/2 cups) – about 10 minutes – then stir in the mint jelly and heat until dissolved.
3. Spoon 4 tbsp of this liquid into a bowl and when it has stopped steaming, sprinkle on the gelatine. Heat it very gently either in the microwave (40 seconds on full power) or over a steaming kettle until the liquid clears.
4. Add to the reduced liquid together with the chopped fresh mint, stir well, then add lemon juice to taste – there should be an even balance between sweet and sour.
5. Transfer to a shallow dish and chill for 20–30 minutes or until the consistency of unbeaten egg white.
6. To assemble the dish, arrange the cutlets side by side on a fairly shallow dish and spoon over the half-set aspic. Allow to set overnight.

TO SERVE
Decorate with lemon sections and sprigs of fresh mint.

ON SKEWERS

Use *flat* rather than round stainless metal skewers: the latter do not hold the ingredients firmly and instead allow them to twist round.

Use *damp* rather than dry wooden skewers: the latter might become charred by the heat of the grill before the kebabs were sufficiently cooked.

KEBABS GREEK-STYLE

This alternative vinaigrette is fragrant with all the perfumes of a Greek hillside in June – it's all due to the rigani it contains. It is excellent for a marinade for chunks of lamb as well as meatballs: leave the meat in it to tenderise for 2–24 hours, the longer the better.

Purée together in a food processor or blender 1 medium peeled onion cut in 1 inch (2·5 cm) cubes, 3 fl. oz (75 ml/⅓ cup) olive oil, 3 tbsp fresh lemon juice, 1 large bayleaf, 2 level teasp dried rigani (or leaf origano), 2 level teasp sea salt, 20 grinds black pepper.

Kefta Kebabs

(Skewered lamb with courgettes)

Serves 6

The raw meat mixture will keep for 24 hours under refrigeration

To achieve just the right texture for these little meatballs, we prefer to buy the lamb cubed rather than minced, then pulse it together with the other ingredients on the food processor. These kebabs make superb party fare: they can be served either hot off the grill, or at room temperature.

small bunch parsley, approx. 1½ oz (40 g)
1 clove garlic
1½ lb (675 g) cubed lean lamb
1 large slice brown or white bread, torn up
1 medium (5 oz/150 g) onion, quartered
1½ teasp dried mint
salt
½ teasp ground allspice
3 tbsp pine kernels, toasted
1 lb (450 g) large courgettes

FOR THE VINAIGRETTE
4 tbsp olive oil
2 tbsp wine vinegar
½ teasp made mustard
10 grinds black pepper
pinch sugar

1. To make the meatballs, put the parsley and garlic in the food processor and process until finely chopped.
2. Add the trimmed meat, bread, onion, mint, 1 teasp salt and the allspice, then pulse until it just clings together. Turn into a bowl, and stir in the pine kernels. Chill, covered, for at least 1 hour.
3. Make the vinaigrette by whisking all the ingredients together in a bowl for 1 minute, adding ¼ teasp salt.
4. Score the courgettes lengthwise with a cannelle knife, blanch whole for 2 minutes in a saucepan of boiling water, then drain and refresh with cold water. Pat dry, then cut into twelve slices and toss in the vinaigrette. Leave to marinate for 45 minutes.
5. Form the chilled lamb mixture into eighteen balls. Thread three meatballs and two slices of courgette alternately on each of six skewers. Lay on a wire cake rack and chill until required.
6. To cook the kebabs, brush with the remaining vinaigrette marinade and grill briskly for 15 minutes, turning once or twice.

POULTRY PLUS

Take a fine young bird or two and create a quartet of poultry dishes, each with its own special appeal, be it a stuffing, a sauce or a glaze. Alternatively, joint your bird first and serve it later, hot from the oven without any last-minute attention. Other Master Class dishes we have selected use cooked chicken and turkey in imaginative ways, so you would never know that the meat was 'second time around'. We end with centrepiece salads: exotic flavours and dramatic colours combining to make beautiful salad 'compositions' that can serve as a main summer dish or a winter starter.

Poulet Fendu Farci au Four

(Spatchcock chicken stuffed with chicken livers and walnuts)

Serves 8

Cooked chicken will keep for 2 days under refrigeration

The chicken liver and walnut pâté that is cunningly tucked under the skin not only perfumes the flesh but also helps to produce a rich, mahogany-brown bird. The technique is simple if you follow the words and pictures. And as the birds are split before cooking, they are very easy to portion at the table.

2 × 3½ lb (1·75 kg) chickens
5 tbsp olive oil
2 teasp dried Herbes de Provence
sea salt
black pepper

FOR THE STUFFING
4 oz (125 g/½ cup) butter or margarine
1 large (8 oz/225 g) onion, finely chopped
1 large clove garlic, finely chopped
8 oz (225 g) chicken livers, lightly grilled
6 oz (175 g/3 cups) fresh breadcrumbs
2 tbsp chopped fresh tarragon
2 eggs, beaten
4 oz (125 g/1 cup) walnuts, finely chopped

1. To make the stuffing, heat the fat and sauté the onion and garlic until soft and golden brown, then tip the contents of the pan into the food processor with all the remaining ingredients (except the walnuts), adding 1 teasp salt and 20 grinds black pepper.
2. Process until puréed then pulse in the walnuts, and turn into a bowl.
3. To prepare the birds, using poultry shears or kitchen scissors, split them the entire length of the back as near as possible to the centre of the backbone.
4. Turn the birds over with breast uppermost and, using the heel of the hand, flatten them. Don't be gentle as you want to break the internal bones so as to accommodate the maximum amount of stuffing.
5. Starting at the neck, slip your fingers between the skin and the flesh over one side of the breast and work them towards the tail to loosen the skin, then gently free the skin a little at a time from around the leg, leaving skin attached at tip of drumstick. Do the same with the other side of the bird.
6. To stuff the birds, allow half the 'pâté' for each bird. Take a handful of stuffing at a time and force it into place, pushing with the fingers of one hand beneath the

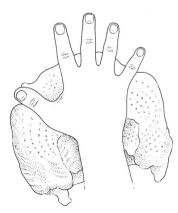

Cut along the backbone of the chicken.

Open the bird out and break the breastbone with your hand.

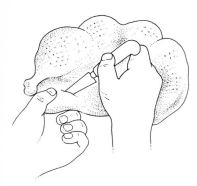

Cut a slit in the flap of skin.

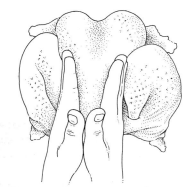

Push end of leg through slit and reform bird.

skin while moulding and forcing with the other from the outside. Stuff the drumstick and thighs well before worrying about the breast.

7. When all of the stuffing is in place, fold the neck skin flap over the throat opening and tuck it beneath the bird.

8. With a small, sharp pointed knife, pierce the web of skin and thin flesh between the inside of the thigh and the tip of the breast, making a slit just large enough to receive the drumstick tip, then force the drumstick gently up and push its tip through the slit to the underside, 'pinning' it in place. Repeat on the other side.

9. Place the birds in a roasting tin and mould the surface with your hands to force the skin and stuffing into a plump version of its natural form.

10. Rub the chickens on both sides with the olive oil, then sprinkle with the herbs. Leave for 1–2 hours.

11. To cook the birds, sprinkle them with sea salt and black pepper and roast in a preheated oven at Gas 8 (450°F, 230°C) for 10 minutes. Turn the oven down to Gas 5 (375°F, 190°C) for a further 40–50 minutes.

12. About 30 minutes after you have put the birds in the oven, start basting every 10 minutes. The birds are cooked when the juices run clear when the thigh is pierced with a skewer.

TO CARVE AND SERVE

Split the bird in two using a very sharp knife, cutting gently through the skin and stuffing. To remove the legs, cut along curved creases between the thighs and the body. Serve (reformed if desired), on a metal or wooden platter. No gravy is necessary. This is also delicious cold.

Canard de Barbarie Roti, Sauce Maçao

(Twice-roasted duck with an apricot and cherry sauce)

Serves 6–8

The duck will freeze for 3 months or keep for 2 days under refrigeration

Before we tried it, we had strong reservations about the very concept of twice-roasted duck. But with the memory still fresh of an epic struggle to carve a recalcitrant duck before our hungry guests, we decided to put it to the test. The results, we can report, were brilliant. The bird is carved at leisure earlier in the day, and then a brief final cook brings it to the table crisp of skin yet moist within. The sauce is superb too.

APPLE AND CALVADOS SAUCE

This is a good alternative sauce for duck.

½ pint (275 ml/1¼ cups) duck stock (see opposite)
2 shallots, finely chopped
2 oz (50 g/½ cup) walnuts, finely chopped
1 tbsp duck fat
½ teasp salt
8 grinds black pepper
2 teasp flour
2½ fl. oz (65 ml/¼ cup) Calvados or brandy
grated rind ½ lemon
2 tbsp lemon juice

FOR THE GARNISH
3 crisp eating apples, peeled, cored and cut into ⅜ inch (1 cm) thick rings
1 tbsp each duck fat and brown sugar

1. After stage 1 of cooking the ducks has been completed, pour off all the fat into a basin.
2. Add the stock to the pan juices, then stir well and set aside.
3. In a small heavy pan sauté the shallots and the walnuts in the duck fat until golden, season then sprinkle with the flour and cook until it turns a pale brown.
4. Stir in the stock and pan juices and simmer for 3 minutes, then add the Calvados, lemon rind and juice and simmer for a further 3 minutes.
5. To complete the garnish, gently sauté the apple rings in the duck fat until tender, sprinkling them on both sides with the brown sugar. Cook until they are tender and caramelised.

2 × 5-5½ lb (2·25–2·5 kg) ducks, excess fat removed, and neck and giblets reserved for stock (see below)
salt
1 orange, quartered
4 eating apples, peeled, cored and thickly sliced

FOR THE DUCK STOCK
reserved giblets
15 fl. oz (425 ml/2 cups) strong chicken stock
1 carrot, sliced
1 whole onion
1 sprig parsley

FOR THE SAUCE
3 oz (75 g/⅓ cup) sugar
4 fl. oz (125 ml/½ cup) white wine vinegar
2 inch (5 cm) piece fresh ginger, peeled and julienned (see page 100)
4 oz (125 g/¾ cup) dried apricots, julienned
15 fl. oz (425 ml/2 cups) duck stock (see below)
4 fl. oz (125 ml/½ cup) dry white wine
3 rounded tbsp apricot jam
1 can cherries, Morello if possible, stoned and drained
black pepper to taste

1. To roast the ducks – Stage 1. On the morning of the day you intend to serve the ducks, dry them thoroughly inside and out with paper towels, then wrap in more towels and leave for 30 minutes.
2. Remove the towels, prick the ducks all over with a sharp fork, and arrange side by side on a rack over a roasting tin. Sprinkle with salt, put two pieces of orange inside each duck, then roast in a moderate oven, Gas 4 (350°F, 180°C), for 2½ hours or until the juices run clear when a leg is pierced.
3. Pour off the fat. (This may be kept for future use, or adds flavour to an alternative sauce, see opposite.)
4. While the ducks are roasting, put the giblets in a pan with the other stock ingredients, cover and simmer for 1½ hours, then strain and bubble the stock until it is reduced to 10 fl. oz (275 ml/1¼ cups).
5. To make the sauce, in a small heavy saucepan, dissolve the sugar in the vinegar and boil, swirling the pan, until it looks syrupy – about 3–4 minutes – then add the ginger, apricots, duck stock and wine, and simmer until it is reduced by about a quarter.
6. Stir in the apricot jam and cherries and season with salt and pepper to taste, then simmer until it has thickened slightly again. Set aside until required.
7. Carve the ducks when they have cooled for about 10 minutes. Halve them, cut out the backbone, then divide in four by cutting diagonally between the breast and the leg so each person gets a portion of the breast.

MASTER CLASS CHICKEN STOCK

Make a gallon of this superb golden 'brew' and you'll never say 'stock cube' again.

3–4 sets of chicken giblets
the last wing joints, previously cut from roasted chickens, then frozen (if available)
any carcases from roast birds in the freezer
1 whole or ½ boiling fowl, with feet
3 large onions, peeled but left whole
6 carrots, each cut lengthwise into four
leaves and top 2 inches (5 cm) of the stalks from a bunch celery
4 very soft ripe tomatoes (or 1 tbsp tomato purée)
2 oz (50 g) bunch parsley, including the stalks
1 tbsp salt
½ teasp white pepper

1. Put the giblets, wing tips, broken-up cooked carcases, fowl and feet into a large soup pan and cover with 8–9 pints (4·5–5 litres/20–22 cups) water – sufficient to come within an inch or two of the top of the pan.
2. Bring slowly to the boil, then remove the scum from the top with a wet metal spoon. Add the vegetables, parsley and seasonings, bring back to the boil, cover and simmer for at least 3 hours on top of the stove, 4 hours in the oven. (An oven set at Gas 2, 300°F, 150°C should keep the liquid at a slow bubble.)
3. At the end of the cooking time, lift out the giblets with a slotted spoon and put in a bowl. Lift out and discard any cooked carcases. Remove the cooked fowl and reserve for another purpose. Place a coarse sieve over a large bowl and pour the stock through to separate it from the vegetables (discard as all their goodness and flavour will be in the stock). If freezer space is at a premium, the stock can be boiled down to half its volume. In any event, chill it

8. Arrange the portions in the cleaned roasting tin on top of the sliced apples. At this stage, the ducks can be refrigerated.
9. To roast the ducks – Stage 2. About 1½ hours before serving, remove the duck portions from the refrigerator and leave to stand for 1 hour.
10. Preheat the oven to Gas 7 (425°F, 220°C) and roast the ducks for 25 minutes until crisp.

TO SERVE
Serve hot with the re-heated sauce.

Chicken Roasted in the French Style

Serves 5–6

The chicken will freeze for 3 months or will keep for 2 days under refrigeration

Roasting a chicken makes it crisp and golden; casseroling it produces a succulent flesh. Trust the canny French to combine these two methods as in this recipe. The chicken is equally good served hot or cold.

1 × 4½ lb (2·25 kg) roasting chicken
small bunch parsley
1 eating apple, quartered
1 medium carrot, finely sliced
1 medium onion, finely sliced
1 pint (575 ml/2½ cups) strong hot chicken stock
sea salt
2 teasp cornflour mixed with 3 tbsp Amontillado sherry

1. Remove the chicken fat from the cavity and insert the bunch of parsley and the quartered apple. Place the bird in a roasting tin just large enough to hold it, and strew the carrot and onion slices around it.
2. Pour the hot stock around the bird (it should half fill the roasting tin), sprinkle lightly with sea salt, and lay the chicken fat on top of the breast.
3. Roast the chicken in a preheated oven at Gas 5 (375°F/190°C), basting it with the stock every 20 minutes. Allow 20 minutes to the pound (450 g), plus 20 minutes – that is, 1 hour 50 minutes for a 4½ lb (2·25 kg) bird. At the end of the cooking time, the bird should be a rich brown and the liquid should have evaporated, leaving only fat and the thickened juices with the browned vegetables in the tin.
4. Transfer the bird to a serving dish and keep hot. Pour the fat from the tin into a small bowl and refrigerate for future use (for roasting potatoes).

overnight so that the congealed fat can be removed next day. Strip the meat from the giblets and wings and refrigerate or freeze for a chicken soup.

Divide the defatted stock into convenient amounts, allowing 2 pints (1·25 litres/5 cups) for 4–6 servings, or 1 pint (575 ml/2½ cups) if condensed. Portion, label and freeze.

5. To make the sauce, put the roasting tin over medium heat and deglaze it with ½ pint (275 ml/1¼ cups) hot water, stirring it well to release the concentrated juices clinging to the bottom.
6. Pour the contents of the roasting tin through a sieve on to the liquid cornflour in a small pan, pressing down well to get all the juices from the vegetables.
7. Bubble this gravy for 3 minutes, taste and add salt and pepper only if necessary – remember it is made up of concentrated stock.

Duck Oriental

Serves 4

Duck cut in quarters, marinated, then roasted to produce a succulent dish, crispy brown on the outside, tender within.

1 duck, approx 4–5 lb (2½ kg) in weight, quartered

FOR THE MARINADE
3 tbsp soya sauce
3 tbsp soft brown sugar
2 fl. oz (50 ml/¼ cup) dry sherry
3 tbsp lemon juice
2 inch (5 cm) piece fresh ginger, grated
2 tbsp olive oil
3 tbsp water

1. Place the duck portions in a shallow dish.
2. In a small basin, whisk together all the marinade ingredients. Spoon over the duck and leave for at least 4 hours or overnight in the refrigerator, basting occasionally.
3. 1½ hours before you want to serve the duck, pre-heat the oven to Gas 5 (375°F, 190°C). Transfer the duck to a roasting tin and pour over the marinade. Cook for 1¼–1½ hours, basting occasionally, until the duck portions are a rich golden brown.

OLIVE OIL

Olive oil gives a golden hue to both roast and sautéed chicken.

If you find the flavour of the olive oil too pervasive for your taste, use one part to three parts of a flavourless oil such as sunflower.

There is no need to use the most expensive 'extra virgin' olive oil for frying. Use the cheaper 'pure olive oil' which is golden rather than greeny-gold in colour.

Pollo in Pepitoria

(Chicken with white wine and ground almond sauce)

Serves 6–8

The chicken will freeze for 3 months or keep for 2 days under refrigeration

Ground almonds (or almond flour as it was known) was often used as a thickener in medieval cookery, before the invention of the roux-based sauce. The practice has survived to this day in Spanish cuisine as in this superb dish.

*6–8 chicken breast portions on the bone, rib cage trimmed
and skinned
2 oz (50 g/½ cup) flour
1 teasp salt
15 grinds black pepper
3 tbsp olive oil
1 large (10 oz/275 g) onion, finely chopped
1 bayleaf
10 fl. oz (275 ml/1¼ cups) each fairly dry white wine and good
chicken stock
2½ oz (65 g) ground almonds
2 hard-boiled egg yolks
2 cloves garlic, crushed
a few threads (or ¼ teasp powdered) saffron or turmeric*

FOR THE GARNISH
*2 oz (50 g/½ cup) slivered almonds, toasted (see page 126)
1 hard-boiled egg, grated and mixed with 1 tbsp chopped
parsley*

1. Put the flour, salt and pepper into a plastic bag and shake the breasts in it, one at a time, until evenly coated.
2. Fry breasts in the hot oil until a rich golden brown. Drain and transfer to a baking tin large enough to hold them in one layer.
3. To make the sauce, sauté the onion in the same oil (covering the pan) until a rich golden brown and beginning to 'melt'.
4. Add the bayleaf and wine and bubble for 3 minutes to concentrate the flavour, then add the stock, cover and leave to simmer gently.
5. Put the ground almonds, hard-boiled egg yolks, garlic and saffron or turmeric in the bowl of the food processor. Process until pasty, then add a cupful of the simmering liquid and process until a smooth creamy mixture is formed.
6. Return to the sauce pan, stir well and leave to cool until just before serving. This can all be done earlier in the day.
7. To complete the cooking, preheat the oven to Gas 5 (375°F, 190°C), and bake the chicken for 20 minutes.

TO SERVE

Reheat the sauce gently until simmering, then discard the bayleaf. Arrange the chicken breasts on a heated platter and coat with hot sauce. Scatter with the toasted almonds and the egg and parsley mixture.

Pepitoria de Gallina

(Casserole of chicken Spanish style)

Serves 6

The chicken will freeze for 3 months or keep for 2 days under refrigeration

This is a typical Spanish chicken sauté with its garnish of plump green olives.

3 fine young chickens, each 2–2¼ lb (1 kg) net weight, cut in half through the breast
1 heaped tbsp flour seasoned with 1 teasp paprika and 15 grinds black pepper
3 tbsp olive oil
sea salt
1 large (7 oz/200 g) onion, finely chopped
1 fat clove garlic, chopped
10 fl. oz (275 ml/1¼ cups) Passata (sieved tomatoes)
1 tbsp tomato purée
1 fat red pepper, halved, seeded and cut in ½ inch (1·25 cm) squares
5 fl. oz (150 ml/⅔ cup) each chicken stock and red wine (e.g. Rioja)
2 teasp dark brown sugar
15 grinds black pepper
8 oz (225 g/2½ cups) button mushrooms, stalks trimmed level with caps
4 oz (125 g/1 cup) green olives, stoned and roughly chopped
8 oz (225 g) petits pois

1. Thinly coat the chicken halves with the seasoned flour, patting off any excess.
2. Brown the chicken pieces on all sides in the hot oil, lift out and arrange breast side up in a roasting tin. Sprinkle lightly with sea salt.
3. In the same oil, gently sauté the onion and garlic until soft and golden then add the tomatoes, tomato purée, red pepper squares, stock, wine, sugar, pepper and 1 teasp salt.
4. Simmer uncovered until the mixture is thick and juicy – about 15 minutes – then pour over and around the chicken halves. They should be half covered with the liquid. If not, add a little more stock. (The dish can now be refrigerated

WINE FOR THE KITCHEN

With a moderately priced wine it makes good kitchen sense to buy a litre bottle, drink some and use a glass or two of it for cooking. Or buy two normal bottles instead of one. If leftover wine is re-corked and refrigerated, it will keep in good cooking condition (but not for drinking) for up to 2 weeks.

Or use 'wine in a box' which is automatically re-sealed after use and will keep well for both drinking and cooking for up to 2 months. The wine in these boxes is usually a 'vin de pays' – a reliable local wine of moderate price made according to strict regulations, though not as highly rated as VDQS or AC wines.

at this point for several hours. Leave at room temperature for several hours before cooking.)

5. To complete the cooking, preheat the oven to Gas 4 (350°F, 180°C), cover the roasting tin tightly with foil and bake the chicken for 45 minutes, basting once. Uncover, add the mushrooms, olives and peas, and baste again. Re-cover and cook for a further 15 minutes. The dish can now be kept hot for up to 30 minutes in a very low oven, Gas $\frac{1}{2}$ (250°F, 120°C).

TO SERVE

Arrange the half birds on heated plates, surrounded by the sauce.

A DELICIOUS NON-DAIRY NUT CREAM

Put 5 fl. oz (150 ml/$\frac{2}{3}$ cup) very hot water and a nut of margarine into the blender, together with a pinch of sugar and 2 oz (50 g/$\frac{1}{2}$ cup) broken cashew nuts. Blend for 1 minute at maximum speed. Pour into a jug and refrigerate for several hours until thickened. It can be frozen.

To use instead of milk – for a custard, for instance – thin down with water.

Just before serving, add to sauce and reheat but do not let it boil. This can be used for chicken or veal dishes in particular.

Suprêmes de Poulardes Farcies

(Sauté of chicken breasts with a spiced fruit stuffing)

Serves 6–8

Leftovers will freeze for up to 1 month. Keeps under refrigeration for 2 days

This is a brilliant presentation for a special meal. As you cut through the crunchy nut coating, you reveal a juicy filling of spiced fruits. The entire preparation of the dish – including the sauce – can be completed hours ahead, and then it needs only 20 minutes in the oven before bringing to table. Serve on a bed of watercress.

6–8 boned and skinned chicken breasts with the wing attached
2 oz (50 g/$\frac{1}{2}$ cup) flour
1 teasp salt
2 eggs, beaten with 2 teasp water
4 oz (125 g/1 cup) fine dried breadcrumbs
4 oz (125 g/1 cup) dry roasted peanuts, chopped
6 tbsp sunflower oil, for frying

FOR THE STUFFING

1 large (10 oz/275 g) onion, finely chopped
2 oz (50 g/$\frac{1}{4}$ cup) butter or margarine
2 Golden Delicious apples, peeled, cored and diced
$\frac{1}{2}$ teasp each cinnamon, dried tarragon and sea salt
10 grinds black pepper
1 teasp grated lemon rind
8 dried dessert figs, finely chopped

FOR THE SAUCE
2 oz (50 g/¼ cup) butter or margarine
4 shallots (or bulbs of 6 spring onions), finely chopped
8 oz (225 g/2½ cups) button mushrooms, very thinly sliced
4 tbsp Amontillado sherry
6 tbsp white wine
5 fl. oz (150 ml/⅔ cup) chicken stock
1 oz (25 g/2 tbsp) flour
good pinch each of salt, grated nutmeg and white pepper
5 fl. oz (150 ml/⅔ cup) double (or non-dairy) cream
(or nut cream)

1. To make the stuffing, sauté the onion in the fat over moderate heat until soft and golden, then add the apple dice, seasonings and lemon rind. Stir well, cover and simmer for approximately 10 minutes until the apples are tender.
2. Remove from the heat and stir in the chopped figs. Leave until it stops steaming.
3. To prepare the chicken breasts, with the tip of a sharp knife, make a deep slit along the thick edge of each. Insert a tbsp of the stuffing into the 'pocket' then press the edges together to seal.
4. Have the salted flour, beaten eggs and mixed crumbs and nuts side by side in three shallow containers. Lay each chicken breast in turn in the flour and gently turn it over so that it is coated on all sides. Brush with the beaten egg then coat thickly with the mixed crumbs and nuts. Refrigerate for at least 1 hour to set the coating.
5. Fry the breasts in the oil until a rich golden brown on all sides. Drain on kitchen paper.
6. To complete the cooking, arrange the browned breasts side by side in a roasting tin and bake at Gas 4 (350°F, 180°C) for 20 minutes.
7. Meanwhile, to make the sauce, melt half the fat and cook the shallots for 5 minutes until softened and beginning to colour.
8. Add the sliced mushrooms and cook a further 3 minutes until beginning to soften, then stir in 3 tbsp of the sherry and cook until only 1 tbsp of liquid remains.
9. Add the wine and stock and simmer a further 10 minutes, then whisk in the remaining fat, creamed with the flour, a teaspoon at a time, bubbling constantly.
10. Add the remaining tbsp of sherry and the seasonings, and stir in the cream.

TO REHEAT
Slowly bring the sauce to the simmer, but do not boil.

CHESTNUT OPTIONS

1. Whole, canned in brine. Drain and use as required.
2. 'Crème de Marron' – chestnut purée, sweetened heavily and flavoured with vanilla.
3. 'Purée de Marron Nature' – puréed then canned with a little glucose. The solid pack needs mashing down with a large fork or processing on a food processor until like thick mashed potato.
4. Dried chestnuts – 12 oz (350 g), soaked overnight in water to cover, is equivalent to 2 lb (1 kg) fresh chestnuts in the shell.
5. Fresh chestnuts – 2 lb (1 kg) in the shell is approx. $1\frac{1}{2}$ lb (675 g) shelled weight.

To shell, with a small pointed knife, cut through the skin round the top of the nut. Drop into boiling water. As soon as the cut widens to show the flesh take out one at a time and remove the inner and outer skin – very easy if nuts are fresh.

Suprême de Poulet à l'Ardèche

(Marinated chicken breasts on a bed of chestnut purée)

Serves 6

The prepared raw dish will keep for 24 hours under refrigeration

The genesis of this innovative dish lies in a recent visit to the Ardèche region of France, famous for its magnificent chestnuts, in particular the marrons glacés which are perhaps the world's most expensive sweetmeats.

6 × 4 oz (125 g) chicken breasts, boned and skinned
2 oz (50 g/$\frac{1}{2}$ cup) plain flour
1 small can chestnuts in brine, drained

FOR THE MARINADE
1 medium onion, grated
1 clove garlic, crushed
1 tbsp light soy sauce
2 tbsp each Amontillado sherry and fresh lemon juice
2 tbsp light brown sugar
3 rounded tbsp mango and ginger chutney

FOR THE CHESTNUT PURÉE
1 × 15 oz (425 g) can natural chestnut purée
2 oz (50 g/$\frac{1}{4}$ cup) butter or margarine
1 medium (5 oz/150 g) onion, finely chopped
$\frac{1}{2}$ teasp salt

FOR THE GARNISH
1 large ripe mango, cut into segments

1. At least 2 hours before cooking, put the flour in a plastic bag and coat each breast in turn by shaking it in the bag.
2. Arrange the breasts in a shallow dish and slash the flesh at 1 inch (2·5 cm) intervals. Lay the chestnuts on top.
3. Whisk all the marinade ingredients together then spoon over the chicken and chestnuts. Leave to marinate, basting once or twice.
4. To prepare the chestnut purée, turn the contents of the can into a basin and mash down with a fork.
5. Melt the fat and sauté the onion until soft and golden, then gradually blend it into the purée together with the salt, until it has the consistency of mashed potato (this can also be done in the food processor).
6. Spread the purée on the bottom of an oven-to-table casserole large enough to hold the chicken breasts in one layer.
7. Lay the breasts and chestnuts on top and spoon over the marinade. (May be left until 1 hour before the meal.)
8. To cook, preheat the oven to Gas 4 (350°F, 180°C), and bake the chicken, covered, for 30 minutes, then uncover,

baste with any free juices, and allow to caramelise for a further 10 minutes.

TO SERVE

Serve each breast sitting on a bed of the chestnut purée, decorating each with mango segments and two or three whole chestnuts.

THREE-CHEESE FEUILLETON

Serves 6

Make and bake exactly as for the Turkey Feuilleton, but use the filling below.

6 oz (175 g/1½ cups) Cheddar
   cheese, grated
8 oz (225 g/1 cup) low fat soft
   cheese
1 oz (25 g/¼ cup) blue cheese,
   crumbled
1 egg, beaten
½ teasp paprika pepper
1 tbsp fresh chopped parsley (or
   fresh coriander)
1 tbsp fresh snipped chives (or
   1 teasp dried chives)

Put the cheeses into a bowl, then stir in the egg, paprika and herbs.

Turkey Feuilleton

Serves 6

Serve freshly baked

This is a variation on the turkey pie theme. Layers of puff pastry are filled with a tasty turkey (or chicken) filling. A slice of the feuilleton makes a delicious informal starter. For a more formal presentation, shape each little feuilleton into a 4 × 2 inch (10 × 5 cm) rectangle.

*1 lb (450 g) puff pastry
1 egg yolk, mixed with 1 teasp water
2 tbsp sesame seeds*

FOR THE FILLING
*8 oz (225 g) tiny button mushrooms, stalks removed
4 oz (125 g) haricots verts
2 tbsp sesame oil
salt
8 grinds black pepper
12 oz (350 g) cooked turkey, cut in bite-sized pieces
½ small (4 oz/125 g) onion, finely chopped
1 oz (25 g/2 tbsp) butter or margarine
2 tbsp flour
5 fl. oz (150 ml/⅔ cup) each strong chicken stock and dry
white wine
good pinch nutmeg
⅛ teasp white pepper
1 tbsp chopped fresh parsley*

1. For the filling, stir-fry the mushrooms and haricots verts in the sesame oil for 3–4 minutes or until barely tender. Season with ½ teasp salt and the black pepper, then turn into a bowl with the turkey.
2. Sauté the onion in the fat until soft and golden then stir in the flour, followed by the stock, wine, nutmeg, white pepper and ½ teasp salt, whisking constantly until thickened. Bubble for 3 minutes, then stir in the parsley and mix with the turkey, stirring gently. Allow to cool.
3. Divide the pastry into two and roll each half into a rectangle measuring approx. 14 × 8 inches (35 × 20 cm). The pastry should be thin.

4. Lay one rectangle on a baking tray and spread with the filling, leaving 1 inch (2·5 cm) of pastry clear all the way round.

5. Dampen this margin with cold water, then lay the second rectangle carefully on top. Seal the pastry all the way round by pressing down on it with the side of the hand, then flake the edges with the back of a knife blade. Make cuts through the top layer at 2 inch (5 cm) intervals to allow steam to escape. Chill until ready to bake. (The feuilleton can now be refrigerated for up to 6 hours.)

6. Preheat the oven to Gas 8 (450°F, 230°C). Paint the egg yolk and water glaze all over the top of the feuilleton and scatter with the sesame seeds.

7. Bake for 15 minutes then turn the temperature down to Gas 6 (400°F, 200°C) for a further 15–20 minutes, when the feuilleton should be well risen, crisp to the touch and richly browned. Serve in slices.

SOY SAUCE

This essential flavouring is made from fermented soy beans with wheat or barley, salt, sugar and yeast. The words 'naturally fermented' or 'naturally brewed' on the bottle tell you that it has been prepared by the traditional time-consuming fermentation method which gives the sauce its characteristic flavour, rather than being artificially coloured and flavoured with added ingredients.

Light soy sauce: looks pleasing with chicken, fish and veal.

Dark soy sauce: is more suitable for beef.

Master Class Chicken Spring Rolls

Serves 6–8   Makes 12 spring rolls

Pancakes will freeze for 3 months

We can't guarantee the authenticity of their pedigree, but we can say without fear of contradiction that these delicate crêpes, stuffed and fried in the Chinese style, are utterly delicious. The filling is also good to spoon on rice and pasta.

4 oz (125 g/1 cup) plain flour
2 eggs
oil
8 fl. oz (225 ml/1 cup) water
2 level teasp salt

FOR THE FILLING
2 tbsp oil
2 tbsp cashew nuts (or almonds), coarsely chopped
1 medium onion, peeled, halved, then sliced paper thin
1 large green pepper, halved, seeded, pith removed and thinly sliced
1 small (8 oz/225 g) can pineapple titbits or pieces in juice
8–10 oz (225–275 g) cooked chicken or turkey breast, cut in bite-sized chunks
2 tbsp sultanas (or raisins)
1 level tbsp cornflour
2 tbsp vinegar
1 level tbsp soft brown sugar
2 tbsp light soy sauce

SETTING THE SEAL

Reserve a little batter to use as a 'glue' to seal each spring roll.

THE BAKING OPTION

Perhaps not as crisp as deep-frying, but certainly more convenient for large numbers, spring rolls can be baked most successfully in the oven. Preheat the oven to Gas 5 (375°F, 190°C. Arrange the spring rolls 1 inch (2.5 cm) apart on oiled trays. Brush all visible surfaces with hot oil (heated for 3 minutes in a small pan), then bake for 25–30 minutes until crisp and golden.

1. Make and cook the 'spring roll' crêpes as described on page 30, using flour, eggs, 2 teasp oil, water and salt. The recipe should make 12 crêpes.
2. To make the filling, heat the oil and cook the nuts until golden. Lift out with a slotted spoon and drain on absorbent paper.
3. In the same oil cook the onion until softened but not brown – about 5 minutes – then add the pepper and cook a further 3 minutes, stirring. Add the drained pineapple (keep the juice), chicken and sultanas and heat through gently.
4. Put the cornflour in a small bowl, and stir in the vinegar, 5 fl. oz (150 ml/$\frac{2}{3}$ cup) pineapple juice, sugar and soy sauce. Stir into the contents of the pan and simmer 3 minutes, then stir in the nuts. Allow to go cold. (The filling can now be used at once, or refrigerated.)
5. To stuff the pancakes, lay each pancake in turn, browner side uppermost, on a board. Put a rounded tablespoon of the filling in a long strip 1 inch (2·5 cm) away from the edge of the pancake nearest you. Turn in the sides to seal in the mixture and roll into a cylinder.
6. Repeat until all twelve pancakes are stuffed. They can now be refrigerated until required (maximum 12 hours).
7. To deep-fry the spring rolls, put as many pancakes as will fit into a frying basket and lower into a pan one-third full of oil, heated until it will brown a cube of bread in 40 seconds (375°F/190°C) – the same temperature as for frying chips.
8. Fry steadily until a rich brown, then drain on crumpled kitchen paper. Fry the remainder of the pancakes.
9. Transfer the cooked spring rolls to a shallow serving dish and keep hot in a low oven, Gas 1 (275°F, 140°C), for up to 30 minutes.

Chicken and Avocado Exotica

Serves 6–8

COLD CHICKEN

A 4 lb (2 kg) roast or poached chicken will yield about 1½ lb (675 g) meat – enough to make this unusual chicken salad for eight people. For a special meal, however, we prefer to use only the white meat.

The 1½ lb (675 g) of raw chicken flesh can be cooked in 10 minutes on full power in a microwave oven, or in 35 minutes at a moderate setting in a conventional oven. It should be sprinkled with a little lemon juice, and covered with clingfilm for the microwave or with foil for a regular oven. The cooked chicken should be quite cold before mixing with the other ingredients.

This doesn't freeze but leftovers may be kept for 2 days under refrigeration

With an accompaniment of honey and walnut knots (see page 21), this is a good dish to come home to after the cinema or theatre.

1½ lb (675 g) chicken flesh
1 large or 2 medium, ripe avocados
2 tbsp fresh lemon juice
½ pint (275 ml/1¼ cups) mild mayonnaise
1 tbsp medium-strength curry powder
2 rounded tbsp mango and ginger chutney
1 teasp grated fresh ginger root

FOR THE RICE SALAD
8 oz (225 g/1⅓ cups) Basmati (Indian long-grain) rice
15 fl. oz (425 ml/2 cups) chicken stock
4 tbsp Master Class vinaigrette dressing (see page 122)
1 large red pepper, seeded and finely diced
3 rounded tbsp seedless raisins
2 oz (50 g/½ cup) dry-roasted peanuts, chopped

TO GARNISH THE SALAD
2 fresh grapefruit, peeled and sectioned
1 bunch watercress

1. Remove any skin from the chicken and cut the flesh into 2 × 1 inch (5 × 2.5 cm) strips.
2. Peel, halve, and stone the avocado, cut it into thick slices and mix gently with the lemon juice.
3. In a large bowl, mix the mayonnaise, curry powder, chutney and fresh ginger, then gently stir in the chicken and avocado, cover and chill until required.
4. To make the rice salad, cook the rice (covered) in the chicken stock for 15 minutes. Remove from the heat but leave covered to steam for a further 15 minutes. Fluff up with a fork.
5. Put the hot rice into a bowl and mix gently with the vinaigrette, using a large fork and spoon.
6. Stir in the red pepper dice, raisins and nuts, then refrigerate in a covered container for several hours.

TO SERVE
Spoon the rice salad round the edge of an oval platter and pile the chicken salad in the centre. Just before serving, decorate with the grapefruit segments and sprigs of watercress.

RIGHT: *Suprêmes de Poulardes Farcies (page 90), a Timbale of Saffron Rice (page 120) and Ribbons of Courgette and Carrot in a Lime and Coriander Glaze (page 105)*

SESAME OIL AND THE CHINESE CUISINE

The haunting flavour of this aromatic oil enhances almost any dish that is cooked in the Chinese fashion. But it should be used sparingly as it has a particularly powerful flavour – similar in its pervasiveness to huile de noix (walnut oil) – that can rather overwhelm the other ingredients in a dish. Chinese chefs will use just a scant tablespoon of it (together with rather more of a tasteless oil such as peanut) to fry chicken or rice; or they will spoon a little over meat or fish as part of a marinade. More often they will use it as a 'garnish', sprinkling a little of it just before serving on to cooked noodles or a vegetable soup, or together with some toasted sesame seeds, into a stir-fry of delicate vegetables.

LEFT: *Carré d'Agneau aux Beaux Champs* (*page 67*), *Courgettes en Barque* (*page 107*), *Pommes de Terre au Cidre* (*page 113*) and *Stir Fry of Mangetout and Petits Pois* (*page 100*)

Fettucine alla Nizza

(Noodle, chicken and fresh basil salad)

Serves 6–8

The salad will keep for 1 day under refrigeration

Like all pasta salads, this needs several hours in the refrigerator to mature in flavour, but always bring back to room temperature before it is served.

$1\frac{1}{2}$ *lb* (675 g) *boned and skinned chicken breast meat*
freshly ground black pepper
3 teasp each sesame oil and light soy sauce
marinade of 4 tbsp sunflower oil mixed with 2 tbsp red wine vinegar and $\frac{1}{2}$ teasp salt
1 lb (450 g) *aubergine*
olive oil
8 oz (225 g) *fresh fettucine, cooked then rinsed in cold water and well drained*
4 oz (125 g/1 cup) *Calamata or Provençal black olives*
1 × 14 oz (400 g) *can red peppers in brine, drained and cut in narrow strips*

FOR THE DRESSING
3 fl. oz (75 ml/$\frac{1}{3}$ cup) *virgin olive oil*
3 tbsp red wine vinegar
1 clove garlic, crushed
1 teasp salt
3 rounded tbsp cut fresh basil (or 3 teasp dried basil plus 3 tbsp coarsely chopped fresh coriander)

1. Lay the chicken on a foiled grill pan and season with black pepper. Mix the oil and soy sauce, then paint over the top surface of the chicken.
2. Grill chicken gently for 8 minutes, turn, sprinkle with more black pepper, brush with oil again and cook for a further 8 minutes. Allow to cool a little then cut in narrow strips and leave in the marinade for 30 minutes.
3. To cook the aubergines, slice them $\frac{1}{4}$ inch (6 mm) thick, arrange on the grill pan, brush with olive oil and grill until golden. Turn, brush again and grill until tender.
4. To assemble the salad, put the cooked fettucine in a large mixing bowl. Mix the dressing ingredients together, adding 10 grinds black pepper, and pour over the fettucine. Mix thoroughly using two spoons, then add the chicken and marinade, aubergine slices, olives and red pepper strips. Toss well and refrigerate for several hours.
5. Leave at room temperature for 1 hour before serving – in a large glass or wooden salad bowl.

TO PEEL A FRESH MANGO

If it is ripe but firm, and depending on the variety,
● either peel with a swivel-type potato peeler
● or with a small sharp knife
● or by making four or five cuts from top to bottom at equal intervals, then stripping off the skin as from an avocado.

If, however, the fruit is squashy ripe, cut it open and spoon out the flesh, which will be ideal to purée for a sauce, sorbet or mousse.

TO CUT THE PEELED FLESH FROM THE STONE, READY FOR SLICING

● take a slice of flesh as near as possible to the stone off each of the two broader sides above and below the stone then cut off any remaining flesh clinging to it. Slice, dice or purée the fruit as required.

Chicken, Fresh Mango and Pasta Salad

Serves 8 as a main course, 12 as a buffet dish

The salad will keep for 2 days under refrigeration. Do not freeze

This is cool on the tongue, with a variety of fruits adding colour and flavour to the bland chicken in its lightly curried dressing.

2 lb (1 kg) boned chicken breast meat
10 fl. oz (275 ml/1¼ cups) chicken stock
salt and white pepper
1½ cucumbers
6 spring onions
3 ripe but firm mangoes
9 oz (250 g) pasta shapes (e.g. spirals)
8 oz (225 g) strawberries, halved

FOR THE DRESSING
10 fl. oz (275 ml/1¼ cups) lemon mayonnaise
2 tbsp medium strength curry paste
2 tbsp lime juice

FOR THE GARNISH
2 bunches watercress
2 fresh limes
8 oz (225 g) strawberries

1. Poach the chicken breasts in the stock for about 10 minutes, then sprinkle lightly with salt and white pepper. Allow to cool, then cut in bite-size strips.
2. While the chicken is cooling, cut the unpeeled cucumbers in 1 inch (2·5 cm) lengths and then into ½ inch (1·25 cm) matchsticks. Lay in a salad spinner or colander, sprinkle with salt and leave for 30 minutes to remove excess moisture. Rinse with cold water and spin or dab dry.
3. Trim the spring onions then slice very finely and cut in 2 inch (5 cm) lengths.
4. Peel the mangoes with a sharp knife or potato peeler then carefully remove the flesh and cut into strips.
5. Cook the pasta according to the packet instructions, drain, rinse with cold water and drain again.
6. Put all the dressing ingredients into a bowl and whisk to blend, then add all the other ingredients and mix gently with a salad spoon and fork until evenly coated.

TO SERVE
Just before you are ready to eat, arrange in a low mound on a large dish, surround with the sprigs of watercress and decorate with lime twists and strawberries.

A VEGETABLE SELECTION

From our Master Class repertoire we have chosen vegetable presentations that are particularly complementary to the main dishes in the book, but with the needs of the single-handed cook/host or hostess firmly in mind. Included are three recipes – Strudel Printanier, Tourte Forestière and Spanokopita – which combine vegetables and pastry and make unusual and excellent companions for the most elegant main dish.

PREPARING INGREDIENTS FOR STIR-FRYING

The Chinese chef always uses a one-handed cleaver to slice food in preparation for a stir-fry. He will choose one of a size and weight to match his physique and keep it constantly at razor-sharpness by honing it on a stone. Unless you are prepared to learn the cleaver technique in a Chinese kitchen, it's more practical to use an 8 inch (20 cm) cook's knife, and keep it sharp by whatever method you prefer. We favour the type of sharpener that has a pair of milled steel rollers set at an angle to each other, against which the blade is stroked until it reaches the desired degree of sharpness.

Cutting techniques

Diagonal cutting: The food is cut across the grain at a slant. This creates a larger cooking surface for firmer vegetables such as asparagus, broccoli, carrots, celery and string beans.

Strip cutting: The food is first cut into diagonal pieces as above, then each piece is cut into two or three strips. This method is used when an extra thinness is required.

Shred (or julienne) cutting: The food is cut into strips as above, then each strip is cut at an angle, producing two tapered slivers. This is excellent for tender vegetables such as spring onions.

Stir-Fry of Mangetout and Petits Pois

Serves 6–8

A pinch of sugar helps to bring out the natural sweetness of the petits pois.

1 oz (25 g/¼ cup) sesame seeds
1½ tbsp sesame oil
8 oz (225 g) small mangetout
1 lb (450 g) frozen petits pois
1 teasp each caster sugar and salt
15 grinds black pepper

1. In a 9 inch (22·5 cm) lidded frying pan or a wok, dry fry the sesame seeds until golden brown – about 3 minutes. Remove and set aside.
2. In the same pan, heat the oil well and stir-fry the mangetout for 2 minutes, then add the petits pois and seasonings. Stir constantly until they are well coated with the fat and have lost their icy appearance.
3. Cover and steam in their own juice for 5 minutes, then uncover and cook briskly to evaporate any free liquid.

TO SERVE
Sprinkle with the toasted seeds, toss well, then serve at once.

Stir-Fried Mangetout and Mushrooms

Serves 6–8

The nutty flavour of the sesame oil goes well with the mushrooms and mangetout in this simple 'stir-fry'.

1 tbsp sunflower oil
2 teasp sesame oil
1 clove garlic, finely chopped
1 inch (2·5 cm) piece fresh ginger peeled and cut in slivers
12 oz (350 g/3¾ cups) tiny white button mushrooms
1 lb (450 g) small mangetout, strings removed
1 teasp light soy sauce
8 grinds black pepper

1. Heat the oils for 2 minutes with the garlic and ginger in a deep 9 inch (22·5 cm) frying pan or wok, then add the mushrooms and stir-fry briskly for 3–4 minutes.
2. Add the mangetout and stir-fry for a further 3 minutes or until barely tender.
3. Sprinkle with the soy sauce and pepper and serve at once.

Tomates Provençales

Serves 6

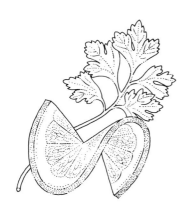

The flavour of this simple but aromatic dish depends on finding the ripest possible tomatoes. Rarely are tomatoes sent to market fully ripened on the plant, so we usually give them two or three days at room temperature to complete the process.

3 firm, ripe, red beef tomatoes, about 3 inches (7·5 cm) in diameter
salt and freshly ground black pepper
1 can rolled anchovies with capers
4 tbsp olive oil

FOR THE FILLING
3 tbsp chopped shallots or spring onions
1 fat clove garlic, crushed
4 tbsp fresh chopped parsley
1 teasp dried Herbes de Provence
6 large basil leaves, torn or shredded (or 1 teasp dried basil)
$1\frac{1}{2}$ oz (40 g/$\frac{1}{3}$ cup) dry breadcrumbs

1. Cut the tomatoes in half and gently squeeze out the juice and seeds. Sprinkle lightly with salt and pepper and turn upside down on to kitchen paper to drain.
2. To prepare the filling, gently heat 3 tbsp of the oil and sauté the shallots until soft and golden. Add all the remaining ingredients, seasoning with a pinch salt and 15 grinds black pepper, and mix well.
3. To assemble, lay a rolled anchovy fillet in the base of each tomato half then spoon in the filling. Sprinkle with a few drops of the remaining olive oil, then arrange on a heatproof platter or dish. The tomatoes can be refrigerated for up to 6 hours at this point.
4. Preheat the oven to Gas 6 (400°F, 200°C), and bake the tomatoes for 15 minutes until they are tender but still hold their shape.

TO SERVE
Serve hot or cold.

Vegetable Fritto Misto with a Hazelnut Sauce

(Assorted vegetable fritters with a hazelnut sauce)

Serves 6–8

Although these vegetable fritters are generally served at room temperature in Italy and Spain, we prefer them hot and crisp.

1½ lb (675 g) *mixed young vegetables – cauliflower, broccoli, courgettes, Jerusalem artichokes, celeriac*

FOR THE SAUCE
3½ oz (100 g) *packet white hazelnuts*
2 oz (50 g/1 cup) *fresh breadcrumbs*
2 *cloves garlic, crushed*
4 fl. oz (125 ml/½ cup) *each olive and sunflower oil*
2 tbsp *wine vinegar*
1 teasp *salt*

FOR THE BATTER
4 oz (125 g/1 cup) *bread flour*
pinch salt
2 tbsp *any oil*
5 fl. oz (150 ml/⅔ cup) *beer*
1 *egg white*

1. To make the sauce, grind the nuts in the food processor or blender then pulse in the breadcrumbs, garlic and 1 tbsp water.
2. Add the oils as for mayonnaise, in a thin stream, then gradually add the vinegar. Stir in the salt and chill until required.
3. Prepare the vegetables. Divide the cauliflower and broccoli into florets, trimming off any tough stalks. Cut the unpeeled courgettes in diagonal slices ⅜ inch (1 cm) thick. Peel and slice the artichokes and celeriac ½ inch (1·25 cm) thick.
4. Put all the ingredients for the batter (except for the egg white) into the blender or food processor and blend until smooth – 1 minute.
5. When ready to cook, whisk the egg white until it holds stiff but glossy peaks, then fold into the batter.
6. To cook the fritters, have ready a deep fryer heated to 350°F/180°C.
7. Using tongs, draw each piece of vegetable through the batter, shaking off any excess, and lower into the hot oil. Don't crowd the pan. Cook until golden – about 4 minutes. Drain on crumpled kitchen paper.
8. Transfer the fritters as they cook to a shallow dish and leave in a slow oven, Gas 1 (275°F, 140°C). They will keep crisp for 1 hour.

TO SERVE

Serve three or four hot fritters on each vegetable plate, accompanied by the chilled sauce (which may need to be thinned by 3–4 tbsp water).

OLIVE OIL AND THE VEGETABLE RAGOÛT

One of the great pleasures of eating in Italy is to choose an antipasto from a huge variety of stewed and stuffed vegetables – courgettes, peppers, aubergines and mushrooms, to name but a few – which are always served at room temperature rather than hot from the oven. Unlike other dishes that have been cooked with one of the more 'refined' oils such as corn oil or sunflower oil, or indeed with butter, they remain equally palatable when cold because the olive oil does not congeal or develop any off odours, but makes its own special fruity contribution to the dish.

The use of olive oil in antipasti – starters – was pioneered by the cooks of the Roman empire who found that in addition to improving the flavour of the particular dish, the oil acted as a 'lining' to the stomach of the diners which slowed down the effects of too much alcohol earlier in the meal.

French Bean, Pepper and Tomato Ragoût

Serves 6–8

Unlike butter, olive oil does not congeal when cold so it means that this kind of ragoût can be served both hot (as a vegetable) and cold (as a starter).

$1\frac{1}{2}$ lb (675 g) whole shoestring green beans (fresh or frozen)
salt
4 tbsp olive oil
1 large (8 oz/225 g) onion
1 clove garlic, crushed
2 medium green peppers, seeded and cut in $\frac{1}{2}$ inch (1·25 cm) strips
14 oz (400 g) can chopped tomatoes in juice
10 grinds black pepper
2 teasp sugar
$\frac{1}{2}$ teasp Italian seasoning
1 tbsp torn fresh basil leaves

FOR THE GARNISH
1 tbsp chopped parsley
4 tbsp grated Parmesan cheese

1. Blanch the beans in a large pan of water with 2 teasp salt for 4–5 minutes or until barely tender. Turn into a sieve and refresh under the cold tap to set the colour, then drain and set aside.
2. Heat the oil, and sauté the onion and garlic for 5 minutes or until softened, then add the pepper strips and continue to cook for a further 5 minutes until the onion turns golden.
3. Add all the remaining ingredients, with $1\frac{1}{2}$ teasp salt, stir well and simmer for a further 5 minutes until thick and juicy. Add the blanched beans and cook for another 3 minutes or until they are tender. Set aside. The ragoût can now be refrigerated for up to 24 hours.

TO SERVE
Just before serving, reheat gently until heated through. Turn into a hot dish and scatter with the parsley and the cheese.

To make a vegetable purse

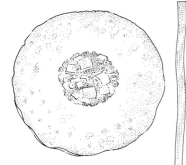

Crêpe with filling and leek tie.

Basque Vegetable Purses

Serves 6–8

Freeze unfilled crêpes for 1 month. Filled crêpes may be kept for up to 12 hours under refrigeration

These juicy little 'purses' make a decorative addition to an individual arrangement of vegetables or as a garnish for a roast or a braise.

FOR THE PURSES
2 eggs
3 oz (75 g/¾ cup) strong white flour
½ teasp salt
1 oz (25 g/2 tbsp) butter or margarine, melted
good pinch nutmeg
5 fl. oz (150 ml/⅔ cup) milk (or water)

FOR THE FILLING
1 large green and 1 large red pepper
2 tbsp olive oil
1 medium (5 oz/150 g) onion, finely chopped
1 large clove garlic, chopped
1 large tomato, cubed
½ teasp salt
10 grinds black pepper
good pinch brown sugar
1 tbsp chopped parsley

TO TIE THE PURSES
2 leaves of leek

1. For the purses, make the batter and fry as in the crêpe recipe on page 30.
2. For the filling, grill the peppers fiercely until the skin is charred, then put in a plastic bag for 5 minutes to steam. The skin can then easily be removed. Discard seeds and core and cut in ½ (1·25 cm) cubes.
3. While the peppers are grilling, heat the oil and sauté the onion and garlic until golden brown, then add the tomato and pepper cubes. Stir well and add the seasonings and parsley. Allow to cool.
4. To prepare the leek ties, blanch the long leaves in boiling water for 1 minute, refresh with cold water and dab dry. Cut in twelve very thin strips.
5. To assemble, arrange each crêpe on a board and put a tablespoonful of the vegetable mixture in the centre. Gather up into a purse shape and tie with a strip of leek.
6. Arrange the purses on a greased tray. (They can be refrigerated for up to 12 hours at this point.) Bake in a hot oven, Gas 7 (425°F, 220°C), for 10–12 minutes until crisp. Keep warm in a low oven until required. They will stay crisp for up to 30 minutes.

THE TWO-SPOON TOSS

We usually use cooking spoons made of a high density plastic to move food about in the pan so that it is evenly cooked and heated through. A spoon (or, if preferred, a matching fork) is held in each hand then used to lift and toss the food in a gentle, even action. This particular kind of material will tolerate fat temperatures up to (but not including) 375°F/190°C, which means that the utensils can be used for any cooking process other than deep-frying. This information is normally given on the label so check before you buy.

Ribbons of Courgette and Carrot in a Lime and Coriander Glaze

Serves 6–8

This is really an elegant stir-fry, with the vegetables cut in wide strips rather than the conventional julienne. The blend of colours makes it a very decorative dish.

1 lb (450 g) young carrots, scraped, then topped and tailed
1 lb (450 g) courgettes, topped and tailed
salt
$1\frac{1}{2}$ oz (40 g/3 tbsp) butter or margarine
2 teasp caster sugar
$\frac{1}{2}$ teasp ground coriander
zest of 1 lime, cut into fine julienne
$1\frac{1}{2}$ tbsp lime juice
1 tbsp fresh chopped coriander

1. Cut both vegetables lengthwise into 'ribbons' using a swivel-bladed peeler.
2. Cook the carrots in boiling salted water until barely tender – about 4 minutes. Drain well and refresh under cold water. (The courgettes do not need this preliminary blanching.)
3. Just before serving, heat the butter or margarine in a wok or large frying pan until sizzling, add the vegetables and sprinkle with the sugar, $\frac{1}{2}$ teasp salt and the ground coriander.
4. Toss over high heat until glazed then add the lime rind and juice. Toss a moment or two more then serve scattered with the chopped fresh coriander.

Gingered Parsnip Purée

Serves 6–8

1½ lb (675 g) parsnips, peeled and cut in 1 inch (2·5 cm) pieces
2 medium potatoes (about 12 oz/350 g in total), peeled
and quartered
salt
2 teasp ground ginger
2 oz (50 g/¼ cup) butter or margarine
speck white pepper
1 rounded tbsp mild honey

1. Cook the vegetables in a large pan of boiling salted water until tender – about 20 minutes. Drain well.
2. Purée the vegetables through a food mill or ricer (not a food processor as this makes the mixture gluey).
3. Return to the pan, add the remaining ingredients plus 1 teasp salt, and use a balloon whisk to incorporate evenly.

Minted Carrot Purée

Serves 6–8

1½ lb (675 g) carrots, peeled and cut in 1 inch (2·5 cm) pieces
salt
1 teasp dried mint (or 1 tbsp fresh chopped in season)
2 oz (50 g/¼ cup) soft margarine or butter
1 teasp sugar
¼ teasp white pepper

1. Prepare as for the parsnip purée, adding a little of the hot cooking liquid if necessary to make a creamy consistency.

Courgette Purée

Serves 6–8

Prepare as for the purée in Courgettes en Barque (opposite).

IDEAS FOR SERVING
1. Pile and fork into a gratin dish.
2. Use as a garnish for a roast.
3. Spoon into tiny individual cocottes – using one or two of the purées side by side.

Courgettes en Barque

(Courgette boats filled with a courgette purée)

Serves 6–8

These are simple to make by a method that's difficult to explain in words. But our diagrams say all. They look stunning surrounded by the Carré d'Agneau aux Beaux Champs (see page 67).

6 × 5 inch (12·5 cm) courgettes, topped and tailed

FOR THE PURÉE
2 oz (50 g/¼ cup) butter or margarine
1½ lb (675 g) courgettes, topped, tailed and thinly sliced
1 teasp salt
10 grinds black pepper
¼ teasp grated nutmeg

To make a courgette boat

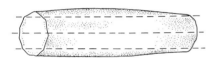

Cut into ½ inch (1·25 cm) slices.

Cut each slice horizontally through the middle.

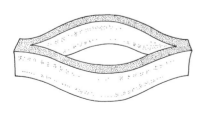

Open out to form a hollow boat.

1. To make the boats, cut the whole courgettes lengthwise into slices ½ inch (1·25 cm) thick (use the two curved outer slices from each courgette for the purée).
2. Blanch the slices in boiling water for 1 minute, then drain in a colander, refreshing with cold water. Pat dry.
3. Lay the slices flat on a board and with a sharp pointed knife make a horizontal incision on one side of each slice, ½ inch (1·25 cm) from each end, then cut through to the other side.
4. Stand the slices on their sides and open up to form bottomless boats (see drawing). Leave at room temperature until required.
5. To make the purée, melt the fat in a heavy pan, add the sliced courgettes together with the unused outer slices from the boats, and season with the salt, pepper and nutmeg. Cover and cook gently until absolutely tender – 10–15 minutes. Then simmer uncovered to evaporate any remaining liquid. Purée the contents of the pan in a blender or food processor.
6. To assemble, arrange the boats on a baking sheet lined with silicone paper, then fill with the purée. These can now be loosely covered and refrigerated for up to 12 hours.
7. Reheat (covered with foil) in a moderate oven, Gas 4 (350°F, 180°C), for 20 minutes.

TO SERVE
Use a fish slice or wide spatula to transfer the hot boats on to each plate or use to garnish the main dish.

FILLO AND FAT

Only a small proportion of fat –
usually oil – is worked into the fillo
dough, so to achieve the
characteristic crisp and puffy
texture, extra liquid fat – it can be
melted butter, good quality block
margarine or oil – must be brushed
on each layer. Only a thin coating
of the liquid fat need be applied –
too much makes it greasy and may
stop the top of the baked pastries
from browning properly.

To apply this fat we use a bristle
brush, approximately 1 inch
(2·5 cm) wide – a brush that is too
large and thick may take up too
much fat and make 'puddles' on
the pastry. Use a back and forward
stroke – rather like applying
paint – so that the fat goes on in
an even layer that moistens the
pastry without saturating it. In this
way one can achieve a similar
result to puff pastry, using only
half the quantity of fat.

Strudel Printanier, Mayonnaise Chantilly

Serves 6–8

This strudel makes an unusual vegetable accompaniment.

1 lb (450 g) fillo pastry
3 oz (75 g/⅓ cup) butter, melted
2 tbsp sesame seeds

FOR THE FILLING
1 oz (25 g/2 tbsp) butter
1 lb (450 g) frozen stir-fry vegetables
8 oz (225 g) fresh broccoli, florets only
4 oz (125 g) mangetout, trimmed and cut in half lengthwise
½ teasp salt and 10 grinds black pepper
1 tbsp finely chopped fresh parsley
6 oz (175 g/1½ cups) sharp Cheddar cheese, grated
2 eggs, beaten

FOR THE MAYONNAISE
8 oz (225 g/1 cup) strained Greek-style cow's yoghurt (or fromage frais or creamed Smetana)
3 rounded tbsp mild mayonnaise
1 teasp caster sugar
1 tbsp chives, snipped
pinch each salt and white pepper

1. Preheat oven to Gas 5 (375°F, 190°C), and melt the butter for the filling in a wok or frying pan. Stir-fry all the vegetables until bite-tender – about 3–4 minutes – then cool.
2. Add the seasonings, parsley, cheese and eggs and mix gently together.
3. Open the packet of pastry and take out twelve sheets. Overlap two of them so that you have a layer 17 inches (42·5 cm) wide. (You may need only 1½ sheets depending on size.)
4. Brush lightly with melted butter, then repeat with five more layers, stacking them on top of each other.
5. Spoon the cooled filling on to the edge of the pastry nearest to you, making a mound about 3 inches (7·5 cm) across, and leaving a 1 inch (2·5 cm) border all round.
6. Turn in the sides to enclose the filling, then roll up into a flattened Swiss roll.
7. Arrange, seal side down, on a greased baking tray, then brush the top with melted butter and scatter with sesame seeds. Bake for 35 minutes or until golden.
8. To make the mayonnaise, stir all the ingredients together.

TO SERVE
Slice the strudel and serve within 30 minutes of baking, with the mayonnaise at room temperature.

THE THIRSTY MUSHROOM

Mushrooms are very porous so that as soon as they are put into a frying pan they appear to absorb all the fat. However do not be tempted to add more; simply keep shaking the pan so that they cook evenly and in 2 or 3 minutes your patience will be rewarded as the fat reappears on the surface of each mushroom. After 2 or 3 more minutes (keep tossing them in the pan) they will have browned to perfection and be cooked.

Note: To sauté 8 oz (225 g) mushrooms, heat 1 oz (25 g) butter and 2 teasp flavourless oil over moderate heat. The minute the butter foam has subsided, add the mushrooms and proceed as above.

Tourte Forestière

(Sherried mushroom tart)

Serves 8

The tourte will freeze for 1 month. The raw pastry will freeze for 3 months. Keep under refrigeration for 3 days

Creamy mushrooms are baked in a savoury brown crust, combining in the smooth and satisfying filling the best features of the French quiche and the English savoury flan. Serve it in wedges as a vegetable accompaniment. The filling must be allowed to go cold before it is used, otherwise it makes the bottom of the tart soggy and may curdle in the heat of the oven. It will come to no harm even if left overnight before use.

FOR THE PASTRY
8 oz (225 g/1 cup) butter or firm margarine, cut in 1 inch (2·5 cm) cubes
6 oz (175 g/1½ cups) each fine-milled wholemeal flour and white self-raising flour (or 6 oz (175 g/1½ cups) plain flour and 1½ teasp baking powder)
½ teasp salt
3 teasp soft brown sugar
1½ teasp dry mustard
2 teasp dried Herbes de Provence
1 egg beaten with 1 teasp wine vinegar and 3 tbsp cold water

FOR THE FILLING
2 oz (50 g/¼ cup) butter
1 large onion, very finely chopped
1 small clove garlic, crushed
1 lb (450 g/5 cups) pinky mushrooms, very thinly sliced
12 fl. oz (350 ml/1½ cups) milk
1 oz (25 g/4 tbsp) cornflour
½ teasp salt
pinch white pepper
¼ teasp ground mace (or nutmeg)
2 egg yolks, beaten
4–6 tbsp double cream
3 tbsp Amontillado sherry
1 tbsp chopped fresh parsley (or fresh coriander)

FOR THE TOPPING
3 tbsp each sesame seeds and grated Parmesan cheese

1. To make the pastry, follow the method outlined in Petites Tartes aux Fines Herbes (see page 39).
2. Take one-third of the pastry and shape into a 1 inch (2·5 cm) thick block, wrap in film and freeze for 1 hour.
3. Roll out the remaining pastry to fit a 9–10 inch (22·5–25 cm) loose-bottomed or ceramic flan tin, approx. 1½

PARMESAN

At the heart of Italian cooking lies the unique flavour of Parmesan cheese. This particular cheese has the ability to act as a 'catalyst' to all the other foods in a particular dish, and for this reason it is widely used in many other national cuisines as well. Yet it has never been successfully copied outside of Italy, for no-one has been able to reproduce the 'granas' – the tiny grains which develop in the cheese as it matures, and distinguish it in texture from any other cheese made anywhere in the world.

The finest Parmesan, 'Parmigiano Reggiano', is produced in a small area of Northern Italy around Parma (naturally), Reggio Emilia, Modena and parts of Bologna and Mantua. This cheese must be matured for at least two years before it can be sold, when it will be pale yellow in colour with a powerful aroma. However, for serving as part of a cheeseboard it is better to buy a younger, softer type of Parmesan – known as 'Parmigiano Padano' which is whitish in colour and is only one year old when it is offered for sale.

As mature Parmesan is so hard and dry in texture – it has to be hacked from the whole cheese with a special knife rather than with a wire like other pressed cheeses – it's tempting to take the easy option and buy it ready-grated in a cardboard or plastic tub. But as with pepper and coffee, its flavour is at its peak at the moment of grating, and then gradually fades a little as time goes by. So if you have a Parmesan grater attachment on your food processor, it's worth buying the cheese by the piece and grating it yourself for a special dish.

inches (3·75 cm) deep. Prick all over and freeze while the filling is prepared.

4. To make the filling, melt the butter over gentle heat then sauté the onion and garlic for 5 minutes or until soft and golden.
5. Add the mushrooms, cover and cook for a further 5 minutes then uncover and bubble for 2–3 minutes to evaporate any free liquid.
6. Add the milk slowly to the cornflour, mixing all the time, then add to the pan with the seasonings and bring to the boil, stirring constantly with a wooden spoon. Simmer for 3 minutes.
7. In a small bowl, whisk the egg yolks, cream, sherry and parsley, then add to the pan and reheat until steaming but do not allow to boil. Leave until cold.
8. To assemble the tourte, preheat the oven to Gas 6 (400°F, 200°C), and spoon the cold filling into the frozen pastry case. Grate the block of frozen pastry all over the top.
9. Sprinkle evenly with the sesame and cheese mixture, and bake for 30 minutes or until a rich golden brown.

TO SERVE
Serve warm but not hot. May be reheated.

Spanakopita

(Greek spinach and cheese spiral)

Serves 6–8

Freeze the raw spiral for 1 month

Rolls of pastry, stuffed with a creamy mixture of spinach and feta cheese, are wound round each other to make one giant spiral. Serve it cut in wedges like a pie for a vegetable accompaniment, a vegetarian summer lunch or alfresco supper.

12 sheets (approx. 12 oz/350 g) fillo pastry
4 oz (125 g/½ cup) butter, melted

FOR THE FILLING
2 × 8 oz (225 g) packets frozen leaf spinach (or 2 lb/1 kg fresh spinach)
butter
2 small bunches spring onions, including 2 inches (5 cm) of the green tops, finely sliced
2 eggs, beaten
8 oz (225 g/2 cups) feta cheese (or crumbly Lancashire cheese)
3 tbsp fresh chopped dill (or 1 tbsp dried dill)
½ teasp salt
20 grinds black pepper
½ teasp grated nutmeg

FOR THE SAUCE

8 oz (225 ml/1 cup) strained Greek-style cow's yoghurt
2 teasp fresh snipped dill (or ½ teasp dried dill)
½ teasp salt
8 grinds black pepper

1. To make the sauce, mix all the ingredients together and chill for several hours.
2. To make the filling, prepare and cook fresh spinach in the usual way, drain well and chop finely. Defrost frozen spinach, squeeze well in a sieve to remove the moisture, and chop finely. Put in a large mixing bowl.
3. Heat 1½ oz (40 g/3 tbsp) butter in a frying pan and gently sauté the spring onions until soft – about 5 minutes.
4. Add to the spinach together with the beaten eggs, crumbled cheese, herbs and seasonings. Mix well, then spoon into a 14 inch (35 cm) piping bag fitted with a 1 inch (2.5 cm) plain nozzle.
5. To assemble, grease an 11–12 inch (27.5–30 cm) pizza pan or the base of a loose-bottomed flan tin, sitting on a baking tray. Stack the sheets of fillo one on top of the other and cover loosely with a teatowel to prevent them drying out.
6. Place a fillo sheet on a board with the long edge towards you and brush lightly all over with melted butter then cover with a second sheet of fillo and brush with butter in the same way.
7. Leaving 1½ inches (3.75 cm) of pastry nearest to you clear, pipe a long strip of the filling from one edge of the sheet of pastry to the other. Fold the lower edge of the pastry to enclose this filling, then roll up like a narrow Swiss roll.
8. Repeat this with the remaining sheets of fillo – there will now be six long rolls.
9. Take one roll and brush it lightly all over with butter, then carefully curl it into a spiral and place it in the centre of the baking tin.
10. Take another roll, brush that in the same way then curl it round the outside of the first spiral. Continue buttering and curling the rolls in the same way, until you have made a giant spiral that completely covers the base of the pan or flan tin. (At this stage the Spanakopita can be frozen or chilled overnight.)
11. To cook, preheat the oven to Gas 5 (375°F, 190°C), and bake for 40–45 minutes or until a rich golden brown.

TO SERVE

Transfer on to a circular wooden board or glass platter, leave to cool for 15 minutes, then serve in wedges with the dilled yoghurt.

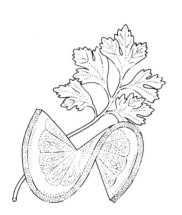

A NOODLE RING

1. Press seasoned and buttered and cooked noodles tightly into a buttered ring mould and smooth the top. (May now be left to go cold.)

2. Reheat freshly cooked noodles in a slow oven, Gas 1 (275°F, 140°C) for 30 minutes. Reheat cold noodles at Gas 3 (325°F, 160°C) for 25 minutes or until warm to the touch.

To serve

Turn out on to a heated platter and fill the ring with freshly cooked vegetables such as broccoli florets, tiny French beans or mangetout.

Nussnudeln

Serves 6

These flavourful nut noodles go well with fish.

butter
12 oz (350 g) fresh wholemeal noodles (tagliatelle), boiled
until tender
½ teasp sea salt
15 grinds black pepper
2 oz (50 g/½ cup) walnuts, finely chopped
2 oz (50 g/½ cup) Parmesan cheese, finely grated
2 oz (50 g/½ cup) dried breadcrumbs

1. To make a beurre noisette, melt 2 oz (50 g/¼ cup) butter in a small pan and cook over medium heat until it turns pale fawn.

2. Melt 1½ oz (40 g/3 tbsp) butter in a large pan and add the hot noodles, tossing until they are coated and glistening, then stir in the salt, pepper, walnuts, cheese and bread-crumbs which have been thoroughly mixed together.

3. Turn into a hot serving dish and pour over the beurre noisette. Serve at once.

Nouilles au Basilic

Serves 6–8

Do not freeze

These savoury noodles go well with a braised joint such as the Veau Poêlé au Vermouth (see page 70).

12 oz (350 g) fresh noodles (tagliatelle)
meat stock (or salted water)
3 oz (75 g/⅓ cup) margarine or butter
4 tbsp fresh chopped parsley
2 tbsp torn fresh basil leaves (or 2 teasp dried basil)
plenty of black pepper

1. Cook the tagliatelle in the water or stock according to packet instructions.

2. Turn into a colander and dredge with cold water to remove any excess starch. Drain thoroughly.

3. In the same pan, melt the fat and add half the parsley, the basil and pepper.

4. Add the tagliatelle and continue to heat over a low light, tossing thoroughly until the tagliatelle is well coated with the herbs and is piping hot. The dish may be kept hot, covered, for up to 30 minutes, either on top of the stove or in a low oven, Gas 1 (275°F, 140°C). Sprinkle to serve with the remaining parsley.

TO COOK IN THE MICROWAVE

Arrange the ingredients in a microwave-safe dish, cover with a lid or pierced film and cook on 100% power for 30 minutes. Leave to stand for 5 minutes then brown under a hot grill.

Pommes de Terre au Cidre

Serves 6–8

In the tiny hilltop village of Antraigues, tucked away in a corner of the Ardèche (the beautiful region of France bordering the Rhône), chef Helen Baissade prepares a wonderful peasant dish of local potatoes cooked in cider. As the potatoes bake, they turn a tawny gold and develop a glorious fruity flavour.

2½ lb (1·25 kg) small potatoes, peeled and sliced wafer thin
2 oz (50 g/¼ cup) butter, melted, mixed with ½ teasp
garlic granules
sea salt
white pepper
8 oz (225 g/2 cups) Edam (or Emmenthal) cheese, grated
10 fl. oz (275 ml/1¼ cups) dry cider

1. Preheat the oven to Gas 5 (375°F, 190°C), and grease an oval gratin dish about 2 inches (5 cm) deep.
2. Arrange a third of the potatoes in an even layer, then drizzle a third of the garlic butter over them. Sprinkle lightly with sea salt and pepper.
3. Cover with a third of the cheese, and repeat with the remaining potatoes, butter, seasonings and cheese, ending with a layer of cheese.
4. Gently pour the cider down the side of the dish, and cover with a piece of greaseproof or silicone paper.
5. Bake in a preheated oven for 1¼ hours or until tender and golden. If necessary, brown under the grill. (May be kept hot in a low oven for 30 minutes.)

TO REHEAT
Place in a hot oven for 15–20 minutes or in a microwave for 5 minutes on 100% power.

GEROSTETE KARTOFFELN
Sauté potatoes in the Viennese fashion

These slices of golden potatoes, gently flavoured with caraway seed, are a favourite accompaniment to a wiener schnitzel.

Peel and thinly slice 6 medium potatoes, then soak in salted water to cover for 30 minutes. Drain and dry thoroughly with a teatowel. In a heavy frying pan heat enough sunflower oil with 1 oz (25 g/2 tbsp) butter to come to a depth of $\frac{1}{2}$ inch (1.25 cm) then sauté finely chopped onion in it until soft and golden. Add the potatoes and cook over medium heat for 12 minutes, turning carefully two or three times to allow them to brown evenly. Sprinkle with 1 teasp caraway seeds, $\frac{1}{2}$ teasp ground sea salt and a little chopped parsley, and serve piping hot.

Pommes Lyonnaise à Romarin
Serves 6–8

The partly-fried potatoes will keep for up to 24 hours under refrigeration

It is difficult to fry a large quantity of potatoes to an even gold on top of the stove. This recipe solves the problem by dividing the cooking in two parts. The potatoes are first softened on top of the stove and then they are spread out in a roasting tin and crisped in the oven.

3 lb (1·5 kg) potatoes, scrubbed
salt
3 oz (75 g/$\frac{1}{3}$ cup) butter or margarine
3 tbsp oil
2 medium onions, chopped
2 teasp finely chopped rosemary spikes (or 1 teasp caraway seeds and 1 tbsp chopped parsley)

FOR THE GARNISH
sea salt
black pepper

1. Boil the whole potatoes in their skins in salted water for 25–40 minutes, depending on their size. (Test with the point of a sharp knife.)
2. Drain the potatoes, return to the empty pan and dry off over a low heat. Leave until cool enough to handle, then skin and cut into cubes or slices $\frac{3}{8}$ inch (1 cm) thick.
3. Put the butter and oil in a heavy frying pan. When they start to foam put in the potatoes and cook very gently, shaking the pan occasionally so that the potatoes absorb the fat rather than fry in it.
4. After 10 minutes, add the onions, and continue to cook at a slightly higher temperature until the potatoes are golden all over and are crisp.
5. Sprinkle with the rosemary, shake the pan to coat all the potatoes, and transfer to a baking tin approx. $14 \times 10 \times 2$ inches ($35 \times 25 \times 5$ cm). A roulade tin is ideal. The potatoes can be refrigerated at this point for up to 24 hours.
6. To re-crisp, 40 minutes before serving, put the potatoes in a pre-heated oven, Gas 7 (425°F, 220°C), and cook until crisp and golden, shaking occasionally.

TO SERVE
Turn into an entrée dish and season with a few grinds of salt and black pepper.

Rösti Forestière

Potato Pancake with Mushrooms

Serves 6

This is a delicious variation on the traditional Swiss 'potato pancake'. We have found that parboiling the potatoes before grating them is the real secret of the successful rösti.

2½ lb (1·25 kg) potatoes (Desirée if possible)
2 oz (50 g/¼ cup) butter or margarine
1 onion, finely chopped
8 oz (225 g/2½ cups) mushrooms, finely sliced
pinch each dried marjoram, thyme and rosemary
4 tbsp oil
1½ teasp salt
15 grinds black pepper
good pinch grated nutmeg

1. Peel the potatoes, leave whole, then put in a pan of cold, unsalted water and bring slowly to the boil. Boil for 6 minutes until they can be pierced with a sharp knife but are still firm and waxy. Drain and allow to go quite cold.
2. Using the coarsest grater – with ½ inch (1·25 cm) holes – grate the potatoes into a bowl.
3. Heat the butter in a 9 inch (22·5 cm) pan and sauté the onion, mushrooms and dried herbs for 3–4 minutes until soft and golden. Remove with a draining spoon and gently mix with the grated potatoes, using two forks.
4. Add 3 tbsp of the oil to the pan and heat for 3 minutes. Put in the grated potato mixture and pat into an even layer to form a cake that just fills the pan.
5. Cook over moderate heat for 7 minutes until the bottom is a rich brown. Sprinkle the top with salt, pepper and nutmeg, then dribble the remaining oil over.
6. Take a plate of slightly larger diameter, lay it on top of the pan and flip the rösti into it. Then slide the rösti back into the pan so that the uncooked side is to the bottom.
7. Continue to cook slowly but steadily for a further 5 minutes until the bottom is crisp and brown also.

TO SERVE

Cut in wedges like a quiche.

Golden New Potatoes and Parsnips

Serves 6–8

This method of cooking without water is a very good way to conserve the delicate flavour of young vegetables.

$1\frac{1}{2}$ lb (675 g) even-sized new potatoes
$1\frac{1}{2}$ lb (675 g) even-sized young parsnips
2 oz (50 g/$\frac{1}{4}$ cup) butter or margarine
1 tbsp oil
sea salt

1. Scrape the potatoes (or simply scrub well to remove all soil), and dry thoroughly in a towel.
2. Peel the parsnips, slice off the root and cut in half lengthwise.
3. Put the butter and oil in a 9 inch (22·5 cm) lidded frying pan and melt it over moderate heat.
4. The minute the fat starts to foam add the potatoes and shake them gently in the fat until well coated on all sides. Cover and cook very gently for 15 minutes, shaking the pan occasionally.
5. Add the parsnips, cover and continue to cook until the vegetables are golden brown outside and very tender when pierced with a sharp knife.
6. If required, the vegetables can be kept hot on a tiny light for up to 30 minutes, then re-crisped just before serving.

TO SERVE

Lift from the pan, discard any remaining fat and scatter with sea salt.

Sweet Potatoes Duchesse

Serves 6–8

This is our favourite way of serving this delicious vegetable, and the addition of some ordinary potatoes gives it a particularly creamy texture.

$2\frac{1}{2}$ lb (1·25 kg) sweet potatoes
12 oz (350 g) Maris Piper (or other mashing) potatoes
3 oz (75 g/$\frac{1}{3}$ cup) butter or margarine
2 teasp salt
$\frac{1}{8}$ teasp white pepper
4 egg yolks

1. Wash both types of potatoes, prick all over, and bake in a quick oven, Gas 6 (400°F, 200°C), for 1 hour until tender.

(Or bake in the microwave for 25 minutes on 100% power then rest for 5 minutes.)

2. Scoop the potato flesh into a warm bowl and, using an electric whisk or large balloon whisk, beat in all the remaining ingredients (reserving half an egg yolk for the glaze). The mixture should be smooth and pipeable.
3. Grease two oven trays, then pipe the mixture into 2 inch (5 cm) mounds using a coarse rose nozzle. Chill for 1 hour then glaze all over with the reserved egg yolk mixed with 2 teasp water.
4. Just before serving, bake in a quick oven, Gas 7 (425°F, 220°C), for 15 minutes or until a rich gold in colour.

RICE WITH A PERSIAN ACCENT

Everybody has their favourite way of cooking this most ancient of foods. The first record of its cultivation dates from the reign of the Chinese emperor Shen Nung in about 3000 BC. Since we discovered the Persian way – soaking the raw rice for 30 minutes, boiling it until 'al dente' and then allowing it to steam to firm yet tender perfection – we have abandoned most of the other methods we have practised through the years.

For providing you use a good quality long-grain rice you cannot fail to achieve fluffy, nutty-textured rice. We favour Basmati rice – grown in the foothills of the Himalayas – which never goes puddingy and in addition has a particularly delightful aroma ('basmati' actually means 'the fragrant one').

When rice was bought from the sack, it was often of uneven quality and contaminated with stones and foreign bodies. But now even the most unusual varieties of rice are sorted and cleaned before sale. If you are a real rice 'freak' look out for 'Delta' rice which has been aged for two years before sale and is claimed to be the ideal variety for cooking in the Persian fashion.

Chilau Rice with a Crisp Potato Layer

Serves 6–8

Do not freeze

One of those simple dishes that are particularly relished by the true gourmet – in fact the crispy layer is often reserved for the most honoured guest, rather like the 'grillon' that clings to the bottom of the fondue dish.

12 oz (350 g/2 cups) Basmati rice
2 tbsp salt
3 tbsp sunflower oil
1 oz (25 g/2 tbsp) butter or margarine
1 lb (450 g) potatoes, peeled and very thinly sliced

1. Soak the rice in water to cover. After 30 minutes pour the rice into a sieve and rinse under the cold tap until the water runs clear.
2. Bring a large heavy-based pan of water to the boil, add the salt and the rice and boil uncovered for 5 minutes. Immediately turn the rice into the sieve and rinse under the hot water tap.
3. Dry the pan then melt 2 tbsp of the oil and the butter. Cover with overlapping slices of potato – this will become the crusty top of the dish.
4. Carefully spoon the rice on top of the potatoes, sprinkle the surface with the remaining oil, then cover the pan top with a dry folded teatowel, and press the lid firmly into place – making sure there is no material near the heat.
5. Steam very gently for 30 minutes. The cooked rice and potato dish may be kept hot over a tiny light for up to 30 minutes.

TO SERVE
Turn out on to a heated oval platter.

THE PERSIAN POLO

Sauté a large chopped onion in 2 tbsp sunflower oil until golden, then add 1½ lb (650 g) lamb cut in 1 inch (2.5 cm) cubes and cook until the onion and meat are richly brown. Add 4 oz (125 g) dried apricots, 2 oz (50 g) muscatel raisins and 1 pint (575 ml/2½ cups) hot water, a teasp each cinnamon and salt and 15 grinds black pepper. Simmer on top of the stove or in the oven until the lamb is meltingly tender, about 1½ hours. Serve on a bed of plain chilau rice, without the carrots. Garnish with 2 oz (50 g) toasted pine kernels

Chilau Rice with Gingered Carrots

Serves 6–8

Every grain of rice, when cooked in this classic Persian style, stays separate and chewy. Salt is added by the tablespoonful, but it's mostly washed out by the time this dish is ready for the table. The carrots not only add a sweetness to the dish, they also bring a touch of colour.

12 oz (350 g/2 cups) Basmati rice
salt
oil

FOR THE GINGERED CARROTS
1 onion, finely chopped
12 oz (350 g) carrots, grated
2 teasp honey
½ teasp ground ginger
10 grinds black pepper

1. Soak and cook the rice as in steps 1 and 2 of the previous recipe.
2. Dry the pan then cover the base with 2 tbsp of the oil. Add the rice, sprinkle with a little more oil, then cover with teatowel and lid as before. Replace and allow rice to steam on a very low light for 20 minutes.
3. The rice can be refrigerated at this point for up to 2 days, then left at room temperature for 1 hour.
4. To cook the carrots, sauté the onion in 1 tbsp oil until golden. Add the grated carrots and cook with the lid on until tender.
5. Add the honey, ginger, 1 teasp salt and the black pepper, then stir gradually into the rice with a large fork.
6. Reheat in a moderate oven, Gas 4 (350°F, 180°C), for 20 minutes (or 30 minutes if the rice is cold).

TO SERVE
Serve on a heated oval platter.

Vermicelli Rice Ring with Nuts

Serves 6–8

This dish will freeze for 1 month or will keep for 2 days under refrigeration

A simple dish, but presented in a rather stylish ring, topped with sautéed pine kernels.

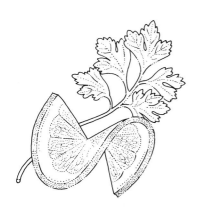

12 oz (350 g/2 cups) Basmati rice
30 fl. oz (850 ml/3¾ cups) chicken stock or water
1 oz (25 g/2 tbsp) butter or margarine
2 tbsp sunflower oil
2 oz (50 g/½ cup) pine kernels
1 onion, finely chopped
6 oz (175 g) vermicelli
1 teasp salt
15 grinds black pepper

THE CHEAPER ALTERNATIVE

Omit the pine kernels. Instead, substitute an equal quantity of broken cashew nuts (less expensive than whole ones) or use dried roasted peanuts straight from the packet

1. Rinse the rice in a colander under the cold tap until the water runs clear. Leave to soak in the measured stock.
2. In a large ovenproof casserole, melt the butter and oil and sauté the pine kernels over gentle heat until pale gold. Drain on crumpled kitchen paper.
3. Add the onion to the fat and sauté until soft and golden.
4. Stir in the broken vermicelli and continue to cook until it has taken on a little colour.
5. Pour in the rice and stock, bring to the boil over moderate heat, stirring, then season with the salt and pepper.
6. Cook in a moderate oven, Gas 4 (350°F, 180°C), for 30 minutes. Fluff up with a fork.
7. Thoroughly grease a 2½ pint (1·5 litre) ring mould and scatter the base with the nuts.
8. Spoon in the cooked rice mixture, packing it down well, and cover with foil. Either refrigerate at this point or return to the oven for 15 minutes.
9. To reheat from cold: sprinkle the surface with 2 tbsp water, cover and bake at Gas 3 (325°F, 160°C) for 20 minutes.

TO SERVE
Turn out on to a heated platter.

TO BRING RICE BACK TO LIFE

To defrost frozen rice in a covered container:
1. Leave overnight in the refrigerator.
   or
2. Cook in the microwave on 50% power for 4–5 minutes until steaming, stirring half way through with a fork.

To reheat rice in a covered container:
First sprinkle lightly with water (to create steam), then either:
1. Cook in the microwave on 100% power for 2–3 minutes until steaming, stirring half way through with a fork.
   or
2. Reheat in a moderate oven, Gas 4 (350°F, 180°C) or over moderate heat on top of the stove, for 15 minutes.

Note Always fluff up rice with a fork, never stir it with a spoon which crushes the grains together.

Timbales of Saffron Rice

Serves 8

This dish will freeze for 2 months or will keep under refrigeration for 2 days

Cardamom, cumin and cinnamon are classic flavourings in many rice cultures. The 'timbale' is a French conceit – we keep just one timbale in the kitchen. Each serving takes only 10 seconds to be moulded in it and then turned out to decorate the dish. If you don't have saffron, add about $\frac{1}{2}$ teasp turmeric to the pan in step 3 to give the rice a pale golden colour.

$\frac{1}{2}$ *teasp saffron threads or* $\frac{1}{2}$ *teasp ground turmeric (see above)*
$1\frac{1}{4}$ *pints (725 ml/3 cups) very hot water*
1 teasp salt
1 lb (450 g/$2\frac{2}{3}$ cups) Basmati rice
1 teasp whole cumin seeds
1 cinnamon stick
seeds from 2 cardamon pods
1 bayleaf
3 oz (75 g/$\frac{1}{3}$ cup) butter or margarine
2 medium onions, finely chopped

1. Add the saffron threads to the water and salt and allow to steep for 5 minutes.
2. Wash the rice in a sieve until the water runs clear (to remove the starch), then add to the saffron water and leave to soak for 30 minutes.
3. In a flameproof casserole cook the cumin seeds, cinnamon stick, cardamom seeds (turmeric if using) and bayleaf in the fat over moderate heat, swirling the pan for 2 minutes to release the perfume.
4. Add the onion and cook, stirring occasionally, until soft and golden.
5. Add the rice and saffron water, bring to the boil, stirring constantly, then cover with a round of silicone paper, then the lid and bake in a moderate oven, Gas 4 (350°F, 180°C), for 20 minutes or until the liquid is absorbed and rice is tender. (This can be done on top of the stove if preferred.)
6. Let the rice stand for at least 10 minutes, then discard the bayleaf and cinnamon stick and keep warm. Alternatively the rice can be refrigerated and then reheated and treated as newly cooked.

TO SERVE
Just before serving, pack into timbale moulds, then gently unmould on to each serving plate.

SOPHISTICATED SALADS

Here are some salads to toss and fragrant dressings to shake up. We start with five salads in varying shades of green, and then travel south to the sun for inspiration. Finally, we let pasta – fusilli and fresh fettucini – give an added dimension of importance to two innovative salads.

GARLIC

We particularly like the purple garlic grown around the Mediterranean and often to be bought from wayside stalls or markets, particularly in Provence (although it is now widely available in supermarkets and greengrocers). This is at its best in late summer and autumn when the bulbs have fat juicy cloves, the flavour is pungent yet sweet, and the papery skin is easy to remove.

We are wary of buying it, however, in early spring because by then many of the garlic cloves will have dried out and you may find when you get it home that you've actually bought a collection of empty husks. Then we sometimes resort to dried 'garlic granules'. These are particularly useful in a salad dressing – $\frac{1}{4}$ teasp of the granules is the equivalent of 1 fresh clove – as they soften and disintegrate if left in it for several hours. Prepared garlic purée is also available, but while this 'does' for emergency use, it does not have the lively pungency of the fresh cloves. We generally avoid commercial garlic salt as it's usually made from the poor-quality remnants that are otherwise unsaleable and tends to develop 'off' odours very quickly.

If you only want a hint of garlic in a dressing, leave half a peeled clove in it for several hours whilst the dressing matures then remove it before tossing the salad. The truly timid garlic-eater can ensure that only a suspicion of the flavour reaches a salad by spearing half a clove on a fork and rubbing it round the inside of the salad bowl, then discarding it.

Master Class Vinaigrette

Sufficient for 3 salads, each serving 6

The vinaigrette will keep for 1 week under refrigeration

We always keep this dressing on hand for both green and cooked vegetable salads. There is a good oil/acid balance which can always be sharpened if necessary with a little extra vinegar. You may prefer to leave out the parsley and onion from the basic mixture – and add them only when necessary – which improves the keeping qualities so that the vinaigrette can be stored for up to a month. Mustard helps the mixture to emulsify so that it will coat the salad ingredients with a thin layer of the dressing. We have found that a ratio of one part to three allows the olive oil to flavour the dressing without overwhelming it, but you can alter the proportion – or use only sunflower oil if you prefer.

9 fl. oz (250 ml/1 cup + 2 tbsp) sunflower oil
3 fl. oz (75 ml/$\frac{1}{3}$ cup) virgin olive oil
3 fl. oz (75 ml/$\frac{1}{3}$ cup) wine vinegar
3 teasp lemon juice
3 teasp caster sugar (or synthetic substitute)
1$\frac{1}{2}$ teasp prepared whole-grain mustard
1$\frac{1}{2}$ teasp sea salt
15 grinds black pepper
2 medium cloves garlic, halved
3 tbsp parsley, chopped
1 small onion, finely chopped (or 3 oz/75 g spring onion bulbs or shallots, finely chopped)

1. Put all the ingredients in a large screw-top jar or bowl and shake or whisk well until thickened.
2. Leave in the refrigerator to mature for several hours.

THE GREENING OF THE SALAD BOWL

'Frisée' is the new French name for what has long been known by the British as 'curly endive'. The French *used* to call it 'chicorée' thus totally confusing cooks on the other side of the Channel to whom 'chicory' is the oval white vegetable first cultivated by the Belgians. They in their turn call it 'witloof' – white leaf. Perhaps if we all use the word 'frisée' for this curly lettuce it will eventually make for an improved 'entente cordiale'!

Many greengrocers are now selling only the pale green, delicately flavoured hearts of frisée without the bitter, dark green leaves which are unusable in a salad. But it must be said that though the texture is a great improvement on a flat lettuce, the colour is a little insipid and the flavour a touch feeble. To brighten up the salad bowl one needs a selection of other salad greens as well. Perhaps the intriguingly shaped golden brown 'oak leaf' ('chêne') lettuce; or the curly edged Batavia lettuce (or 'escarole') or the solid-hearted iceberg or Webb lettuces; or the long, sweet-hearted 'Cos' or 'London' lettuce (known as 'romaine' in the United States). For a greater contrast of size and texture, there are the dark green leaves of watercress or the pale ones of lamb's lettuce ('mâche' or 'cornsalad') and perhaps just a hint of the rose-pink 'radicchio' – known in Italy as 'rosso di Verona' – which, to bring this saga full-circle, is actually first cousin to chicory or 'witloof'!

Garden Salad with Summer Herbs

Serves 6–8

Serve the same day

The concept of herbs treated as a salad vegetable rather than a garnish was introduced to us at a memorable lunch one hot Athens afternoon. We find it gives visual as well as textural interest to a mixed salad. The raw courgettes have a delicious nutty flavour.

1 Batavia lettuce
1 Cos lettuce
1 bunch watercress, leaves only
1 fine bulb of fennel, trimmed
2 tbsp fresh lemon juice
6–8 red radishes, thinly sliced
8 oz (225 g) small courgettes, topped, tailed and very thinly sliced
1 small handful fresh parsley
1 small handful basil leaves

FOR THE DRESSING
5 fl. oz (150 ml/⅔ cup) Master Class vinaigrette (see opposite)

1. Wash, spin dry then wrap the lettuces and watercress in a dry teatowel and leave in the refrigerator to crisp for at least 2 hours.
2. Slice the fennel (discarding the tough base) and leave in a bowl sprinkled with the lemon juice. This prevents browning and also lessens the strong flavour of aniseed.
3. One hour before the meal, tear the lettuces into bite-sized pieces and arrange with all the remaining ingredients in a salad bowl large enough to allow the contents to be later tossed with the dressing. Cover and refrigerate again until required.

TO SERVE
This is dressed at the table! Shake the vinaigrette well and pour over the salad, tossing until all the ingredients are glistening.

SUMMER HERBS IN WINTER

Our herb bed pays us dividends at every season of the year. In late spring and summer it is sheer delight to pick the growing herbs – the spiky chives (we leave one plant uncut so it will develop its charming blue flowerheads), the golden lemon thyme, the green-tasselled dill and fennel, the scented pot marjoram and vigorous mint (spreading everywhere if we let it) and, in the unheated greenhouse (to protect the tender leaves from any unseasonal chills), the sweet and spicy basil. Right through the season we harvest our garden herbs, to use fresh or to freeze or dry for winter use.

Chives are cut in 6 inch (15 cm) lengths (usually three times during the season), then tied into 'faggots' with string before being enclosed in plastic bags and frozen. Out of season we chop or cut off as much as we need of the frozen herb then return the remainder to the freezer for later use.

Dill responds well to drying, particularly in a forced-air or fan oven. We put as much freshly picked dill as will make a layer 1–2 inches (2·5–5 cm) deep on a wire cake tray, then leave it in a very low oven, Gas $\frac{1}{4}$ (225°F, 110°C) for 50 minutes, turning it occasionally. It is ready when it feels absolutely bone dry and can be crumbled in the fingers. We rub it through a coarse metal sieve – to separate the stalks from the leaves, then store in an airtight container in a cool dry cupboard.

French Winter Salad

Serves 6–8

Serve the same day

Marinating the avocado in advance not only prevents it browning but also greatly enhances its flavour.

1 ripe avocado
1 green pepper
1 head frisée
1 oak leaf (or Batavia) lettuce (or 6 inch/15 cm length of Chinese leaves)
1 pack watercress leaves
1 oz (25 g/$\frac{1}{4}$ cup) toasted sesame seeds

FOR THE DRESSING
5 fl. oz (150 g/$\frac{2}{3}$ cup) Master Class vinaigrette (see page 122)

1. Several hours before serving, peel and stone the avocado and cut into thin crescents. Halve and deseed the pepper and cut into similar-sized pieces.
2. Put both into a bowl, cover with the dressing and refrigerate.
3. Wash and dry the different salad leaves and put into a large salad bowl lined with a teatowel. Cover loosely with a towel and refrigerate.
4. Half an hour before serving, lift out the leaves, tear into bite-sized pieces and return them to the bowl.
5. Add the avocado and pepper slivers together with the dressing and toss gently together so that the leaves are coated.

TO SERVE
Sprinkle with the sesame seeds.

At the first foretaste of winter, we bring the **bay tree** into the porch (we also keep a **rosemary** bush in a tub there as well), so that the leaves can be picked throughout the entire year. However, any leaves that are removed when the bush is pruned can be dried on paper towels in the microwave. A handful will probably take 2 minutes on full power before they begin to curl.

Parsley is washed, dried and bagged before freezing, then crumbled still frozen into soups, stews, casseroles and dressings.

Mint is best made into mint jelly or sauce, or dried like dill.

Basil will keep all its pungency and colour if made into pesto (see page 126) and refrigerated. The leaves go black in the freezer but they can still be used to flavour any dish that contains liquid, then removed before serving.

TO SAVOUR THEIR FLAVOUR

Chop: parsley, marjoram, thyme and mint

Tear: basil

Snip: dill, fennel, chives and lovage

A Country Garden Salad with a Blue Cheese Dressing

Serves 6–8

Serve the same day

Pecans have a sweeter, less assertive flavour than walnuts which makes them ideal partners for a simple salad of mixed green leaves. The addition to the vinaigrette of a little crumbled blue cheese sharpens the flavour without overwhelming it.

hearts of 2 Cos lettuces
1 head radicchio
1 bunch watercress, stalks discarded
2 fat heads chicory, leaves separated and left whole
1 bunch lamb's lettuce
2 tbsp tiny parsley sprigs
4 oz (125 g/1 cup) pecans, shelled and broken

FOR THE DRESSING
5 fl. oz (150 ml/$\frac{2}{3}$ cup) Master Class vinaigrette (see page 122)
3 oz (75 g/$\frac{3}{4}$ cup) Danish Blue cheese (or Stilton, or Bleu de Bresse), crumbled

1. Wash, spin dry, then wrap all the salad greens in a tea-towel and leave in the refrigerator to crisp for at least 2 hours.
2. An hour before the meal, tear the Cos lettuces and radicchio into bite-sized pieces and arrange in a large salad bowl with the other ingredients. Cover and refrigerate.
3. Just before serving, gently shake the vinaigrette and cheese together in a screw-top jar.

TO SERVE
Gently spoon the dressing over the salad, tossing until the leaves are glistening.

TO SLIVER AND TOAST ALMONDS

Soak whole blanched almonds for 15 minutes in boiling water to cover. Drain, blot dry, then cut in strips with a cook's knife. Toast in a moderate oven, Gas 4 (350°F, 180°C) for 10 minutes, shaking once or twice, until golden brown and crisp.

You could also brown them under a gentle grill, or toss in a non-stick frying pan set over moderate heat until golden brown.

Chicory, Frisée and Black Grape Salad with Toasted Almonds

Serves 6–8

Serve the same day

A refreshing salad to serve after a hearty main course such as the roast beef Dijonnaise (see page 69).

8 oz (225 g) chicory
1 head frisée
5 fl. oz (150 ml/⅔ cup) Master Class vinaigrette (see page 122)
1 tbsp finely snipped chives
1 teasp dried Herbes de Provence
8 oz (225 g) black grapes, halved and pipped
2 oz (50 g/½ cup) split blanched almonds, toasted and lightly salted

1. Cut the stems from the chicory and discard any damaged outer leaves. Separate the leaves, then wash and spin dry.
2. Discard the root and the tough green outer leaves of the frisée. Separate the leaves then wash and spin dry.
3. Put the vinaigrette in a small bowl, add the chives and the Herbes de Provence and whisk until the mixture emulsifies again.

TO SERVE

In a salad bowl, combine the prepared chicory and frisée with the halved grapes and the toasted salted almonds. Pour on the herbed vinaigrette and toss until the leaves are well coated and glistening.

INSTANT PESTO FOR A SALAD DRESSING

Into the food processor, put a small handful of basil leaves, a tablespoon each of pine kernels, olive oil and Parmesan cheese. Process to a purée then add the remaining dressing ingredients, process until thickened to an emulsion and use as required.

Bean, Pepper and Artichoke Salad with Pesto

Serves 6–8 or 10 at a buffet

The salad will keep for 2 days under refrigeration

The pesto dressing gives this interesting salad an unexpected – and very satisfying – flavour. Serve it with a platter of cold roast meat or chicken.

1 × 15 oz (425 g) can red kidney beans, drained
1 × 15 oz (425 g) can cannellini (haricot) beans, drained
1 large (8 oz/225 g) red pepper, cut in ⅜ inch (1 cm) dice
1 × 15 oz (425 g) can artichoke hearts, drained and sliced in four
small bunch spring onions, trimmed and finely sliced
8 oz (225 g) cherry tomatoes

FOR THE DRESSING
4 tbsp olive oil
3 teasp (1 oz/25 g) pesto
2 tbsp red wine vinegar
½ teasp salt
10 grinds black pepper

FOR THE GARNISH
a few sprigs fresh basil

1. Put the drained beans into a bowl, and add the red pepper dice, the artichoke heart slices and the spring onions.
2. For the dressing, put the oil in a small bowl and whisk in the pesto followed by the remaining dressing ingredients.
3. Pour over the salad, toss gently and chill for at least 2 hours.

TO SERVE
Just before serving, add the tomatoes, toss gently again and arrange in a shallow serving dish. Garnish with the sprigs of fresh basil.

THE SALAD TOMATO

Tomatoes ripened under a hot Southern sun are the essential ingredient for all those simple but utterly delicious Greek, Italian and French salads which linger in the holiday memory. Back home, you have a choice: either grow your own – the tiny cherry tomatoes such as 'Gardener's Delight' seem to develop the best flavour in Northern climes, and are available by name in some shops – or buy larger tomatoes then allow them to ripen at kitchen temperature for 2 or 3 days when the orange colour of the skin will turn a deep red and the juices inside it sweeten. (Sunshine, or even daylight, is *not* essential.) Refrigerate the ripe tomatoes to stop them over-ripening – when the skin will begin to shrivel – but always leave them at room temperature for at least an hour before eating.

Mangetout and Tomato Salad

Serves 6–8

Serve the same day

The barely-cooked mangetout add the crunch element to this minty tomato salad. Serve it with a rich and saucy meat dish such as Veau Poêlé au Vermouth (see page 70).

1 lb (450 g) medium mangetout, strings removed
1 lb (450 g) medium well-ripened tomatoes
1 large green pepper

FOR THE DRESSING
6 tbsp extra virgin olive oil
3 tbsp white wine vinegar
1 level teasp each caster sugar and sea salt
15 grinds black pepper
1 tbsp chopped spring onion
1 tbsp chopped parsley
1 tbsp snipped chives
3 teasp mint jelly

1. Cook the mangetout in a large pan of rapidly boiling salted water, with the lid off, until just bite-tender.
2. Immediately turn into a colander or salad spinner and drench with cold water until steaming stops – this will 'set' the colour. Drain thoroughly, or spin dry.
3. Shake all the dressing ingredients together in a screw-top jar until thickened to an emulsion.

4. Cut the tomatoes into six or eight wedges (depending on their size). Halve and deseed the pepper and cut into very fine dice.
5. Put the dressing into a mixing bowl, add all the vegetables and toss gently to coat, using two spoons.

TO SERVE

Half an hour before the meal, transfer the dressed salad to a shallow serving dish and leave at room temperature.

THE MELLOW MELON

It used to be easy to tell when a particular melon was ready to eat. With a honeydew melon, you gently palpated the neck (blossom) end and softness equalled ripeness. Or you put your nose to a canteloupe or Charentais type melon and judged its maturity by the strength of its musky perfume. Now, however, the melon market is flooded with many newly developed varieties, some of which need different tests for ripeness.

A counsel of good sense, therefore, is to buy *any* variety of melon at least 3 days in advance. If it passes the ripeness test when you get it home it can be held in that condition under refrigeration for up to 4 days. If not, it can be allowed to ripen at room temperature.

The two most interesting new varieties of melon, the Galia and the Ogen, are of the Charentais type, whose perfume indicates their degree of ripeness. In addition the green skin of the Galia must turn yellow before it can be used.

Remember, however, you don't have a second chance. As with the avocado and the pear, once a melon is cut its ripening cycle comes abruptly to a halt.

Melon and Cherry Tomato Salad

Serves 8–10

The salad will keep for 1 day under refrigeration

Very pretty and refreshing for a summer buffet.

1 large ripe Galia (or Ogen) melon
1 lb (450 g) cherry tomatoes

FOR THE DRESSING
3 tbsp sunflower oil
1 tbsp huile de noix (walnut oil)
3 tbsp raspberry vinegar
½ teasp salt
speck white pepper
2 tbsp lemony mayonnaise
1 tbsp finely chopped fresh mint

FOR THE GARNISH
a few tiny sprigs fresh mint

1. Use a melon baller to scoop out the melon.
2. If tomatoes are too large for a mouthful, cut in half.
3. Put all the salad dressing ingredients into a screw-top jar and shake together very thoroughly until thickened – about 2 minutes.

TO SERVE

An hour before serving, combine the tomatoes and melon balls, and mix gently with the dressing. Arrange in a bowl and chill. Garnish with the mint leaves just before setting on the table.

A VARIETY OF VINEGARS

Raspberry vinegar – one of the more useful clichés of nouvelle cuisine – is the modern descendant of the fruit vinegars of Victorian times which were really fruit cordials to be diluted for summer drinks. Because it is sweetened, raspberry vinegar goes particularly well in the dressing for savoury fruit salads – it's an excellent partner for strawberries, and also for the vinaigrette used to dress avocados. But there are many other interesting unsweetened fruit and herb vinegars, which are made simply by steeping the flavouring ingredient in them for a week or so. You can buy these from the more adventurous kind of grocer. Currently we have in stock wine vinegars flavoured variously with lemon, tarragon, lime, blackcurrant and 'fruits of the forest' (dark berries) – plenty of room here for the adventurous salad-maker to experiment.

Melon and Strawberry Mélange with a Raspberry Vinegar Dressing

Serves 6–8

Serve the same day

A salad for early summer to serve in tart contrast to the rich and smooth Sole Lautrec (see page 64).

> 6 inch (15 cm) piece cucumber
> salt
> 3–4 very small melons (Galia or Ogen type)
> 1 lb (450 g) strawberries

FOR THE DRESSING
> 2 tbsp caster sugar
> 4 tbsp hot water
> 1½ tbsp raspberry vinegar (or red wine vinegar)
> 4 tbsp coarsely chopped fresh mint

FOR THE GARNISH
> 3 oz (75 g/¾ cup) toasted split almonds
> 6–8 tiny sprigs mint

1. First prepare the cucumber. Score the skin with a cannelle cutter, slice thinly, then cut the slices in half. Put in a salad spinner sprinkled with salt and leave for 30 minutes. Rinse and spin dry.
2. Cut the melons in half by the vandyke method (see page 28). Remove the seeds and scoop out the flesh with a baller. Keep the shells. Put the balls in a strainer over a bowl and leave until required (can be overnight).
3. Slice the strawberries and leave until required.
4. To make the dressing, put the sugar in a large heatproof bowl, pour on the hot water and stir to dissolve. Stir in the vinegar and then the chopped mint.

TO SERVE
Half an hour before dinner, put the strawberries, melon balls and cucumber into the dressing and stir lightly. Divide between the melon shell halves. Chill. Just before serving, sprinkle with the toasted nuts and garnish with a mint sprig.

PLEASE COMPOSE YOURSELF

As usual, the French have the right word for it. For a 'Salade Composée' is just that – a still life composition in the classic style. The Italian salad on the right is in this tradition – the ingredients arranged in a symmetrical fashion with the dressing lightly spooned on top. But the newest version of the genre – the 'Salade Tiède' of the nouvelle cuisine – though composed with equal skill, has its bouquet of salad leaves and slivers of poultry or fish arranged more like an abstract painting than an Old Master.

A Salad of Avocado, Mozzarella and Tomatoes in a Fresh Herb Dressing

Serves 6–8

Serve within 2 hours

This classic Italian salad is enlivened with slices of ripe avocado. It can be served as a light main course as well as on the buffet table

8 oz (225 g/2 cups) buffalo milk Mozzarella (or Gouda) cheese, chilled and then sliced $\frac{1}{4}$ inch ($\frac{5}{8}$ cm) thick
1$\frac{1}{4}$ lb (575 g) fully ripe salad tomatoes, sliced $\frac{1}{4}$ inch ($\frac{5}{8}$ cm) thick
2 fat, ripe but firm avocados, halved, peeled and sliced $\frac{1}{4}$ inch ($\frac{5}{8}$ cm) thick

FOR THE DRESSING
3 tbsp extra virgin olive oil
3 tbsp sunflower oil
2 tbsp bottled sun-dried tomatoes (or 1 extra tbsp each olive oil and vinegar and 1 teasp tomato purée)
1$\frac{1}{2}$ tbsp lemon vinegar (or lemon juice)
2 tbsp snipped chives
1 tbsp parsley, chopped
1 tbsp fresh basil (or $\frac{1}{2}$ teasp dried basil)
1 medium clove garlic, finely chopped
15 grinds black pepper
$\frac{1}{2}$ teasp sea salt

FOR THE GARNISH
sprigs of fresh herbs
4 oz (125 g/1 cup) black Provençale olives

1. Two hours before serving, arrange the sliced cheese, tomatoes and avocado on a large flat platter, $\frac{1}{2}$ inch (1$\frac{1}{4}$ cm) deep, or on 6–8 small individual dishes.
2. Shake all the dressing ingredients together until thickened, then drizzle over the salad, making sure the avocado slices are well coated.

TO SERVE
Just before serving, garnish with the fresh herbs and olives, and serve with granary bread or Honey and Walnut Knots (page 21).

MAKING THE TOSS

A correctly dressed salad should have every surface of each ingredient lightly coated with dressing. To achieve this result you either follow the Italian fashion and put the dressing in the bowl first and then lay the greens on top, or you arrange the salad in the bowl first and then sprinkle and toss. To perform either technique efficiently, you need a bowl – be it shallow or deep – with sides wider than the base. This enables you to toss the salad thoroughly but lightly with a spoon and fork, without scattering any of it on the table.

A Salad from the Sun

Serves 6–8

Serve the same day

Green and fruity, with a creamy dressing, this would be an ideal 'chaser' to the Poulet Fendu au Four (see page 83).

2 large mangos
2 medium avocados, ripe but still firm
1 heart of celery, about 8 sticks
2 crisp green-skinned eating apples
8 oz (225 g) black grapes
1 head frisée
4 tbsp dry roasted cashews

FOR THE DRESSING
2 rounded tbsp of a lemony mayonnaise
3 tbsp sunflower oil
1 tbsp huile de noix (walnut oil)
2 tbsp raspberry vinegar
$\frac{1}{2}$ teasp salt
10 grinds black pepper
1 tbsp fresh dill, snipped

1. Four hours before the meal, put all the dressing ingredients into a large bowl and whisk together until smooth.
2. Peel the mangos and cut away from the stone, then cut in sections about $1\frac{1}{2}$ inches ($3\frac{3}{4}$ cm) long.
3. Halve, stone and peel the avocados, and cut into crescents of a similar size.
4. Core the apples, halve, then cut into segments of a similar size.
5. Cut the celery into half inch ($1\frac{1}{4}$ cm) lengths.
6. Halve and deseed the grapes.
7. Add all these ingredients to the dressing, stirring gently until evenly coated. Refrigerate.
8. Wash and spin dry the frisée, wrap in a tea towel and chill.

TO SERVE
An hour before serving, line a shallow bowl with the frisée (torn into bite-sized pieces), then spoon in the dressed fruits and vegetables. Scatter with the cashews. Serve chilled.

Cucumber and Orange Segments in a Minted Cream Dressing

Serves 6–8

This salad will keep for 1 day under refrigeration

A light, refreshing salad to serve after a fish dish.

2 large cucumbers, thinly sliced
1 tbsp salt
3 large navel oranges, segmented

FOR THE DRESSING
8 oz (225 g/1 cup) strained Greek-style cow's yoghurt
2 teasp each fresh lemon juice, white wine vinegar and caster sugar
$\frac{1}{2}$ teasp salt
10 grinds black pepper
1 small clove garlic, crushed
1 tbsp chopped mint leaves (or 1 teasp dried mint)

FOR THE GARNISH
tiny sprigs fresh mint

1. Several hours before the meal put all the dressing ingredients into a large basin and whisk lightly together. Refrigerate.
2. Put the slices of cucumber in a salad spinner or colander, sprinkle with the salt and leave for 30 minutes then rinse and dry.
3. Remove the cucumber to one bowl and the orange segments to another, cover and refrigerate.
4. An hour before serving add cucumber and orange to the dressing and turn to coat, using two spoons.

TO SERVE
Transfer to a shallow dish, such as a pottery quiche dish.

Piperies Salata

(Toasted Pepper Salad)

Serves 6

Keeps 48 hours under refrigeration

A wonderful pepper salad in green, scarlet and gold, which can be prepared the day before. Delicious with something like the pasteles on page 42.

1 large green pepper and 1 large yellow pepper
2 × 14 oz (400 g) cans red pimentos in brine
6 oz (175 g/1$\frac{1}{2}$ cups) fine black olives

ROASTED PEPPERS

Actually a misnomer – at least in Western terms – because they're really grilled or, if you like, 'roasted' over charcoal. By the time the skin has become black and charred, the flesh inside will be deliciously tender.

To remove the skin, simply put the whole peppers in a large plastic bag and allow the trapped steam to soften it so it can be easily stripped off with the fingers.

FRUIT FROM A TREE A THOUSAND YEARS OLD

That's the olive – to which you'll notice we're rather partial at Master Class. Black – or ripe – olives in particular. Our favourites are the Calamata and the Provençale. Greek Calamata are oval in shape with a meaty texture and a particularly delicious flavour imparted by the mixture of olive oil and wine vinegar in which they're canned. They are excellent as a garnish or with pre-dinner drinks. Olives from Provence, on the other hand, which are round and tender-fleshed, can be easily separated from their stone so they are ideal for slicing into a salad or stew.

A CULINARY SPIN DRYER

The principle of centrifugal force which is utilised to dry clothes – as well as to separate the cream from the milk – is used in the salad spinner to dramatic effect. It removes every drop of moisture from salad greens of every variety and is particularly useful in drying aubergines, courgettes and cucumber slices that have been salted to draw out unwelcome moisture. We also use it to dry washed parsley which can then be kept fresh and crisp in an airtight container for as long as 10 days. We think that drying lettuce in a spinner is the only way to ensure that, whatever the variety, it stays fresh and crisp for up to 24 hours. (Wrap the leaves in a soft absorbent teatowel, lay this in a bowl and refrigerate until needed.)

FOR THE DRESSING
6 tbsp virgin olive oil
1 large clove garlic, crushed
2 tbsp finely chopped fresh coriander (or parsley)
1 teasp dried mint (or 1 tbsp fresh, chopped, in season)
1½ tbsp lemon juice
10 grinds black pepper
1 teasp sea salt

1. Grill the fresh peppers under or over fierce heat until the skin has blackened and feels papery all over (10–15 minutes). Leave until cool enough to handle then remove the skin and seeds.
2. Drain the canned peppers then cut all the peppers into strips ½ inch (1·25 cm) wide and place in a shallow (e.g. gratin) dish with the olives.
3. Whisk the remaining ingredients together in a small bowl then spoon over the peppers. Cover and refrigerate overnight.

Strawberry and Cucumber Salad

Serves 6–8

Serve the same day

The sweetened vinegar dressing – a Scandinavian notion – makes a light and refreshing salad to serve with a whole salmon (see page 50) or to accompany a rich chicken dish such as Pollo in Pepitoria (see page 88).

1 fat cucumber
1 lb (450 g) strawberries

FOR THE DRESSING
2 level tbsp caster sugar
2 tbsp boiling water
2 tbsp each raspberry vinegar and wine vinegar
1 tbsp snipped fresh dill (or chopped mint leaves)

FOR THE GARNISH
sprigs dill (or mint)

1. Make the dressing 2 hours before dinner. Dissolve the sugar in the boiling water then stir in the vinegars and dill (or mint). Allow to cool.
2. Finely slice the unpeeled cucumber and thickly slice the hulled strawberries.

TO SERVE
Arrange cucumber and strawberries in concentric circles in a shallow dish and pour over the dressing. Garnish with the fresh herbs.

PASTA PERFECT

This depends on the quality of the pasta and the manner in which it is cooked. If possible we buy chilled fresh pasta as it is lighter and more delicate on the tongue. However, dried pasta will do very well in a salad as it's difficult to tell the fresh from the dried when the pasta is cold. Here the cooking method is all important to ensure that the pasta still has some 'bite' to it even when it is dressed.

To cook pasta, we allow it to 'swim' in a very large pan of rapidly boiling salted water, stirring it occasionally with a wooden spoon or fork to keep it on the move. As the pasta enters the boiling water it will lower the temperature. Immediately cover the pan to allow it to come back to the boil as quickly as possible, then just as quickly uncover it to complete the cooking. (A covered pasta pan inevitably overflows.)

One cannot abandon a pan of bubbling pasta as it's essential to keep on testing it for doneness every minute or so. The cooking time varies with the shape of the pasta as well as with the freshness, so start testing fresh pasta after 3 minutes, dry pasta after 8. It must be cooked 'al dente' – when there is no suspicion of uncooked starch, but still a little resistance as the teeth bite into it. Now the cooking must stop at once, so take it off the heat and add a cup of cold water, then drain and use according to the recipe.

A Salad of Fusilli and Smoked Salmon in a Lightly Curried Dressing

Serves 6

Serve the same day

An elegant main-dish salad or starter – to serve with plenty of light and crusty granary bread or the honey and walnut knots on page 21.

8 oz (225 g) smoked salmon, cut in julienne
9 oz (250 g) fusilli (pasta twists or spirals), cooked until 'al dente'
8 oz (225 g) fresh (or frozen) all-green asparagus, cooked until tender and cut in 1 inch (2·5 cm) pieces

FOR THE DRESSING
2 cartons strained Greek-style cow's yoghurt (or 2 × 5 fl. oz/150 ml/⅔ cup cartons soured cream)
5 fl. oz (150 ml/⅔ cup) whipping cream
1 clove garlic, crushed
1 teasp curry powder
15 grinds black pepper
2 tbsp finely grated onion
1 tbsp capers, drained

FOR THE GARNISH
a few reserved asparagus tips
paprika pepper

1. Earlier in the day, mix all the dressing ingredients in a bowl and lay the smoked salmon julienne on top. Cover and refrigerate.
2. An hour before serving, cook the pasta then refresh under cold water and drain well.
3. Turn the pasta into the dressing and gently toss until the pasta and smoked salmon are evenly coated.
4. Stir in the asparagus, reserving some of the tips for garnish. Leave at room temperature.

TO SERVE
Gently spoon the salad into a glazed earthenware dish. Garnish with the reserved asparagus tips and a light dusting of paprika.

HUILE DE NOIX

This exquisite if highly flavoured oil is pressed from the magnificent walnuts that grow in the Dordogne region of France. (Although we usually translate *'noix'* as plain and simple 'nuts', in France the word is specific to walnuts.)

At Master Class we are very frugal with our walnut oil, not only because of its price – it is even more expensive than many olive oils – but also because its intriguing flavour can become overpowering when added with too prodigal a hand. In our recipe for Walnut Knots, only 3 tbsp are needed to flavour 20 bread rolls. When you see it specified in a salad dressing – it goes particularly well with avocados – you will notice that it is used with a much larger quantity of a flavourless oil such as sunflower.

Because it has not been 'purified' or 'deodorised' like many of the cheaper cooking oils, it can quickly become rancid when exposed to light and heat, so it's best stored in the refrigerator where it will stay sweet for up to six months.

A Fresh Pasta Salad with an Anchovy, Aubergine and Green Coriander Dressing

Serves 6–8

Serve the same day

Ideal for a light summer lunch, with a cheese board on the side and fresh peaches to follow.

$\frac{3}{4}$–1 lb (350–450 g) *fresh fettucini*
3 tbsp olive oil

FOR THE SAUCE
1 lb (450 g) aubergine
1 tbsp salt
1 tbsp huile de noix (walnut oil)
1 tbsp sunflower oil
1 tbsp light soy sauce
black pepper
1 bunch fresh coriander (or 2 oz/50 g flat parsley), finely chopped
3 tbsp sesame seeds, toasted
1 can flat fillets of anchovy, cut in $\frac{1}{4}$ inch (6 cm) pieces

1. Cook the pasta until 'al dente', then drain thoroughly and immediately mix in a bowl with the olive oil. Set aside to cool completely.
2. To make the sauce, peel the aubergine and cut in $\frac{3}{4}$ inch (2 cm) cubes. Arrange in a salad spinner and sprinkle with the salt. Leave for 30 minutes then rinse and spin dry.
3. Heat the oils in a heavy frying pan, add aubergine cubes and cook over fierce heat, stirring, until tender – about 4–5 minutes. Stir in the soy sauce and black pepper.
4. Pour the hot aubergine mixture over the pasta and, using two forks, toss with the coriander leaves, sesame seeds and anchovies. Leave for at least 30 minutes (longer does no harm) for the pasta to soak up the seasonings.

TO SERVE
Serve the salad at room temperature.

LES GRANDS DESSERTS

We offer you every opportunity to indulge your guests – but with small servings please – with our luxurious chocolate desserts. Alternatively, tempt them with something frozen and fruity.

For a dramatic finish, guaranteed to impress, we have included two stunning desserts from the crêperie. And, for individual servings, we suggest you fill 'petit pots' with various delectable mixtures.

You will also find that it is easy to devise a spectacular finale to your meal with a little help from the pâtissier. It's all a matter of assembly.

SCHWARTZWALD KIRSCH ROULADE

Serves 8

Make the roulade exactly as opposite, but fill instead with a ganache (chocolate cream) and cherries.

1 can pitted Morello or black cherries, drained very well

FOR THE GANACHE
3 oz (75 g) plain chocolate, broken into pieces
1 tbsp water
1 oz (25 g/2 tbsp) caster sugar
8 fl. oz (225 ml/1 cup) whipping cream
2 tbsp Kirsch

1. For the ganache, in a small pan, melt the chocolate with the water and sugar (see page 141).
2. Add the cream and bring to the boil, either on top of the stove or on 100% power for 2½ minutes in the microwave.
3. Put in a shallow container and freeze for 45 minutes. Add the Kirsch and whisk until it is thick enough to hang on the whisk. Chill until required.
4. Spread the roulade with the ganache mixture and scatter with the well-drained cherries. Roll up, chill well, and dust thickly with icing sugar.

Chocolate and Chestnut Roulade

Serves 8

The roulade will freeze for 1 month or will keep for 2 days under refrigeration

There really is no need for any flour in this delicate sponge – the chocolate acts as a 'binder' instead. It is advisable to make it the day before, to make it easier to slice. However, it's the wise hostess who makes it even earlier and tucks it away in her freezer.

FOR THE ROULADE
6 oz (175 g) plain chocolate, broken into pieces and melted (see page 141)
2 tbsp hot water
6 oz (175 g/¾ cup) caster sugar
5 × no. 3 eggs, separated

FOR THE CHESTNUT FILLING
1 × 15 oz (425 g) can natural chestnut purée
3 oz (75 g/½ cup) icing sugar
2 tbsp any orange-flavoured liqueur (Cointreau, Curaçao, or Grand Marnier)

FOR THE CREAM
5 fl. oz (150 ml/⅔ cup) whipping (or non dairy) cream
1 teasp caster sugar
1 teasp grated orange rind

TO DREDGE THE CAKE
sifted icing sugar

1. To make the chestnut filling, beat all the ingredients together until a smooth cream.
2. To make the cream, whisk the cream until it stands in soft peaks, then stir in the sugar and orange rind.
3. To make the roulade, preheat the oven to Gas 4 (350°F, 180°C). Line a roulade tin approx. 12 × 8 × 1 inch (30 × 20 × 2·5 cm) with silicone paper, mitreing the corners to make a snug fit.
4. Stir the melted chocolate and hot water together to make the chocolate more liquid.
5. Add the sugar to the egg yolks in a small bowl and beat with a balloon whisk until pale and creamy.
6. Whisk the egg whites in a larger bowl until they hold stiff, glossy peaks.
7. Stir the melted chocolate into the yolk and sugar mixture then stir in a large tablespoon of meringue. Pour the chocolate mixture down the side of the bowl holding the beaten whites, then use a rubber spatula to fold the two gently together.
8. Coax this fluffy mixture into the tin and spread it evenly, particularly into the corners. Bake for 20 minutes, until

a skewer comes out clean from the centre of the cake.

9. While the cake is cooking, have ready two sheets of greaseproof or silicone paper (one thickly dusted with sifted icing sugar) and also a dry teatowel.

10. Remove the cooked roulade from the oven, transfer to a cooling tray and cover lightly with one sheet of paper and the teatowel. When quite cold, turn on to the icing-sugar paper, ease out of the tin, then slowly peel away the baking paper.

11. Spread first with an even layer of the chestnut mixture and then with the flavoured whipped cream.

12. With the help of the sugared paper, roll up the roulade carefully, then transfer to a serving dish. Chill thoroughly for several hours or, preferably, overnight.

TO SERVE
Dust thickly with more icing sugar just before serving.

MERINGUES IN MINIATURE

The same meringue that is used for a large torta can be miniaturised to serve with coffee, or as part of a pâtisserie display on a buffet table.

For dessert, the meringue should be piped into the shape of a nest about 3 inches ($7\frac{1}{2}$ cm) in diameter (remember that Pavlova-type meringues increase in size during the cooking period). This is most easily made using a $\frac{3}{8}$ inch ($\frac{3}{4}$ cm) wide plain or star nozzle, piping first the circle, then piping a 'rope' of meringue round the edges until the nest is about $1\frac{1}{2}$ inches (4 cm) high.

To serve as pâtisserie, use the same tube but pipe a succession of smaller and smaller blobs, each one depressing the previous one, to form a 'conch shell'. Sandwich two of these shells together and place in paper cases.

Bake either shape until they are crisp to the touch and can easily be lifted off the lining paper.

Torta di Cimabue Genoa

(Chocolate meringue layer with a chestnut liqueur filling)

**Serves 9–10 (12 with other desserts)
or 6–8 (10 with other desserts) (see opposite)**

This dessert will freeze for 1 month or keep for 3 days under refrigeration

We don't know how it got its name but this is a brilliant confection in any language. It is so good that we give two sets of quantities!

FOR THE CHOCOLATE MERINGUE LAYERS
*6 egg whites
$\frac{1}{4}$ teasp cream of tartar
12 oz (350 g/$1\frac{1}{2}$ cups) caster sugar
2 teasp cornflour
2 teasp vanilla essence
6 oz (175 g) plain chocolate, melted (see page 141)
6 oz (175 g/$1\frac{1}{2}$ cups) walnuts, finely chopped*

FOR THE FILLING
*1 × 15 oz (425 g) can natural chestnut purée
2 oz (50 g/$\frac{1}{3}$ cup) icing sugar
4 tbsp chocolate-flavoured liqueur (Sabra, Crème de Cacao)
4 tbsp cooled coffee (made with 4 teasp coffee granules)
15 fl. oz (425 ml/2 cups) double (or non dairy) cream*

FOR THE GARNISH
$3\frac{1}{2}$ oz (100 g) plain chocolate curls (see page 157)

1. To make the meringue layers, preheat the oven to Gas 2 (300°F, 150°C), and whisk the egg whites and the cream of tartar until they form soft peaks.

CREAM FOR WHIPPING

We generally use 'whipping cream' which has a fat content of between 35% and 42%. This whips easily and seems to enclose more air – thus producing a lighter-textured mixture – than 'double cream'. Double cream has a legal minimum fat content of 48% so its use is recommended when it is to be diluted before whipping with a liquid flavouring such as coffee, liqueur or fruit juice. Take care, however, as it is much easier to overwhip than whipping cream. If whipping cream is unavailable you can create your own by mixing together equal quantities of double cream and single cream (which has a minimum fat content of 18%).

Rules for successful whipping
1. Put the well-chilled cream in a well-chilled bowl.
2. Whisk quickly at first by hand or machine until the cream thickens, loses its gloss and begins to cling to the whisk.
3. Now whip more slowly until it reaches the consistency needed for the particular recipe. Go warily for the last few seconds, however, as overbeaten cream will separate into butter and whey and can never be brought back to the cream state again.

Whipping or double cream will double in volume when whipped – thus 5 fl. oz (150 ml/$\frac{2}{3}$ cup) cream in the carton equals 10 fl. oz (275 ml/$1\frac{1}{4}$ cups) when whipped.

If you wish to lower the fat content of the creamy element in a recipe, you can substitute an equal *volume* of strained Greek-style cow's yoghurt, which comes out of the carton already having the texture of a whipped cream. Thus 10 fl. oz (275 ml/$1\frac{1}{4}$ cups) of the yoghurt can replace 5 fl. oz (150 ml/$\frac{2}{3}$ cup) unwhipped double or whipping cream.

2. Add the caster sugar and cornflour a tablespoon at a time, whisking until stiff again after each addition. Whisk in the vanilla essence.
3. Stir one-quarter of this meringue into the slightly cooled melted chocolate then add to the remainder of the meringue together with the chopped walnuts. Gently whisk the two mixtures together until the colour is even.
4. Have ready three baking trays at least 10 inches (25 cm) wide, lined with silicone paper. Draw a 9 inch (22·5 cm) circle on each tray using a round baking tin or pan lid as a guide.
5. Pipe the meringue through a $\frac{1}{2}$ inch (1·25 cm) plain nozzle on to each of the three trays, in a spiral pattern.
6. Bake the meringues for 50 minutes until the top is crisp to the touch and a spatula can easily be inserted between the base and the paper. Allow to go cold still on the baking trays.
7. To make the filling, put the chestnut purée, icing sugar, liqueur and coffee into the food processor and process until smooth and creamy.
8. Whisk the cream until it holds firm peaks, then pulse 2 tbsp of it in to lighten the chestnut purée mixture. Fold both mixtures together. Chill until the meringue layers are quite cold.
9. To assemble the torta, carefully turn one layer on to a large serving dish or silver tray and spread a third of the chestnut cream all over it. Cover with the second meringue and spread with a further third of the cream.
10. Lay the final meringue on top, cover with the remaining cream piped in a spiral, and decorate with chocolate curls. Leave for 24 hours in the refrigerator before serving.

Quantities to serve 6–8 (10 with other desserts)

FOR THE CHOCOLATE MERINGUE LAYERS
4 egg whites
pinch cream of tartar
8 oz (225 g/1 cup) caster sugar
$1\frac{1}{2}$ teasp cornflour
1 teasp vanilla essence
4 oz (125 g) plain chocolate, melted (see page 141)
4 oz (125 g/1 cup) chopped walnuts

FOR THE FILLING
1 × 15 oz (425 g) can natural chestnut purée
2 oz (50 g/$\frac{1}{3}$ cup) icing sugar
3 tbsp chocolate-flavoured liqueur
3 tbsp cooled coffee (made with 3 teasp coffee granules)
10 fl. oz (275 ml/$1\frac{1}{4}$ cups) double (or non dairy) cream

Prepare and bake everything as before, but the meringue layers should be 7–8 inches (17·5–20 cm) in diameter.

WHEN IT'S TEATIME IN VIENNA

The ladies of modern-day Vienna (and many of the gentlemen too) sit at their marble-topped tables in the Café Demel – as the Viennese have done since the heyday of the Habsburghs in the nineteenth century – enjoying their afternoon slice of torte and their coffee with 'Schlagobers', the whipped cream that is the trademark of the Konditorei (tearooms) of Austria. It is a reflection of the importance that the Viennese attach to their cakemakers that a firm such as Demel, founded during the days of the 'ancien regime' and rejoicing still in the title of 'Imperial Royal Court Confectioner', takes its role in the life of the city so seriously that it actually stamps the bottom of its 'own brand' tins of cocoa with the Imperial Eagle, symbol of the lost Empire.

To the Viennese, their 'Gebäck, kuchen and torten' (pastry, plain cakes and gâteaux) are important matters of state. But just as much fun in our opinion as a sedate afternoon tea at Demel's, is to buy a 'takeaway' cake from a stall in the 'Nasch' (food) market, then stand in the street by the flower stalls eating a slice of a creamy pastry, a relic of a time of nutritional innocence when the word cholesterol had not yet been heard in the land.

There are, however, other kinds of Viennese cakes – moist nut cakes – that can be enjoyed without great helpings of cream. In the list of ingredients for such cakes – as for instance in the foundation for the 'Mohr in Hemd' – flour has been omitted and nuts ground to a similar texture are used instead. These cakes may be served topped with a rum icing, but in our opinion they do not need this kind of embellishment but can stand alone, unadorned, the perfect contemporary accompaniment to a good cup of coffee.

Möhr in Hemd

Serves 12–15

Freeze the complete cake for up to 1 month; refrigerate for 3 days. Cake alone will freeze for 3 months

This is a brilliant example of the pastry chef's art, from Austria.

FOR THE CAKE
8 oz (225 g/1 cup) caster sugar + 1 teasp vanilla essence (or 7 oz/200 g/1 cup caster sugar + 1 oz/25 g/2 tbsp vanilla sugar)
7 oz (200g) plain chocolate, grated
7 oz (200 g/1¾ cups) ground almonds
4 level tbsp fine dry breadcrumbs
6 eggs, separated
2 tbsp lemon juice

FOR THE TOPPING
5 fl. oz (150 ml/⅔ cup) each whipping cream and double cream
2 teasp icing sugar

FOR THE ICING
3 oz (75 g) plain chocolate, melted
1 oz (25 g/2 tbsp) butter, melted
1 tbsp brandy (or rum)

1. To make the cake, preheat the oven to Gas 4 (350°F, 180°C). Grease a 10½ inch (26 cm) springform round tin and line the bottom with silicone paper.
2. Divide the sugar into two equal portions. Mix the chocolate with the ground almonds and breadcrumbs.
3. Whisk the egg whites until they hold floppy peaks, then add one portion of the sugar, a tablespoon at a time, whisking until stiff after each addition.
4. Whisk the egg yolks until creamy, add the other portion of sugar gradually, followed by the lemon juice, then whisk until light and creamy.
5. Stir a few tablespoons of the meringue into the yolk mixture first, then fold the yolk mixture into the meringue, using a rubber spatula.
6. Finally, fold in the chocolate mixture, spoon into the tin, and spread level.
7. Bake for 30–35 minutes until the top is firm to a gentle touch, and a skewer or toothpick plunged into the centre comes out clean. Leave on a cooling tray for 30 minutes, then gently ease out of the tin. (The cake will keep moist in a plastic container for at least a week.)
8. To make the topping, whisk all the ingredients together until the mixture forms shiny peaks. *Do not overbeat.*

9. Spread evenly over the cake, then put in the freezer until solid – about 2 hours.
10. To make the icing, mix all the ingredients until smooth, then pour over the frozen cream. Chill until required.

Gâteau 'Queen of Sheba'

Serves 8

The cake will freeze for up to 3 months

The potato flour – or 'fécule' as it is known in France – gives this superb cake a particularly moist texture. It can be served plain, but is especially delicious accompanied by a fairly tart fruit compote – such as the nectarine one on page 148.

4 oz (125 g/$\frac{1}{2}$ cup) unsalted butter
6 oz (175 g) plain chocolate, broken into pieces
4 oz (125 g/$\frac{1}{2}$ cup) caster sugar
4 eggs, separated
1 teasp vanilla essence
2 oz (50 g/$\frac{1}{2}$ cup) potato flour
1 level teasp baking powder
pinch salt

FOR DREDGING THE CAKE
sifted icing sugar

1. Preheat the oven to Gas 4 (350°F, 180°C), and prepare either an 8 inch (20 cm) moule à manqué (shallow tin with sloping sides) or an 8 inch (20 cm) loose-bottomed tin: oil and bottom line with silicone paper.
2. Put the butter in a large heavy-based pan and melt it gently, then add the broken chocolate and sugar. Stir over very gentle heat until everything is melted together.
3. Take from the heat and stir in the egg yolks, vanilla, sifted potato flour and baking powder.
4. Finally, fold in the egg whites, beaten with the salt until they hold stiff but still glossy peaks.
5. Turn the mixture into the prepared tin and bake for 40–45 minutes until well risen and firm to a very gentle touch.
6. Leave on a cooling tray for 5 minutes then turn out and leave until cold. Dredge with icing sugar.

TO SERVE
Serve in slices accompanied by spoonfuls of compote.

MELTING CHOCOLATE

Break it into small pieces, then melt in a basin over a pan of very hot water.

You can also melt it in the microwave – 4 oz (125 g) will take 1½ minutes on 100% power. Stir well. If chocolate is melted with a liquid such as coffee it will probably take 30 seconds less.

WINES FOR DESSERT

With the possible exception of dishes containing citrus fruits or chocolate, one can usually find a wine to match even the most luscious dessert. The sweetness of the wine must, however, always equal that of the dessert or all that will come through on the palate will be its acidity.

Those fruits which themselves tend to develop 'winey' overtones as they mature will go happily with a sweet dessert wine such as Sauternes. These include apples, apricots, peaches, mangoes, papayas, passion fruit, figs and melons.

Some other partnerships:

● Apfelstrudel with a well-balanced German or Austrian white wine.

● Custards, cream and sweet mousses, fruit tarts and flans with Sauternes or Monbazillac (from the Dordogne).

● Christmas pudding with a fairly sweet sparkling wine.

● Fruit compotes with a sweet Muscatel such as Muscat de Beaumes de Venises.

● Hot soufflés (not lemon or orange) with a sweet wine from the Loire such as a Vouvray petillant (very slightly sparkling).

● Luscious gâteaux and torten with an Eiswein (rich and rare German wine).

● Icecreams and sorbets with a matching liqueur.

● Rich plain cakes (without filling or frosting) with a Madeira or a fairly sweet sherry.

Biscuit Tortoni

Serves 8–10

This icecream will freeze for up to 1 month

This smooth and creamy icecream – which is always served by tradition in little cups or pots – owes its delicious flavour of Jordan almonds to a combination of Amaretto liqueur and the famous Italian Amaretti biscuits. We know from our researches that this is an Italian/American classic, but we have yet to uncover the true story of Signor Tortoni!

3 eggs, separated
pinch salt
2½ oz (65 g/⅓ cup + 1 tbsp) icing sugar
10 fl. oz (275 ml/1¼ cups) whipping (or non dairy) cream
2 tbsp Amaretto liqueur
½ teasp vanilla essence
1 × 85 g (approx.) packet of Amaretti (or ratafia) biscuits, crushed to a coarse powder
2 oz (50 g/½ cup) toasted almond nibs

FOR THE GARNISH
8 oz (225 g/1½ cups) each raspberries and loganberries
3 tbsp caster sugar

1. Whisk the egg whites with the salt until they hold stiff peaks, then add the icing sugar a tablespoon at a time, whisking until stiff after each addition.
2. Whisk in the egg yolks, just enough to blend the colours evenly.
3. Whisk the cream with the liqueur and essence until it holds soft peaks.
4. Mix the biscuit crumbs and then the toasted almonds together, and reserve 2 rounded tbsp for garnish.
5. Fold the whipped cream into the meringue mixture together with the almond and biscuit mixture.
6. Divide between individual containers – demitasses, petit pots or soufflé dishes – and sprinkle the tops evenly with the reserved nut mixture.
7. Freeze for at least 12 hours.

TO SERVE
Sprinkle the raspberries and loganberries with the caster sugar just before serving. Place each container on a dessert plate and garnish with the sugared berries.

SOFT SCOOP ICECREAM

Most factory-made icecreams achieve their 'soft from the freezer' texture by the addition of stabilisers, emulsifiers and other additives. It is easy, however, to achieve exactly the same effect with a home-made icecream, using nothing other than normal household ingredients. The secret lies in the recipe – really a frozen mousse mixture – which we use for all the icecreams in this book. This contains a high proportion of egg yolks and cream – and it is globules of fat from these ingredients which surround the developing ice crystals and prevent them from growing too large and in the process coarsening the texture of the mixture. These home-made 'soft scoop' icecreams do not need to be either beaten or whisked as they freeze, yet even when they are served straight from the freezer, they feel smooth and creamy on the tongue.

Chestnut Mocha Bombe

Serves 10

The bombe will freeze for 1 month

A rich and smooth chocolate icecream is 'injected' with a liqueur-flavoured chestnut purée to provide an unusual contrast of both taste and texture.

FOR THE ICECREAM
3 eggs, separated
3 oz (75 g/½ cup) icing sugar
1 teasp vanilla essence
4 oz (125 g) plain chocolate, grated
1 tbsp dark roast instant coffee, dissolved in 1 tbsp hot water
10 fl. oz (275 ml/1¼ cups) whipping (or non dairy) cream
(save 2 fl. oz/50 ml/¼ cup for garnish)

FOR THE CHESTNUT FILLING
1 × 7 oz (200 g) can sweetened chestnut purée (crème de marron)
2 tbsp coffee (or chocolate)-flavoured liqueur

FOR THE GARNISH
the reserved cream (see above), *whipped until stiff*
chocolate curls (see page 157)
sifted icing sugar
sifted cocoa powder

1. To make the icecream, whisk the egg whites until stiff then add the icing sugar gradually, whisking until stiff again after each addition.
2. Add the vanilla and the chocolate (melted in the coffee) to the yolks, then whisk gently into the meringue.
3. Finally, whip the cream until it holds soft peaks then fold into the egg mixture. Turn into a 2 pint (1·25 litre) basin and freeze for 6 hours or until firm.
4. Remove from the freezer and, using the handle of a wooden spoon, make 'tunnels' in an even pattern from the top, stopping just short of the base.
5. To make the filling, thin the chestnut purée with the liqueur, then spoon into the 'tunnels' from a teaspoon. Return to the freezer for a further 2 hours or until firm.
6. To unmould the bombe, soak a kitchen cloth in hot water, then wring out and wrap around the outside of the basin. Run a knife round the inside of the bowl to help release the bombe, then turn out at once on to a serving dish.
7. Quickly decorate with the reserved whipped cream and scatter with the chocolate curls, then return to the freezer.

TO SERVE
Just before the meal, transfer the bombe to the refrigerator to help it soften slightly. Just before serving, dust the chocolate curls with the icing sugar and cocoa powder.

SOME ICECREAM EXTRAS

Glazed Kumquats Cut 4–6 oz (125–175 g) fresh kumquats into slices $\frac{1}{4}$ inch (6 mm) thick then arrange side by side in a shallow dish. Sprinkle with a thin layer of caster sugar and leave at room temperature overnight when the sugar will have liquified and glazed the fruit. Serve as a garnish for orange or lemon icecream or sorbet. Good with lemon icebox cake.

Frosted Grapes Whisk the white of an egg with a large fork until it begins to froth. Wash and dry about 12 oz (350 g) seedless black or green grapes. Using a $\frac{1}{4}$ inch (6 mm) painting brush, paint each grape with a thin layer of egg white then shower with caster sugar from a sifter. Arrange side by side on a wire cake rack and leave to dry and develop some sparkle either in an airing cupboard or a cooling oven. Use as decoration for a mild-flavoured icecream.

Glazed Pineapple Fingers Make the glaze by dissolving 3 oz (75 g/$\frac{1}{3}$ cup) granulated sugar in 4 fl. oz (125 ml/$\frac{1}{2}$ cup) water over gentle heat. Stir in 3 fl. oz (75 ml/$\frac{1}{3}$ cup) fresh orange juice, then bring to the boil. Mix 2 teasp cornflour with 2 tbsp fresh lemon juice then stir into the bubbling liquid. Simmer for 3 minutes until clear, then take off the heat and stir in 2 tbsp Cointreau or Kirsch. Pour over fingers of fresh pineapple and leave for at least 2 hours before arranging on individual plates and topping with icecream.

RIGHT: *Zuccotto* (*page 158*) and *Dolce alla Piemontese* (*page 159*)

Luscious Lemon Icebox Cake

Serves 10

The cake will freeze for 1 month

The best of all lemon icecreams is layered with ginger-flavoured crumbs.

FOR THE CRUST
6 oz (175 g) crisp ginger biscuits, broken
3 oz (75 g/$\frac{1}{3}$ cup) butter or margarine, melted
$\frac{1}{2}$ teasp ground ginger
$1\frac{1}{2}$ tbsp icing sugar

FOR THE LEMON FILLING
4 oz (125 g/$\frac{1}{2}$ cup) granulated sugar
3 eggs, separated
juice and rind of 2 lemons (approx. 5 tbsp)
1 tbsp caster sugar
8 fl. oz (225 ml/1 cup) double (or non dairy) cream

1. To make the lemon filling, put the granulated sugar, egg yolks, lemon juice and rind into the food processor or blender and process until creamy – about 1 minute.
2. Turn into a heavy-based pan and stir over moderate heat until the mixture thickens enough to coat the back of the spoon. Do *not* allow to boil. Transfer to a medium sized basin and leave in the freezer until cold to the touch – about 20 minutes.
3. Meanwhile, whisk the egg whites until they hold soft peaks then add the caster sugar and whisk until the meringue holds stiff peaks.
4. Whip the cream until it holds its shape then fold it into the chilled yolks followed by the meringue.
5. To assemble the icebox cake, line the base of a 2 lb (900 g) loaf tin – 9 × 5 × 3 inches or 11 × 4 × 3 inches (22·5 × 12·5 × 7·5 cm or 27·5 × 10 × 7·5 cm) – with a strip of silicone paper.
6. Process the broken biscuits until fine crumbs then pulse in the remaining ingredients. Turn into a small bowl.
7. Sprinkle a third of the biscuit mixture in an even layer on the base of the loaf tin, cover with half the lemon mixture, then another third of biscuit mixture and then the second half of the lemon mixture. Finally sprinkle the remaining crumb mixture on the top (this will become the base of the dessert).
8. Freeze for 6 hours at least, though longer will allow the flavours to fully develop.
9. Have ready a long serving dish. Run a sharp knife round the edges of the tin, then gently unmould the cake, removing the lining paper. Return to the freezer until required.

THE SESAME SWEETMEAT

Halvah has a particularly seductive flavour and texture that can quickly become an addiction – that is, if you are partial to the taste of crushed sesame seeds and the melt-in-the-mouth-crispness of home-made fudge. An exceptionally fine pistachio-studded halvah is made in the Lebanon, but for the very best selection you need to go to the Duty Free shops at Ben Gurion Airport, Tel Aviv. Failing that, try your neighbourhood Middle Eastern delicatessen or health-food shop. Although this kind of halvah is usually served as a sweetmeat with Turkish coffee, it can also be used most effectively to flavour icecream.

STRAWBERRY COULIS

Process 1 lb (450 g) very ripe strawberries and 4 oz (125 g/$\frac{1}{2}$ cup) caster sugar in a blender or food processor until the sugar has dissolved and a thick purée has formed – it will take approximately 1 minute. Thin down to the required consistency with a little lemon juice or strawberry-flavoured liqueur.

A raspberry coulis is made in a similar way but the berries should first be pushed through a mouli or a sieve to remove the pips. No lemon juice is necessary for the tarter fruit but a little raspberry liqueur may be added instead.

LEFT: *Mango and Ginger Sorbet (page 150), Strawberry and Orange Petits Pots (page 156), Halva and Pistachio Icecream (above), Mamoules (page 178), Danish Nut Crisps (page 176) and Lemon Pecan Spritz Biscuits (page 178)*

Halvah and Pistachio Icecream

Serves 8–10

The icecream will freeze for 1 month

It is a good idea to counterbalance this rich icecream with a garnish of mild-flavoured fruit such as sliced strawberries, lightly sugared redcurrants or poached fresh peaches – or a strawberry coulis. It freezes well for up to a month and the texture is soft enough to serve straight from the freezer. It can be turned out of its tin an hour or two before dinner.

2 oz (50 g/$\frac{1}{2}$ cup) pistachio nuts, shelled
3 large eggs
2 oz (50 g/$\frac{1}{4}$ cup) caster sugar
7–8 oz (200–225 g) halvah (plain or with pistachios)
10 fl. oz (275 ml/1$\frac{1}{4}$ cups) whipping (or non dairy) cream

1. Have ready a loaf tin 9 × 5 × 3 inches or 11 × 4 × 3 inches (22·5 × 12·5 × 7·5 cm or 27·5 × 10 × 7·5 cm).
2. Blanch the pistachio nuts by covering them with boiling water and cooking on 100% power for 30 seconds in the microwave or bubbling for the same time on the top of the stove. Drain well then slip off the skins and set the nuts aside to dry on a paper towel. Chop coarsely.
3. Whisk the eggs and sugar until pale cream in colour, greatly increased in volume and similar in texture to whipped cream. It takes about 5 minutes to reach this stage using an electric whisk.
4. Crumble the halvah in the fingers until it looks like coarse sand.
5. Whisk the cream until it holds soft peaks, then gently fold in the halvah.
6. Fold the eggs gently into the cream mixture together with 1 oz (25 g/$\frac{1}{4}$ cup) of the coarsely chopped nuts.
7. Sprinkle the remaining nuts evenly over the base of the tin then spoon the mixture into the tin. (If you prefer to serve the icecream in scoops, turn it into a large plastic container.)
8. Freeze for an hour then stir gently to redistribute the nuts. Leave undisturbed for at least another 3 hours though it's preferable to leave it to 'ripen' in flavour overnight before serving.

TO SERVE
Serve in slices or scoops, garnishing with the chosen fruit or the coulis.

A DAMP SOLUTION

If you have problems with unmoulding icecreams or savoury mousses, try lining the mould or tin with dampened clingfilm. This works like a charm, particularly with icecream 'bombes' which are notoriously difficult to handle at the unmoulding stage. See also page 157.

Nutty Toffee Slice

Serves 12–15

The icecream will freeze for 1 month

A smooth and creamy-textured icecream with a 'vein' of butterscotch toffee running through it.

FOR THE NUT CRUNCH
2 rounded tbsp golden syrup
$1\frac{1}{2}$ oz (40 g/3 tbsp) butter or margarine
scant 4 oz (125 g/$\frac{1}{2}$ cup) light brown sugar
scant 4 oz (125 g/1 cup) chopped mixed nuts

FOR THE ICECREAM
4 eggs, separated
4 level tbsp icing sugar
10 fl. oz (275 ml/$1\frac{1}{4}$ cups) whipping (or non dairy) cream
$1\frac{1}{2}$ teasp vanilla essence

1. To make the nut crunch, put the golden syrup, butter or margarine and sugar in a heavy saucepan, and stir over gentle heat until melted. Add the nuts.
2. Turn up the heat and continue stirring until the mixture is a rich golden brown (but stop before it turns chestnut colour when it will have caramelised).
3. Immediately pour into a small baking tin lined with silicone paper, and leave to set while you prepare the icecream.
4. To make the icecream, whisk the egg whites until they hold soft peaks then add the icing sugar a tablespoon at a time, whisking until stiff after each addition.
5. Whisk in the egg yolks until just blended.
6. Whisk the cream and the vanilla until the mixture holds soft peaks, then fold it into the meringue. Leave in the bowl and put in the freezer.
7. As soon as the toffee is set hard, break it up into approx. 1 inch (2·5 cm) chunks and process on the food processor until a coarse powder.
8. After the icecream has been in the freezer for 30 minutes, take it out and carefully stir in the toffee.
9. Spoon into a loaf tin and return to the freezer. Leave overnight.

TO SERVE
Unmould on to a long serving dish, cut in slices, and accompany with a basket of a crisp biscuit such as Lemon Pecan Spritz (see page 178).

MARSALA

The pride of Sicily – it's been made in the town of that name ever since it was invented by an Englishman, one John Woodhouse, 200 years ago – Marsala is a fortified wine similar to Madeira. In the 18th century it actually outsold Madeira, sherry and port in this country. Nowadays, it's mostly drunk only by the Italians, but it's used for cooking in this country. As with Madeira, there are varying degrees of sweetness so it's important to match the wine to the dish. For a sweet zabaione or zabaglione, our favourite is Marsala all'uovo, though one marked 'demi secco' or 'fine' is quite satisfactory. However, for a savoury dish such as Vitello al Marsala, choose a dry or semi-dry one (usually marked 'secco' or 'fine') instead.

Mango e Fragole al Zabaione

(Mango and strawberry compote with a fluffy wine sauce)

Serves 6–8

The fruits are marinated in sweetened lemon juice, which draws out their natural juices – an ideal method for fresh fruit salad. (An equivalent amount of high-bulk sugar substitute can be used as sweetener.)

Male chefs use a large balloon whisk to make their zabaione, but for folk with less well-developed muscles, a hand-held electric whisk is a more comfortable – and equally effective – appliance.

FOR THE FRUIT COMPOTE
2 large (10–12 oz/275–350 g) mangoes
1 lb (450 g) choice strawberries
3 tbsp lemon juice heated with 3 tbsp caster sugar

FOR THE ZABAIONE
6 egg yolks
2 oz (50 g/$\frac{1}{4}$ cup) caster sugar
1 teasp cornflour
6 tbsp cream Marsala
10 fl. oz (275 ml/1$\frac{1}{4}$ cups) double (or non dairy) cream

FOR THE GARNISH
approx. 2 oz (50 g) Amaretti or ratafia biscuits, coarsely crushed

1. Not more than 4 hours before serving, slice the mangoes and strawberries, arrange on two separate plates and sprinkle with the lemon syrup. Leave at room temperature, lightly covered.
2. To make the zabaione, put the egg yolks, sugar and cornflour into a basin on top of a double saucepan and whisk by hand or electric whisk until pale and mousse-like. Whisk in the Marsala.
3. Stand the basin over a pan of simmering water and whisk constantly until the mixture becomes as thick as softly whipped cream and has increased two or three times in volume. This takes 5–6 minutes. Remove from the heat and place in the freezer for 10 minutes.
4. Meanwhile, whisk the cream until it stands in soft peaks then fold it into the chilled mixture and refrigerate.

TO SERVE
An hour before serving, divide the fruit and juice between eight tall wine glasses and chill. Just before serving, spoon the chilled zabaione on top of the fruit and sprinkle with the Amaretti.

THE ALTERNATIVE FRUIT COMPOTE

Peaches, pears, apricots and apples all take kindly to a gentle poaching in a sweet and lemony apricot syrup. Peaches and apricots can be left whole (their cooked flesh is more fragrant if the stone is left in), but pears are best peeled and halved, and eating apples such as Cox's should be peeled and cored.

Always turn off the heat just before the fruit is completely tender – it will continue cooking in the steam trapped in the covered pan but without losing either its shape or texture. Fresh berries can be added to any of these compotes just before serving.

Compote of Nectarines

Serves 8

Serve with yoghurt or with a chocolate cake such as Gâteau 'Queen of Sheba' (see page 141).

4 level tbsp apricot jam
1 teasp each grated lemon and orange rind
3 level tbsp granulated sugar
8 fl. oz (225 ml/1 cup) water
10 large nectarines
2 tbsp apricot brandy (or other fruit-flavoured liqueur)
2 tbsp lemon juice

1. Put the jam, rinds, sugar and water into a wide saucepan or lidded frying pan. Stir over gentle heat until the sugar dissolves, then cook gently for about 3 minutes or until the mixture looks syrupy.
2. Drop the fruit into the syrup, cover and cook very gently until just tender – about 5–10 minutes. Test with a knife. Baste once or twice during this time.
3. Take from the heat and lift off the nectarine skins, then leave in the syrup, covered, until cool.
4. Add the liqueur and the lemon juice, and chill thoroughly.

Mirkatan

(Dried fruit compote)

Serves 6–8

This dish will keep for 4 days under refrigeration

This is an ancient Armenian fruit compote. The plump fruits are macerated in a delicately spiced syrup – it is a very versatile dish as it can be served hot or cold at any time of the year. It is often served with a whipped cream flavoured with rosewater, but we favour the Greek-style strained yoghurt lightly sweetened with honey as an accompaniment.

8 oz (225 g/1½ cups) pitted prunes
8 oz (225 g/1½ cups dried apricots
8 oz (225 g/1½ cups) dried peaches or pears
4 oz (125 g/¾ cup) sultanas
freshly brewed tea to cover the fruit
3 oz (75 g/½ cup) walnut halves
water

5 fl. oz (150 ml/⅔ cup) port-type wine
3 strips of orange zest
1 cinnamon stick
3 oz (75 g/⅓ cup) caster sugar
1 tbsp fresh lemon juice
1 tbsp citrus blossom water

1. The day before, put the dried fruit in a bowl and pour the strained tea over it. Cover and leave overnight.
2. Next day, strain into a bowl (reserving the liquor) and insert the walnut halves into the prunes.
3. Make up the reserved tea with water, if necessary, to 8 fl. oz (225 ml/1 cup). Put in a wide pan together with the wine, orange rind, cinnamon stick and sugar. Bring to the boil and simmer uncovered for 3 minutes.
4. Add the dried fruit, cover and simmer for 20 minutes until the fruit is tender and the syrup has thickened. Stir in the lemon juice and citrus blossom water. Serve hot or cold.

Gooseberry Sorbet

The home cook can afford to use far more fruit than the commercial maker, so that it is really worth making your own sorbets. A wonderful texture is easily achieved with one of the moderately-priced domestic sorbetières – a worthwhile investment if you are particularly partial to sorbets. However, if you follow our directions, a very similar texture – albeit with the expenditure of rather more time and effort – can be achieved with a food processor.

1 lb (450 g) fresh (or frozen) gooseberries (or
12 fl. oz/350 ml/1½ cups) unsweetened purée)
water
grated rind and juice 1 lemon
6 oz (175 g/¾ cup) granulated sugar
1 large egg white, whisked until it holds stiff glossy peaks

1. Top and tail the fresh fruit then put in a pan with 3 tbsp water and the lemon rind and juice. Cover and simmer for 8–10 minutes until tender.
2. Leave until the mixture stops steaming then push through a sieve or 'mouli'.
3. Put the sugar and 10 fl. oz (275 ml/1¼ cups) water into a small heavy-based pan and heat, stirring, until the sugar is dissolved. Then bring to the boil and simmer steadily for 10 minutes. Allow to go cold, then add the purée.
4. The mixture can now be put into an electric icecream machine together with the whisked egg white, and frozen according to directions. Otherwise turn into a plastic container and freeze as for the Mango Sorbet (see page 150).

Mango and Ginger Sorbet with a Compote of Mangoes, Strawberries and Kumquats

Serves 8–10

This dessert will freeze for 2 months

No sugar syrup is used in this delicately-flavoured sorbet, so the perfume of the mangoes comes through strong and clear.

FOR THE SORBET
2 large (10–12 oz/275–350 g) ripe mangoes
6 tbsp fresh orange juice
3 tbsp fresh lemon juice
1 teasp grated lemon rind
½ teasp ground ginger (optional)
5 oz (150 g/⅔ cup) sugar
1 egg white

FOR THE COMPOTE
2 large ripe mangoes
8 oz (225 g) kumquats, washed and sliced
3 tbsp caster sugar dissolved in 3 tbsp lemon juice
1 lb (450 g) choice strawberries

1. Set the freezer to 'fast freeze'. Peel the mangoes for the sorbet. Cut the flesh away from the stone, then cut it all in rough 1 inch (2·5 cm) chunks. Purée with the juices, rind, ginger and sugar (using either a blender or a food processor) until the sugar has dissolved – about 1 minute.
2. The mixture can now be put into an electric icecream machine and frozen according to directions. Otherwise, turn the purée into a plastic container and freeze for 3 hours or until semi-frozen.
3. Have the egg white ready, whisked until it holds stiff peaks. Whisk the purée by hand or machine until it lightens in colour – 45 seconds on the food processor or blender, 1 minute with an electric whisk – then immediately fold in the egg white, return to the container and re-freeze until solid – for at least 6 hours.
4. Start making the compote the day before if you like. Peel the mangoes, as above, then slice and arrange flesh in a shallow serving dish with the sliced kumquats. Sprinkle with the lemon syrup, cover with clingfilm and refrigerate.

TO SERVE
About 2 hours before serving, arrange the strawberries, thickly sliced, on the plate and spoon over some of the syrup. Re-cover and leave at room temperature until ready to serve. At the beginning of the meal, transfer the sorbet to the refrigerator to soften. Serve in scoops with the fresh fruit compote.

THE FRENCH WAY TO GLACÉ FRUIT

We have never tasted glacé fruits to compare with those produced by the century-old pâtisserie and confiserie of Henri Auer at the entrance to the famous flower market of Nice in the south of France. For this is a very precise art and one must be a sugar boiler of distinction to achieve the perfect product – when the natural juices of the fruit, and the sugar syrup in which it has been steeped for many days, are indissolubly locked in together. Just how long it takes to achieve this result is the secret of the craft, and how rare it is to find fruit of this quality we can confirm after fruitless searches in other Mediterranean lands. To achieve the distinctive surface, the prepared glacé fruit must be washed and dried then dipped in a high-density syrup that sets with a shine.

To create the crunchy surface characteristic of crystallised fruits (which are prepared up to this point in exactly the same way), the fruit is simply dipped in a coarse-textured sugar.

Preparing glacé and crystallised fruit is a very labour-intensive process, so that it goes without saying that it is also an expensive one. But it is better to use another kind of flavouring altogether than to settle for fruit that is second best.

Crêpes Soufflés Rothschild

Serves 6–8

Freeze uncooked filled crêpes for 1 month

Rich and rare is the filling for these brilliant crêpes soufflés – as befits a dish with such an opulent name. The exotic mixture of glacé fruits, macerated in a fruit brandy, probably dates from the 1880s at a time when, according to Alfred Suzanne, chef to the Duke of Bedford, 'The big hats of finance here [in England] as everywhere will only have French chefs in their kitchen.' And the four families of English Rothschilds headed the list. You will be relieved to note that as the crêpes go direct from the freezer to the oven there is no need to employ a chef of *any* nationality in your kitchen!

FOR THE CRÊPES
4 oz (125 g/1 cup) plain flour
pinch salt
2 eggs
2 oz (50 g/¼ cup) butter, heated until it turns pale fawn
8 fl. oz (225 ml/1 cup) milk
1½ level tbsp caster sugar

FOR THE COULIS
1 × 15 oz (425 g) can choice apricots in their own juice
2 tbsp apricot brandy
1 tbsp fresh lemon juice

FOR THE SOUFFLÉ FILLING
3 eggs separated
finely grated rind of ½ lemon and ½ orange
2 oz (50 g/¼ cup) sugar
1½ oz (40 g/6 tbsp) flour
6 oz (175 ml/¾ cup) milk
nut of butter
4 oz (125 g/½ cup) chopped glacé fruit, marinated for several hours in 3 tbsp Kirsch

TO COAT THE CRÊPES
1 oz (25 g/2 tbsp) butter, melted
3 tbsp each ground almonds and golden granulated sugar

1. Make the crêpes as described on page 30, but only cook the second side for 30 seconds to dry the surface. Set aside until required. (The stacked crêpes can be frozen at this point (see page 33).)
2. To make the coulis, put the fruit and juice into a pan and simmer until thick and mushy. Put in a blender or food processor with the brandy and lemon juice and purée. Taste and add a little sugar if necessary. Chill.
3. To make the soufflé filling, beat the egg yolks, citrus rind and sugar together, then stir in the flour and enough of the milk to make a creamy paste.

4. Heat the remaining milk until it just comes to the boil, then whisk it into the egg mixture. Return to the pan and reheat, whisking gently, then bubble for 2 minutes. Stir in the butter. Cool until it stops steaming.

5. Stir in the glacé fruit and Kirsch.

6. Whisk the egg whites until they hold stiff glossy peaks. *Stir* a quarter into the custard and *fold* in the rest.

7. To fill the crêpes, lay each crêpe, pale side up, on a board and spoon a generous tablespoonful of the soufflé mixture in the centre.

8. Fold the crêpe in half and then in half again. Arrange on greased trays.

9. Paint thoroughly with melted butter and scatter with equal parts of the ground almonds and golden granulated sugar. Put in the freezer for at least 2 hours before baking.

10. To bake the crêpes, preheat the oven to Gas 5 (375°F, 190°C) then, 25 minutes before serving, put the frozen crêpes in the oven. Bake for 15 minutes until puffed and golden. Serve at once.

Topfenpalatschinken, Kirschensauce

(Cream cheese crêpes with a spiced cherry sauce)

Serves 6–8

The cooked crêpes will freeze (unfilled) for up to 3 months

This stunning dessert comes from the rich culinary heritage of the former Austro-Hungarian Empire.

crêpes made as on page 30, but only cook the second side for 30 seconds to dry the surface

FOR THE FILLING
1 lb (450 g/2 cups) curd (medium fat) cheese
1 oz (25 g/2 tbsp) soft butter
3 tbsp caster sugar
1 tbsp lemon juice
1 teasp grated lemon rind
½ teasp vanilla essence
2 tbsp from an 8 oz (225 ml/1 cup) carton strained Greek-style cow's yoghurt (reserve the remainder to serve with the hot stuffed crêpes)

FOR THE MORELLO CHERRY SAUCE
1 × 15 oz (425 g) can pitted Morello cherries and their juice
3 teasp cornflour mixed with 2 tbsp cherry brandy
1 tbsp granulated sugar (if necessary)

TO BAKE THE CRÊPES
1 oz (25 g/2 tbsp) butter, melted

CRÊPES WITHOUT TEARS

The secret lies in the pan which should have a solid base that sits fair and square on the heat. Our favourite crêpe pan – 7 inches (17·5 cm) in diameter – has a sturdy non-stick lining applied in a 'waffle' design. We've never had a dud crêpe since we started to use it.

1. To make the filling, combine all the ingredients together and beat until fluffy.
2. To make the sauce, bring the cherries and their syrup to the boil, stir in the cornflour mixture and allow to bubble for 2 minutes, stirring constantly. Sweeten with sugar if too tart. Pour into a sauce boat and chill.
3. Lay all the crêpes, pale side up, on a board, and pipe or spoon a generous tbsp of the filling across the lower third of each. Turn the sides and roll up into a cylinder.
4. Arrange side by side on a platter or gratin dish. The crêpes can be refrigerated at this point for up to 24 hours.
5. To bake the crêpes, preheat the oven to Gas 5 (375°F, 190°C), and brush the surface of the crêpes with the melted butter. Bake for 15 minutes until golden.
6. Serve accompanied by a spoonful each of cherry sauce and the reserved yoghurt.

THE 'OPEN' FREEZE

Delicate foods that might be crushed by packaging, or soft foods that might stick together if bagged when still raw, should be 'open frozen' without any protective covering until they feel solid to the touch. As this will take no more than 3 hours even for a large gâteau, there is no danger that unwelcome odours from other food in the freezer will be absorbed or that 'freezer burn' will develop on organic produce such as raw meat and fish balls.

It is equally important to take the same precautions when the foods are defrosted. Remove them from the package or bag while still frozen hard and allow to defrost without covering, preferably in the refrigerator.

Coffee Praline Meringue Cups

Serves 8

The cups will freeze for 1 month

The intense coffee flavour in the 'semi-freddo' filling makes a welcome contrast to the airy sweetness of the meringue.

FOR THE MERINGUE
3 egg whites
¼ teasp cream of tartar
1 level teasp cornflour
6 oz (175 g/¾ cup) caster sugar

FOR THE FILLING
10 fl. oz (275 ml/1¼ cups) whipping (or non dairy) cream
1 rounded tbsp instant coffee dissolved in 3 teasp hot water
3 teasp sugar
2 tbsp any chocolate-flavoured liqueur (Sabra, Tia Maria)
1 recipe praline (see page 175)

1. To make the meringue cups, preheat the oven to Gas 2 (300°F, 150°C) and line a tray with silicone paper.
2. Whisk the egg whites with the cream of tartar until they hold soft peaks.
3. Mix the cornflour and sugar together and add to the whites a tablespoonful at a time, beating until stiff after each addition.
4. Put a ½ inch (1·25 cm) nozzle into a large piping bag, fill with the mixture and, starting from the centre of the base, pipe out little cups about 2½ inches (6 cm) across. The cups rise in the oven so leave 2 inches (5 cm) between each one.
5. Put the tray of meringues in the preheated oven and then turn it down to Gas 1 (275°F, 140°C). Bake for 45–60

minutes, or until the cups feel crisp to the touch and lift off easily from the tray. Put on a cooling tray.

6. To make the filling, whisk the cream until thick enough to hang on the whisk, then whisk in the coffee, sugar and liqueur. Don't use boiling hot coffee or it may curdle the cream. Fold in 2 tbsp of the praline.

7. Pipe or spoon the cream into the cups, and freeze until required.

TO SERVE

About 15 minutes before serving, remove from the freezer and sprinkle each cup with a teasp of the remaining praline.

THE FUNNEL-FILLED FLUTE

When the glass is narrow and the mixture is thick and creamy, the easiest way to fill the one with the other without marking the glass is to pour it through a plastic jam funnel which is just a shade narrower than the diameter of the glass.

Khoshab

Serves 6–8

The syllabub will freeze for 1 month or will keep for 2 days under refrigeration

An Armenian version of syllabub with an apricot brandy flavoured syrup whipped into the cream.

3 oz (75 g/$\frac{1}{3}$ cup) caster sugar
8 fl. oz (225 ml/1 cup) water
8–9 oz (225–250 g) tenderised apricots
1 tbsp lemon juice
$\frac{1}{2}$ teasp vanilla essence
3 tbsp apricot liqueur (or apricot brandy)
10 fl. oz (275 ml/1$\frac{1}{4}$ cups) double (or non dairy) cream
the flavoured apricot syrup (see below)
2 oz (50 g/$\frac{1}{2}$ cup) toasted pine kernels (or almond nibs)

FOR THE GARNISH
sprigs fresh mint

1. Bring the sugar and water to the boil in an 8 inch (20 cm) saucepan, add the apricots, then cover and simmer for 15 minutes until tender but not mushy.

2. Take off heat and stir in the lemon juice, vanilla essence and apricot liqueur. Refrigerate for about 40 minutes.

3. Put the cream into a bowl with the syrup drained from the apricots.

4. Whip until it stands in stiff peaks, then fold in the apricots, cut in small cubes, reserving some cubes for garnish. Fold in almost all the pine kernels.

5. Divide the flavoured cream between individual flutes or glass bowls, and decorate with the remaining fruit and pine kernels. Chill until required.

TO SERVE

Just before serving, garnish with sprigs of fresh mint.

SMALL IS BEAUTIFUL

. . . . when it's a tiny
(6 fl. oz/175 ml/¾ cup) soufflé dish
filled with a rich custard such as
crème brûlée.

. . . . when it's a slim champagne
flute filled with a syllabub such as
Khoshab.

. . . . when it's a lidded china
custard pot filled with a cold
soufflé such as the Strawberry and
Orange Petit Pots.

. . . . when it's a triangular
Manhattan glass filled with scoops
of Gooseberry Sorbet.

. . . . when it's a demi-tasse cup
filled with an icecream such as
Biscuit Tortoni.

Fruits of the Forest Brûlée

Serves 6–8

We feel that the pint of cream considered essential to achieve the correct consistency in a classic crème brûlée is somewhat of an anachronism in these cholesterol-conscious days. We have therefore reduced it by half and thickened the mixture with – dare we mention it – custard powder! We think the result is superb. As for the vexed question of how to caramelise the sugar topping using a domestic grill instead of the traditional salamander, we applied a little lateral thinking and caramelised the sugar on top of the stove then poured it over the chilled crème. It set like a golden mirror! Do serve the brûlée the same day, however, or it will begin to 'weep' as it absorbs moisture from the atmosphere.

8 oz (225 g/1½ cups) each raspberries and blackberries
3 tbsp Crème de Framboises

FOR THE CRÈME
8 fl. oz (225 ml/1 cup) milk
1 oz (25 g/4 tbsp) each custard powder and sugar
8 fl. oz (225 ml/1 cup) double cream
1 teasp vanilla essence

FOR THE CARAMEL
8 oz (225 g/1 cup) granulated sugar
2–3 tbsp water

1. Put the fruit in a bowl and sprinkle with the liqueur. Leave at room temperature while the crème is prepared.
2. For the crème, make the milk, custard powder and sugar into a custard in the usual way. Chill until absolutely cold.
3. Whisk the cream with the vanilla essence until it holds stiff peaks. Chill. Whisk the cold custard for 1 minute on the food processor until creamy, then fold in the chilled cream.
4. Take six to eight small soufflé dishes and divide the fruit and juice between them, then cover with the custard cream. Freeze for half an hour.
5. To make the caramel, put the sugar and water in a heavy-based pan, and heat, stirring, until clear, then boil without stirring until a rich brown caramel.
6. Immediately plunge base of pan into a bowl of cold water in the sink to stop the cooking.

TO SERVE
Take the soufflé dishes from the freezer and cover with a thin layer of caramel. Chill until required.

**FROZEN OR BOTTLED
ORANGE CONCENTRATE**

The only way we know to
introduce an intense flavour of
orange into a cold sweet, icecream
or sorbet, is to use the juice in a
concentrated form. If no other
liquid is used in the recipe, you
may want to partially dilute it, but
for most recipes it can be used
straight from the container.

Strawberry and Orange Petits Pots

Serves 12

*This dessert will freeze for 1 month without the strawberries
or will keep for 2 days under refrigeration*

This is the finest orange mousse we know. The concentrated
juice gives it a depth of flavour that's impossible to achieve
with ordinary juice – and just think of the mass of bland
cream and meringue it has to contend with!

*3 whole eggs
2 egg yolks
3 oz (75 g/$\frac{1}{3}$ cup) caster sugar
grated rind and juice of $\frac{1}{2}$ large lemon
6 fl. oz (175 ml/$\frac{3}{4}$ cup) concentrated frozen orange juice, left
at room temperature for $\frac{1}{2}$ hour
$\frac{1}{2}$ oz (15 g) gelatine (or 1 lemon jelly), dissolved in 4 tbsp
water
8 fl. oz (225 ml/1 cup) whipping (or non dairy) cream
2 tbsp Cointreau (or other orange-flavoured liqueur)
1 lb (450 g/2$\frac{3}{4}$ cups) small strawberries*

FOR THE GARNISH
tiny sprigs mint

1. Put the whole eggs and egg yolks into a basin and beat
   until frothy, preferably with an electric whisk.
2. Gradually add the sugar and continue to whisk until the
   mixture becomes thick and mousse-like, and a little of the
   mixture dropped from the whisk remains on the surface
   for a few seconds.
3. Gradually add the lemon juice and grated rind and the
   undiluted orange juice to the egg mixture, whisking all the
   time. Finally add the melted jelly or gelatine.
4. Whisk the cream and liqueur until thick enough to hold
   its shape.
5. Gradually fold the egg mixture into the cream using a
   rubber spatula.
6. Slice the strawberries thinly and fold into the orange
   mixture.

TO SERVE
Divide between twelve little pots or put into a crystal bowl,
and chill for at least 4 hours. Garnish with sprigs of mint.

CHOCOLATE CURLS

The professional chocolatier 'tempers' his chocolate in a special temperature-controlled machine which ensures that it is just the right texture for rolling into decorative curls.

For the limited occasions on which we need chocolate in this condition, we use this rough and ready method which seems to work well:

Pour 6 oz (175 g) melted chocolate on to a marble or plastic slab. Using a long, slim palette knife, gradually spread it into a layer $\frac{1}{8}$ inch (3 mm) thick, working the palette knife back and forward until the surface of the chocolate becomes cloudy. At this stage the chocolate will have a supple texture and be partially set without being brittle.

Using a large cook's knife, press down on the chocolate at an angle, so that it begins to curl on itself, forming chocolate 'cigarettes'. We have also made curls by pulling a metal cheese cutter or long-bladed potato knife over the surface of the chocolate. With some makes of chocolate we have even been able to grate curls from the solid block.

Delice au Chocolat

(Chocolate mousse in a brandied sponge case)

Serves 10

Freeze for 1 month with the cream decoration, 3 months without. Complete, it keeps for 2 days under refrigeration

Another spectacular dessert with a wonderful juxtaposition of tastes and textures.

2 × 8–10 oz (225–275 g) Madeira cakes, sliced $\frac{3}{8}$ inch (1 cm) thick

FOR THE CHOCOLATE MOUSSE
4 eggs, separated
1 teasp granulated sugar
6 oz (175 g) plain chocolate, melted
1 tbsp rum (or brandy)

FOR THE SOAKING MIXTURE
5 tbsp rum (or brandy)
10 fl. oz (275 ml/1$\frac{1}{4}$ cups) strong coffee made with dark roast instant coffee
5 teasp granulated sugar

FOR THE GARNISH
12 fl. oz (350 ml/1$\frac{1}{2}$ cups) double cream
2 teasp instant coffee dissolved in 2 teasp boiling water
3 oz (75 g) chocolate curls (or coarsely grated chocolate)

1. To prepare the mousse, whisk the egg yolks with the sugar then stir in the melted chocolate with the rum.
2. Whisk the egg whites until they hold soft peaks, stir a heaped tablespoon into the chocolate mixture to lighten it, then fold in the rest, using a rubber spatula.
3. For the soaking mixture, add the rum (or brandy) to the coffee and sweeten with the sugar.
4. Take a round cake tin 8 inches (20 cm) in diameter and 3 inches (7·5 cm) deep, brush it out with cold water, then line with clingfilm protruding above the rim.
5. Dip the slices of cake quickly in and out of the soaking mixture then use to line the sides and bottom of the tin.
6. Spoon in the mousse and cover with the remaining cake soaked in the same way.
7. Fold over any clingfilm protruding from the sides to protect it from drying out, then refrigerate for 12 hours.
8. Invert on to a serving dish, carefully removing the cling-film. (If frozen, allow 1 hour to defrost.)

TO SERVE
Whip the cream with the cooled coffee then pipe in rosettes all over the cake, or cover and fork decoratively. Garnish with the chocolate curls.

Zuccotto

Serves 8

The zuccotto will freeze for 1 month or will keep for 3 days under refrigeration

Every time you serve this amazing dessert, you will recall that famous photograph of the cathedral, looking down from the hills above Florence. And it has actually been 'assembled' without any cooking at all.

2 × 8 oz (225 g) bought Madeira cakes
3 tbsp each brandy and Amaretto liqueur
15 fl. oz (425 ml/2 cups) double (or non dairy) cream
1 teasp vanilla essence
5 level tbsp icing sugar
3½–4 oz (100–125 g) plain chocolate
2 oz (50 g/½ cup) blanched almonds, coarsely chopped and grilled until golden
3½–4 oz (100–125 g/¾ cup) white hazelnuts, coarsely chopped and grilled until golden
2 teasp instant coffee, dissolved in 2 teasp hot water

FOR THE DECORATION
5 rounded tbsp reserved cream
12 × 1–1½ inch (2·5–3·75 cm) chocolate dessert wafers

1. Have ready a 2 pint (1·25 litre) mixing bowl. Cut the cake into slices ⅜ inch (1 cm) thick, then cut each slice in two wedges.
2. Line the sides of the bowl with the majority of the wedges, keeping the points to the centre bottom of the bowl and laying the crust edge of one wedge next to the cut edge of the other.
3. Mix the brandy and liqueur and sprinkle half of it on the cake to moisten it evenly.
4. Whip the cream with the vanilla and icing sugar until it holds soft peaks. Remove 5 rounded tbsp and reserve for decoration. Chop half the chocolate into pieces the size of a small pea, and add, with the nuts, to the bulk of the cream.
5. Divide the cream into two portions and spoon one portion on to the cake, spreading it evenly over the surface, cassata style.
6. Melt the remaining chocolate with the coffee and water then fold into the remaining cream. Use to fill the cavity.
7. Cut more cake to fit the top of the bowl, then sprinkle with the remaining liqueur. Press down gently to seal the top of the cake to the sides. Cover with clingfilm and chill overnight. Or freeze, then put in the refrigerator 1 hour before serving.

To prepare the 'dome'

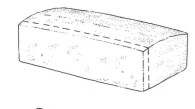

Slice the cake and cut into wedges.

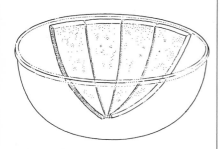

Line the bowl with wedges of Maderia cake.

MANGO COULIS

2 very ripe (10 oz/275 g) mangoes, peeled
3 oz (75 g/⅓ cup) caster sugar
1 tbsp lemon juice

Process the mango flesh with the sugar and lemon juice for 1 minute until thick and smooth. Chill.

TO SERVE

Turn upside down on a serving plate. Complete the decoration of the dome by piping a thick swirl of the reserved cream on the centre top, and spike with the chocolate squares.

Dolce alla Piemontese

Serves 8–10

This dessert will freeze for 1 month or will keep for 2 days under refrigeration

Don't tell anyone how simple this was to prepare! Serve with a speedy mango coulis.

1 packet trifle sponges (approx. 200 g) (or an 8 oz/225 g slightly stale plain sponge cake)
5 fl. oz (150 ml/⅔ cup) each medium dry white wine (such as Riesling) and pineapple juice
1½ tbsp Kirsch

FOR THE CRÈME DIPLOMAT
8 fl. oz (225 ml/1 cup) milk
1 oz (25 g/2 tbsp) each caster sugar and custard powder
1 egg yolk
½ teasp vanilla essence
10 fl. oz (275 ml/1¼ cups) double cream
3 oz (75 g) best quality glacé pineapple, cut in julienne, soaked in 1½ tbsp Kirsch for several hours

FOR THE GARNISH
5 fl. oz (150 ml/⅔ cup) whipping cream
1 oz (25 g) glacé pineapple pieces

1. To prepare the Crème Diplomat, make a custard in the usual way with the milk, sugar and custard powder, but stir in the egg yolk and the vanilla only when it has thickened. Chill for 30 minutes, then turn into the food processor and whizz for 1 minute until light and creamy.
2. Whip the cream together with any liqueur not absorbed by the pineapple. When it hangs on the whisk, fold into the custard together with the pineapple. Chill.
3. Line the bottom of a loaf tin – approx. 10 × 4 × 3 inches or 9 × 5 × 3 inches (25 × 10 × 7·5 cm or 22·5 × 12·5 × 7·5 cm) – with a strip of silicone paper.
4. To assemble the Dolce, cut each trifle sponge horizontally or slice the cake into fingers about ⅜ inch (1 cm) thick and the width of the base of the tin. Divide the pieces into three portions.
5. In a shallow bowl mix the wine, pineapple juice and liqueur, then quickly dip the first third of sponge in and out of the wine mixture. Use to line the bottom of the loaf tin.

6. Spread half the crème on top, cover with a further layer of soaked sponges, yet more crème and finally the remainder of the moistened sponge. Cover with film and chill overnight.

7. Next day, loosen the cake from the edges of the tin with a sharp knife, then unmould it on to a long dish. Whip the garnish cream until it stands in peaks, then fork or pipe in a trellis on top of the Dolce. Decorate with the pineapple pieces. Chill thoroughly.

A DO-IT-YOURSELF BASIC DESSERT SPONGE

This can be used in any dessert that requires a light and absorbent fatless sponge. It can be frozen for up to 6 months.

Have ready a 9–10 inch (22·5–25 cm) loose-bottomed cake tin about 3 inches (7·5 cm) deep, greased and bottom-lined with silicone paper. Preheat the oven to Gas 4 (350°F, 180°C).

In a large bowl, whisk together until stiff and fluffy the whites of 3 eggs and 3 tbsp cold water, then add 5 oz (150 g/$\frac{2}{3}$ cup) caster sugar, a tablespoon at a time, whisking until stiff after each addition. Stir in $\frac{1}{2}$ teasp vanilla essence and 2 oz (50 g/$\frac{1}{2}$ cup) each of self-raising flour and cornflour. (Add $\frac{1}{2}$ teasp baking powder if plain flour is used.) Spoon into the prepared tin and bake for 35–40 minutes until the cake has begun to shrink away from the sides of the tin and the surface feels springy to a gentle touch.

Himbeertopfentorte

(Viennese raspberry and cream cheese gâteau)

Serves 8–10

The gâteau will freeze for 1 month or keep for 2 days under refrigeration

Guests always wonder how on earth the cheesecake got into the centre of the cake!

1 fatless sponge cake, 9–10 inches (22–25 cm) in diameter
(frozen for 30 minutes to facilitate slicing)
sifted icing sugar

FOR THE FILLING
3 oz (75 g/$\frac{1}{3}$ cup) caster sugar
4 fl. oz (125 ml/$\frac{1}{2}$ cup) water
3 fl. oz (75 ml/$\frac{1}{3}$ cup) orange juice
2 tbsp cornflour
2 tbsp lemon juice
2 tbsp Crème de Framboises (raspberry liqueur)
1 lb (450 g/2$\frac{3}{4}$ cups) fresh (or frozen) raspberries

FOR THE CHEESECAKE
$\frac{1}{2}$ oz (15 g) gelatine (or 1 lemon jelly)
3 tbsp lemon juice
1 lb (450 g/2 cups) curd (medium fat) soft cheese
finely grated rind $\frac{1}{2}$ lemon
2 oz (50 g/$\frac{1}{4}$ cup) caster sugar
$\frac{1}{2}$ teasp vanilla essence
5 fl. oz (150 ml/$\frac{2}{3}$ cup) soured cream (or strained Greek-style cow's yoghurt)

THE GENTLE TOUCH

Though their texture seems more fragile, raspberries are more durable than strawberries both in the refrigerator and the freezer, but they still need careful handling.

To store in the refrigerator

Remove from the basket, then arrange in a single layer in a shallow container, cover lightly but securely with clingfilm and refrigerate for up to 24 hours.

To store in the freezer

Lay the berries in one layer on flat trays or baking tins. Allow to freeze until as hard as little bullets – about 2–3 hours – then pack in bags or plastic containers.

To use frozen berries

Add to a fruit salad when still semi frozen and serve within half an hour. If you want to use them as a filling for a gâteau that is to be subsequently frozen, as with the Himbeertopf entorte, use while still frozen. By the time the cake has defrosted the berries will be just the right texture.

1. To make the filling, dissolve the sugar in the water and orange juice over a moderate heat. Mix the cornflour to a cream with the lemon juice, then stir into the hot syrup, bring to the boil and simmer for 3 minutes until clear.
2. Remove from the heat and stir in the liqueur. Leave to go cold, then stir in the raspberries.
3. To make the cheesecake, sprinkle the gelatine on to the lemon juice then heat gently (in the microwave or over hot water) until clear. (If lemon jelly is used, dissolve in the hot lemon juice.)
4. Put the cheese into a bowl then stir in the dissolved gelatine (or jelly) followed by all the remaining ingredients. Chill while you prepare the tin and cake.
5. To assemble the cake, have ready a 9–10 inch (22–25 cm) loose-bottomed cake tin about 3 inches (7·5 cm) deep. It must be large enough to hold the cake.
6. Slice the cake in half horizontally and lay the bottom half in the tin. Spoon the half-set cheese cake on top and cover with the raspberry filling. Lay the other half of the cake lightly on top, and refrigerate for at least 6 hours.

TO SERVE

Dredge the top of the cake thickly with sifted icing sugar. Stand the tin on a canister or jar of smaller diameter and carefully pull down the sides. Lay the cake, still on the base, on a serving dish. Serve well chilled.

A WORLD
OF PATISSERIE

*We have trawled through the pastry repertoires of eight
different cuisines to bring you the best tortes, tartes and
strudels the Continent has to offer. Also in this section are
some beauties for the biscuit barrel – for everyday or a special
day, or to accompany our frozen desserts. There are also some
delicious little mouthfuls for the after-dinner coffee tray and
a couple of biscuits for the cheeseboard, which are certainly
worth any effort involved.*

EGG WHITES IN STORE

When we find we have spare egg whites we simply stockpile them in plastic containers, adding surplus whites as they occur. These whites will keep under refrigeration for a month – and in fact seem to whip to a better volume when they have been in store for a week or two. At the end of the month, smell any remaining whites – they should be completely odourless. If not, throw them away.

When you wish to use only some of the egg whites in the container, count each egg white as 1 fl.oz (25 ml) and measure them out according to the recipe.

Unwhipped egg whites can be frozen for up to six months. After defrosting they will whip up as though newly separated. However, be sure to label how many egg whites are in each container.

Engadine Nusstorte

Serves 10–12

The torte will freeze for 1 month or keep for 4 days under refrigeration

The pride of the Swiss, the meltingly tender pastry holds a honeyed filling of caramelised walnuts. It goes without saying that a little goes a long way.

FOR THE PÂTE SABLÉE
(enough for 1 torte plus 9 tartlet cases)
4 egg yolks
4 oz (125 g/⅔ cup) icing sugar
10 oz (275 g/1¼ cups) butter, softened and cut in 1 inch (2·5 cm) cubes
2 teasp grated lemon rind
1 lb (450 g/4 cups) plain flour
½ teasp salt

FOR THE FILLING
7 oz (200 g/1 cup) granulated sugar
3 tbsp cold water
9 oz (250 g/2¼ cups) walnuts, coarsely chopped
1½ oz (40 g/3 tbsp) butter
5 fl. oz (150 ml/⅔ cup) double cream
1 rounded tbsp mild honey or golden syrup
1 teasp vanilla essence

FOR DUSTING THE TORTE
sifted icing sugar

1. To make the pâte sablée, put the egg yolks, sugar, butter and rind into the food processor, and pulse until the sugar has been absorbed by the butter.
2. Add the flour and salt, pulse until the mixture is beginning to cling together in tiny lumps, then tip into a bowl. Knead the dough into a ball.
3. Roll out one-third of the dough and carefully ease into a 9 inch (22·5 cm) round or square loose-bottomed flan tin approx. 1½ inches (3·75 cm) deep. Trim the edges level.
4. Pat the remaining dough into a square about 2 inches (5 cm) thick, wrap in clingfilm, then put in the freezer together with the pastry case and leave for 1 hour.
5. To make the filling, put the sugar and water in a heavy-based 8 inch (20 cm) pan and cook over moderate heat, stirring until the sugar is dissolved. Stop stirring, but allow the mixture to turn a light caramel, gently tilting the pan occasionally to ensure even cooking.
6. Immediately remove from the heat and stand the pan in a sink or large bowl of cold water – this halts the cooking.
7. Lift out after 2–3 minutes and stir in the walnuts, butter and cream, then return to the heat and simmer, stirring

constantly, for 5 minutes until the mixture is liquid again.

8. Stir in the honey or golden syrup and the vanilla essence, then allow to cool for 10 minutes. Spoon into the frozen crust.

9. Grate an even layer of the frozen pastry over the filling, covering it completely. Reserve any remaining pastry for tartlets.

10. Bake for 50 minutes in a medium oven, Gas 4 (350°F, 180°C), until the pastry is crisp and golden. When cold dust thickly with icing sugar.

TO SERVE

Serve in slim wedges or squares with coffee, or as a dessert with a selection of sliced exotic fruits such as fresh figs, star fruit, mango, strawberries or pineapple.

La Pignola avec le Coulis aux Mures

(Pine kernel tart with a blackberry sauce)

Serves 10–12

The tart will freeze for 2 months or will keep for 1 week under refrigeration

A speciality of Provence, the orange-scented frangipane is covered with a luxurious topping of pine kernels.

FOR THE PASTRY
1 egg
3 oz (75 g/$\frac{1}{3}$ cup) caster sugar
$\frac{1}{2}$ teasp vanilla essence
$5\frac{1}{2}$ oz (165 g/$\frac{2}{3}$ cup) firm butter or firm margarine, cut in 1 inch (2·5 cm) cubes
8 oz (225 g/2 cups) self-raising flour (or 8 oz/225 g/2 cups plain flour plus 2 teasp baking powder)

FOR THE FILLING
butter or margarine
6 oz (175 g/1$\frac{1}{2}$ cups) pine kernels
4 oz (125 g/1 cup) ground almonds
4 oz (125 g/$\frac{1}{2}$ cup) caster sugar
3 eggs
1 oz (25 g/4 tbsp) potato flour (or cornflour)
$\frac{1}{2}$ teasp baking powder
pinch salt
grated rind 1 orange
2 teasp citrus-blossom water
2 tbsp apricot conserve

MAKING THE CASE FOR A SHAPELY FLAN

Whether it's for a flan, a tarte or a quiche, if the pastry case shrinks down in the oven it can only be described as a disaster. The reasons for the shrinkage can be many – too much water in the pastry, overhandling when mixing, stretching when rolling, to mention but three. Here's our surefire formula for success:

Roll the pastry on a board that's been lightly but evenly floured. Aim from the first to roll the pastry into the shape of the flan tin – thus for a round tin start with a ball and give the pastry a quarter turn after each roll so that it takes on the form of a thinner and thinner circle; for a square or oblong tin, start with a square or rectangular piece of pastry.

Put all the pressure on the forward rather than the backward rolling action – this avoids overstretching the dough.

When the dough is the required thickness, lay the rolling pin on top, then roll the dough back on it so that it is wrapped loosely round it. Gently unroll on to the tin, then ease gently into place.

Now for our 'patent' idea. Take a little 'tuck' in the pastry all the way round the bottom edge of the tin so that the case is slightly thicker near the bottom than it is at the top. Roll the rolling pin over the top of the tin to cut off any excess pastry.

To bake 'blind' without filling, prick the bottom and sides of the pastry with a fork then press a large piece of foil into its shape, completely covering the bottom and sides. Freeze for at least an hour before baking according to the recipe.

FOR THE COULIS
12–16 oz (350–450 g) blackberries
3 oz (75 g/⅓ cup) caster sugar
2 teasp lemon juice (or 2 tbsp Crème de Framboises liqueur)

1. To make the coulis, purée the blackberries and sugar in a food processor or blender for 1 minute, then sieve to remove the pips. Stir in the lemon juice (or liqueur) and chill.
2. To make the pastry, put the egg, sugar, vanilla essence and fat into the food processor and pulse until the sugar has been absorbed.
3. Add the flour (and baking powder if used) and pulse until the mixture is beginning to cling together in tiny lumps.
4. Tip into a bowl and gather into a dough, then flatten it into a 1 inch (2·5 cm) thick slab. Wrap in film and chill for 30 minutes.
5. To make the filling, melt 1 oz (25 g/2 tbsp) butter or margarine in a small frying pan and lightly brown the pine kernels. Drain on crumpled kitchen paper then set aside.
6. In a large bowl mix the almonds and sugar, then beat in the eggs one at a time, whisking until smooth and creamy.
7. Mix the potato flour, baking powder and salt in a small basin, then gently stir into the first mixture together with the grated rind, citrus-blossom water and 3 oz (75 g/⅓ cup) butter, melted.
8. To assemble the tart, preheat the oven to Gas 5 (375°F, 190°C), and roll out the chilled dough to fit a 9 inch (22·5 cm) round or square loose-bottomed flan tin 1½ inches (3·75 cm) deep.
9. Spread the case with the apricot conserve, then spoon in the almond mixture. Smooth level, and bake for 10 minutes.
10. Take out and quickly cover the surface with the pine kernels. Return to the oven and bake for a further 20 minutes until the pastry is a golden brown and the pine kernels are a chestnut colour.

TO SERVE
Serve in thin wedges or fingers accompanied by the blackberry coulis.

SAVOURY KATAIFI

This 'shredded wheat' pastry can be deep-fried like Chinese noodles, but without having to go through the tedious process of boiling beforehand. This crispy kataifi is perfectly acceptable served at room temperature several hours after frying, but if you prefer you can reheat it in a quick oven for 5 to 10 minutes until warm to the touch. Serve as a main dish accompaniment or for a savoury 'nibble'.

Defrost 6 oz (175 g) kataifi pastry, then tease the strands apart with the fingers.

Preheat sufficient oil for deep frying in a pan or electric fryer to a temperature of 375°F (190°C). Put a handful of the pastry into a frying basket and cook in the hot oil until golden – about 2 minutes. Drain on crumpled kitchen paper. Repeat with the remaining pastry.

To serve, pile in a heatproof serving dish or basket.

Individual Kataifi

(Greek nut pastries)

Makes 24

The raw or cooked pastries will freeze for 3 months. Cooked pastries will keep for 1 week under refrigeration

Known as 'Konafa' to the Turks, this unusual pastry – which is rather like a tangle of wool – provides a crisp contrast to the nutty, citrus scented filling.

8 oz (225 g) bought kataifi pastry, defrosted
8 oz (225 g/1 cup) butter or margarine, melted

FOR THE NUT FILLING
4 oz (125 g/1 cup) each walnuts and blanched almonds,
coarsely ground
4 oz (125 g/½ cup) caster sugar
1 teasp ground cinnamon
1 egg white
1 tbsp citrus-blossom water

FOR THE SYRUP
1 lb (450 g/2¼ cups) sugar
12 fl. oz (350 ml/1½ cups) water
1 tbsp lemon juice
2 tbsp citrus-blossom water

1. To make the filling, mix all the ingredients together.
2. To make the syrup, dissolve the sugar in the water, add the lemon juice and simmer 15–20 minutes until thick enough to coat the back of a spoon. Stir in the citrus-blossom water and cook for 2 minutes longer. Leave to cool, then refrigerate.
3. To assemble the pastries, place the pastry in a large bowl and gently tease apart with the fingers.
4. Take a small handful of pastry strands and lay on a board. Using a pastry brush dab with melted butter or margarine.
5. Mould a tablespoon of the nut filling into a short sausage shape and lay on one end of the pastry. Roll up firmly into a neat roll, then place in a roulade or Swiss roll tin approx. 12 × 8 × 1 inches (30 × 20 × 2·5 cm).
6. Repeat with the remaining pastry and filling.
7. Brush the tops with the remaining butter. Bake in a moderate oven, Gas 4 (350°F, 180°C), for 55 minutes.
8. Remove from the hot oven and immediately pour the cold syrup over the hot pastries. Leave to go cold, basting with the syrup once or twice.

TO SERVE
Serve as a 'sweetmeat' with after-dinner coffee, or to accompany a sorbet.

A DELIGHT TO BOTH THE TURKS AND THE GREEKS

There's something slightly sinful about Rahat Lokum – the voluptuous sweetmeat invented by the Turks but whose most important ingredient – mastic – is produced only on the Greek island of Chios.

Maybe it's because of the way of life it suggests devoted to the joys of the senses . . . open the box and you are transported to a world of rosewater-scented kitchens and cooks who can find the time to stand and stir the pot for the 3 hours that are needed to bring this mixture of sugar syrup, cornflour and pulverised mastic to the very special texture that makes it such a delight to eat. (The Rahat Lokum eaten in the West is prepared in factories where a mechanical stirrer does the job!)

Genuine Turkish Delight does not contain gelatine, so if you see it listed on the box, do not buy it or you will be disappointed.

Strudel with Eastern Promise

Makes 2 strudels, each cutting into 10–12 slices

The strudel will freeze raw for 3 months or will keep for 2 days under refrigeration

In this Rumanian speciality, the little nuggets of Turkish Delight make an exotic scented filling.

6 sheets strudel (or fillo) pastry (about 6–8 oz/175–225 g)
4 oz (125 g/½ cup) butter or margarine, melted
2 oz (50 g/½ cup) ground almonds

FOR THE FILLING
1 × 12 oz (350 g) box rosewater and lemon Turkish Delight
2 oz (50 g/½ cup) ground almonds
8 oz (225 g/½ cup) walnuts, finely chopped
1 tbsp each citrus-blossom water and lemon juice
grated rind 1 lemon
2 oz (50 g/¼ cup) caster sugar

FOR DUSTING THE STRUDELS
sifted icing sugar

1. For the filling, cut the Turkish Delight into approx. ½ inch (1·25 cm) cubes. Put into a bowl and gently mix with the icing sugar from the box and all remaining filling ingredients. Divide into two, each portion being sufficient for one strudel. Divide the melted fat and ground almonds into two as well.

2. To assemble one strudel, lay one sheet of pastry on a board and brush evenly with melted fat. Scatter lightly with ground almonds, then lay another sheet on top and repeat with fat and almonds.

3. Lay the third sheet on top, brush with the fat, scatter the top half of the pastry furthest from you with the remaining ground almonds, then arrange one portion of the filling evenly over the half nearest to you, leaving ½ inch (1·25 cm) clear all the way round.

4. Fold in the sides of the pastry to seal in the filling, then roll up from the side nearest to you and arrange the strudel, join side down, on a tray lined with silicone paper. Brush the top and sides with melted butter.

5. Make a second strudel with the remaining sheets of pastry, the second portions of filling, fat and almonds.

6. Bake the strudels in a quick oven, Gas 5 (375°F, 190°C), for 30 minutes or until a rich golden brown. Lift carefully on to a cooling tray.

TO SERVE
Just before serving, dust thickly with icing sugar and cut in 1 inch (2·5 cm) wide diagonal slices. Serve with the Halvah Icecream (see page 145) or the Khoshab (see page 154), or as a petit-four with coffee.

OF CHEESE AND CHEESECAKES

Social historians believe that the first cheesecakes were made about 350 BC on the Greek island of Samos – you can find some of these early recipes in *The Deipnosophists*, a book about Greek food of the Classical period which was written by the Egyptian philosopher Athenaeus in the third century AD. The soft curd cheese used in these cakes was made from sour goats' milk which had been allowed to separate into curds and whey in the heat of a Greek summer, then put into a muslin bag to drip until firm, very much as country housewives make it today.

This type of cheese is now made on a commercial scale all over the world, but it varies enormously in taste and texture according to the animal – sheep, cow, goat or buffalo – whose milk is used, the butterfat content and the method of souring; cheese made with rennet or lemon juice as a clotting agent has a different texture from that made with naturally-soured milk. As you would expect, it has many different names; 'fromage blanc' in France, 'quark käse' in Germany, 'ricotta' in Italy, 'myzithra' in Greece and 'labna' in the Middle East. In the United States it may be called 'farmers' cheese', 'pot cheese' or 'cottage cheese', whilst in Britain it's known either as 'curd cheese' or 'cream cheese' (although a true cream cheese, made from set cream – like the French Petit Suisses – is not cheese at all, more a cream dessert.)

We can't say categorically which of these soft cheeses is the best one to use in a cheesecake, as it varies with the recipe. This in turn tends to reflect the kind of soft cheese produced in the country where the cake was first made. But you can't go far wrong using 'curd cheese' which according to present-day labelling laws has to be described as a 'medium fat soft cheese'.

Almond Cheese Torte

Serves 8

The torte will freeze for 1 month or will keep for 3 days under refrigeration

A traditional Russian way with cheesecake: the rich and creamy filling is at its best served slightly warm.

FOR THE PASTRY
6 oz (175 g/1½ cups) self-raising flour (or 6 oz/175 g/1½ cups plain flour plus 1½ teasp baking powder)
4 oz (125 g/½ cup) firm butter cut into 1 inch (2·5 cm) cubes
2 oz (50 g/⅓ cup) icing sugar
1 egg, separated
1 tbsp each cold water and wine vinegar

FOR THE FILLING
3 eggs, separated
caster sugar
12 oz (350 g/1½ cups) low (or medium) fat soft cheese
2 oz (50 g/½ cup) ground almonds
1 oz (25 g/2 tbsp) soft butter
2 tbsp lemon juice
grated rind ½ lemon
1 teasp vanilla essence
5 tbsp sultanas

FOR THE GLAZE AND TOPPING
the reserved egg white, whisked until frothy
1 tbsp granulated sugar
1 oz (25 g/¼ cup) flaked almonds

1. To make the pastry, put the flour, butter and icing sugar into a bowl and rub together, by hand or machine, until the mixture resembles coarse breadcrumbs.
2. Mix the egg yolk with the water and vinegar and sprinkle all over the dry ingredients. Gather into a dough using a knife or fork.
3. Chill for 30 minutes then roll out to fit a 9 inch (22·5 cm) loose-bottomed fluted flan tin, approx. 1½ inches (3·75 cm) deep. Leave in the freezer while the filling is prepared.
4. To make the filling, preheat the oven to Gas 4 (350°F, 180°C), and whisk the 3 egg whites until they hold soft peaks. Whisk in 1 oz (25 g/2 tbsp) of the sugar.
5. Put all the remaining filling ingredients, plus 2 oz (50 g/¼ cup) caster sugar into a bowl and mix until thoroughly blended. Gently fold in the meringue.
6. Remove the pastry case from the freezer, then spoon in the filling, levelling it with a knife. Paint the frothy egg white over the top, sprinkle with the granulated sugar, then scatter evenly with the almonds.

Soft cheeses and their butterfat content:

2–10% butterfat	low fat soft cheese
10–20% butterfat	medium fat soft cheese
20–45% butterfat	full-fat soft cheese
45–65% butterfat	cream cheese
over 65% butterfat	double cream cheese

A VARIETY OF BUTTERS

Sweet butter is made from freshly separated cream. It has a mild delicate flavour and a firm texture. It is especially good for rubbed-in pastry, lemon curd and shortbread. It comes mainly from Australia, New Zealand, Great Britain and Ireland.

Lactic butter has a slightly 'tangy' flavour, similar to that of soured cream. Cream which has been left overnight to mature is added to newly-separated 'sweet' cream before churning. It is especially tasty for bread and butter, for buttering scones and teabreads and, because it creams easily without oiling, it is excellent for rich fruit and 'cut and come again' cakes and for pastries where a 'plastic' textured butter is required. It is produced mainly in France, Holland and Scandinavia.

All butters were once heavily salted as a means of preservation. Today the salt is added mainly for flavour. Both sweet cream and lactic butters are marketed in a salted and unsalted pack.

The colour of butter depends largely on the shade of the butter fat, which in turn varies with the breed of cow and the 'flavour' of the pasture where it grazes – hence the premium one must pay for beurre d'Isserles produced in the lush countryside of Normandy.

7. Bake for 40 minutes until a pale gold in colour and firm to gentle touch around the edges – the filling will set completely as it cools.

TO SERVE
Serve with coffee, or as a dessert accompanied by a compote.

Flaky Nusse Strudel

Makes about 20 slices

The cooked strudel will freeze for 3 months or will keep for 3 days at room temperature in an airtight container

A light and flaky cream cheese pastry – from Israel – covers a refreshing lemon and walnut filling. Make the pastry and filling the day before.

FOR THE PASTRY
4 oz (125 g/½ cup) 'plastic' or lactic butter (see left)
4 oz (125 g/½ cup) fairly dry, low (or medium) fat soft cheese
4 oz (125 g/1 cup) self-raising flour

FOR THE FILLING
1 egg white
3 oz (75 g/⅓ cup) granulated sugar
8 oz (225 g/2 cups) walnuts, finely chopped
1 rounded tbsp thin honey (or golden syrup)
2 teasp finely grated lemon rind
½ teasp vanilla essence

FOR SPREADING ON THE DOUGH
2–3 tbsp apricot (or cherry) conserve

FOR THE GLAZE
1 egg yolk mixed with 1 teasp water

FOR DREDGING THE COOKED STRUDELS
sifted icing sugar

1. The day before, make the pastry as follows. Cream the butter and cheese together using a fork then gradually work in the flour, kneading until a smooth dough is formed. Flatten this dough into a block about 1 inch (2·5 cm) thick, wrap in film or foil and refrigerate overnight.
2. Make the filling the day before too: this allows it time to mature in flavour. Whisk the egg white until it holds soft peaks, then fold in the sugar. Add the remaining ingredients and mix well. Cover and refrigerate.
3. To assemble the strudel, the next day, remove the pastry from the refrigerator and divide in two portions.
4. On a lightly floured board, roll one portion into a rectangle

approx. 12 × 7 inches (30 × 17·5 cm), then neaten the edges with a knife.

5. Spread the dough with a thin layer of half the conserve, leaving a ½ inch (1·25 cm) clear border all the way round, then spread with half the filling.

6. Turn in the short ends to enclose the filling, then roll up into a long cylinder. Repeat with the other portion of pastry and filling.

7. Arrange the strudels side by side on an ungreased baking sheet. The raw strudels may be frozen at this point.

8. To bake, preheat the oven to Gas 8 (450°F, 230°C), and brush the strudels all over with the egg glaze. Prick decoratively with a fork or tweezers (see page 00): this prevents the pastry bursting in the oven, and makes it easier for the icing sugar to cling to the surface after baking.

9. Bake for 5 minutes, then turn the heat down to Gas 5 (375°F, 190°C), for a further 20 minutes until the strudels are a rich brown. Remove to a cooling rack.

TO SERVE

Have the strudels at room temperature. Dredge thickly with icing sugar then cut in 1½ inch (3·75 cm) wide diagonal slices. Serve plain with tea or coffee, or for dessert accompanied with a fruit compote.

Viennese Apfel Torte

Serves 6–8

The raw pastry will freeze for 1 month. Do not freeze the completed torte. Serve the same day

Because the pastry is so fragile, we don't attempt to roll out the top crust; instead we freeze some and then grate it on top, forming an interesting textured covering.

FOR THE PASTRY
9 oz (250 g/2¼ cups) plain flour
pinch salt
1 oz (25 g/¼ cup) ground almonds (or hazelnuts)
3 oz (75 g/⅓ cup) caster sugar
grated rind ½ lemon
6 oz (175 g/¾ cup) butter (or firm margarine), cut in 1 inch
(2·5 cm) chunks
1 egg yolk
2 tbsp single cream (or evaporated milk)

FOR THE FILLING

2 lb (1 kg) baking apples, approx. 1½ lb (675 g) when peeled and cored
4 oz (125 g/½ cup) granulated sugar
1 teasp ground cinnamon
3 tbsp raisins (or sultanas)
2 oz (50 g/½ cup) walnuts, coarsely chopped
2 tbsp lemon juice

FOR SPRINKLING ON THE TORTE

golden granulated (or demerara) sugar

1. To make the pastry, put the flour, salt, nuts, sugar and lemon rind into a bowl. Add the chunks of butter and rub in gently until the mixture resembles dry breadcrumbs.
2. Mix the egg yolk and the cream then sprinkle on the dry ingredients and mix to a dough.
3. Divide the dough in two and knead each piece gently on a floured board until smooth. Flatten each piece until 1 inch (2·5 cm) thick. Wrap in foil, *chill* one half for an hour and *freeze* the other half for an hour.
4. Preheat the oven to Gas 5 (375°F, 190°C), and have ready a 9–10 inch (22·5–25 cm) flan tin, 1½ inches (3·75 cm) deep. Roll the chilled piece of pastry to fit the flan tin, then gently ease into place and trim the edges level.
5. Assemble the torte and filling just before baking or the juicy apples may make the pastry soggy. Coarsely grate or finely slice the apples and mix with all the other ingredients for the filling.
6. Immediately spread in an even layer over the pastry then coarsely grate the frozen pastry over the top. Sprinkle with the sugar then bake for 45 minutes until golden brown.

TO SERVE

Serve warm or at room temperature accompanied by cinnamon cream (see page 199).

GINGER SQUARES

These little Dutch 'bonnes bouches' are very moist and moreish, yet very quickly made.

Use the same pastry as for the Viennese Apfel Torte but substitute soft light brown sugar for the caster sugar in the recipe. Line the tin with half the pastry, then spread it evenly with the contents of a 1 lb (450 g) jar of ginger preserve. Grate the remaining pastry on top as described and scatter with 4 tbsp demerara sugar mixed with 4 tbsp flaked almonds. Bake at Gas 5 (375°F, 190°C) for 40 minutes or until golden brown. Leave to cool for 15 minutes, then cut into 24 or 30 squares. When quite cold, store in an airtight container for up to 2 weeks.

To make the braid

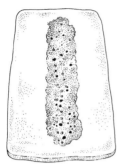

Arrange filling down centre of pastry.

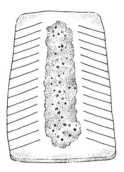

Make diagonal cuts.

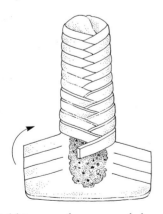

Fold in top of pastry and then overlap strips to form a braid.

Brandied Mincemeat and Almond Braid

Serves 10–12

The raw braid will freeze for 1 month. Ready-to-serve braid will freeze for 1 week

To taste this glorious confection at its best, bake and eat on the same day. You could substitute a compote of well-drained apricots or spiced apples for the mincemeat filling.

1 lb (450 g) puff pastry
2 rounded tbsp apricot conserve

FOR THE ALMOND FILLING
2 oz (50 g/¼ cup) each butter (or margarine) and caster sugar
1 egg
½ teasp vanilla essence
4 oz (125 g/1 cup) ground almonds
1 tbsp flour
1 oz (25 g/¼ cup) almond nibs, toasted

FOR THE MINCEMEAT FILLING
12 oz (350 g) mincemeat
1 tbsp each brandy and ground almonds

FOR THE ICING
3 teasp each orange juice and Cointreau
5 oz (150 g/¾ cup) icing sugar
1 oz (25 g) toasted almonds

1. To make the almond filling, put all the ingredients into a bowl and beat until creamy – about 2 minutes.
2. Preheat the oven to Gas 8 (450°F, 230°C), and roll the pastry into a rectangle measuring 14 × 9 inches (35 × 22·5 cm), when well trimmed.
3. Arrange the almond filling in a strip 2½ inches (6 cm) wide down the length of the pastry, leaving 1 inch (2·5 cm) clear at either end.
4. Mix the mincemeat filling ingredients in a bowl, then spoon this on top of the almond filling.
5. Leaving ½ inch (1·25 cm) of uncut pastry on either side of the filling, cut the pastry into ¾ inch (2 cm) wide diagonal strips – about fifteen strips on each side.
6. Criss-cross the strips of pastry over the filling, covering it almost completely. Finally, turn the ends under and pinch to seal.
7. Lift the braid carefully on to a silicone-lined baking sheet. Bake for 30 minutes until crisp and brown.

8. Meanwhile, mix the icing ingredients into a smooth thick paste.
9. As soon as the braid comes from the oven, carefully brush over with the apricot conserve, followed by half the icing. Cool for 20 minutes, then apply a further coat of icing and decorate with almonds.

TO SERVE

Serve in 1 inch (2·5 cm) slices.

Toasted Hazelnut Shortbread

Makes 24

The biscuits will freeze for 3 months or keep for 1 week at room temperature in an airtight container

The traditional Scottish classic with an added dimension – toasted ground hazelnuts.

3½–4 oz (100–125 g/¾–1 cup) hazelnuts, skinned
8 oz (225 g/1 cup) butter, chilled, cut in rough 1 inch (2·5 cm) chunks
4 oz (125 g/⅓ cup) caster sugar
8 oz (225 g/2 cups) plain flour
½ teasp salt

TO SPRINKLE ON THE BISCUITS
2 tbsp granulated sugar

1. Preheat the oven to Gas 4 (350°F, 180°C). Have ready a roulade tin measuring 12 × 8 inches (30 × 20 cm) and 1 inch (2·5 cm) deep.
2. Toast the hazelnuts in the oven until a rich gold – about 15 minutes – then remove and reduce heat to Gas 3 (325°F, 160°C). Cool the nuts for 10 minutes then grind or process until as fine as sand.
3. Put all the ingredients into a bowl and rub together by hand or machine until like very fine crumbs – stop before the crumbs start clinging together.
4. Spoon into the tin and using the back of a fork, press into an even layer then sprinkle evenly with a tablespoon of the granulated sugar.
5. Bake for 30–35 minutes or until the surface is firm and the shortbread is a pale gold.
6. Place the tin on a cooling rack and leave to firm up for 10 minutes, then sprinkle with the remaining sugar and cut into 2 inch (5 cm) squares.

SOME RULES FOR THE BISCUIT BAKER

Use a quality butter with a 'plastic' texture. The cheaper blended butters tend to produce greasy biscuits.

● Make sure that all the biscuits on a tray are of a similar size so that they will bake in the same time span.

● Buy baking sheets as large as the oven will hold, solidly made, preferably from pressed aluminium. (This material has a ten-year life and when necessary can be burnished like new with soap-filled pads.)

● Save washing up by lining the trays with silicone paper instead of greasing them. The same paper can be used again and again until it becomes too dark and brittle.

● Don't overbake – many biscuits that are soft to the touch when they come out of the oven will firm up on cooling, so follow our instructions to test for doneness.

● Don't store the biscuits in covered containers until they are absolutely cold or any trapped steam will cause them to become soggy.

● Allow biscuits to mature for a day or two if recommended – particularly if they are made with butter. The flavour will then be far superior than when freshly baked.

Chocolate Butterballs

Makes about 24

The butterballs will freeze for 3 months or keep for 1 week at room temperature in an airtight container

A typical American-style 'cookie' with a slightly spongy texture and a rich chocolate flavour.

8 oz (225 g/1 cup) soft butter
4 oz (125 g/½ cup) dark brown sugar
1 teasp vanilla essence
1 egg
8 oz (225 g/2 cups) plain flour
½ teasp salt
2 oz (50 g/½ cup) cocoa powder
4 oz (125 g) plain chocolate, coarsely chopped

1. Preheat the oven to Gas 4 (350°F, 180°C) and line two baking trays with silicone paper.
2. Process the butter until creamy, then add the sugar, vanilla and egg, and process until just absorbed.
3. Pulse in the flour, salt and cocoa, followed by the chocolate.
4. Tip on to a board and form into a rough ball. Chill for 20 minutes.
5. With damp palms roll rounded teaspoons of the mixture into 1 inch (2·5 cm) balls, and arrange 1 inch (2·5 cm) apart on the baking trays.
6. Bake for 20 minutes then *immediately* transfer with a palette knife on to a cooling tray. When quite cold store in an airtight container.

Coconut Chocolate Fingers

Makes about 30

The fingers will freeze for 3 months or keep for 1 week in an airtight container

Spongy coconut biscuits with a built-in chocolate coating.

4 oz (125 g) plain nut chocolate, broken into pieces
3 oz (75 g/⅓ cup) butter
6 oz (175 g/2 cups) desiccated coconut
5 oz (150 g/⅔ cup) caster sugar
2 oz (50 g/¼ cup) glacé cherries, chopped
2 oz (50 g/¼ cup) glacé pineapple, chopped
2 eggs, beaten

THE SCISSORS 'CHOP'

Sticky foods like glacé and dried fruits are most easily 'chopped' with a snip of the scissors. The sharpest cook's knife tends to get caught in their sugary interior, and even the double-bladed knife of the food processor will be unable to cut through them, unless they're chopped with another ingredient – for example walnuts – that is both *unsticky* and dry in texture.

SURE-FIRE PRALINE

This delicious powder, made from caramelised nuts, will keep indefinitely in an airtight container. It adds a glorious flavour to all manner of pâtisserie and icecreams, and also provides a crunchy finish for many kinds of butter biscuits.

To make it, first line a small baking tin with silicone paper. Put 4 oz (125 g/$\frac{1}{2}$ cup) granulated sugar and 2 oz (50 g/$\frac{1}{2}$ cup) flaked almonds into a wide frying pan or heavy-based saucepan and cook without stirring over moderate heat (shaking the pan occasionally) until the sugar and nuts are chestnut in colour. Pour *at once* on to the paper and leave to set – about 15 minutes. When the praline is cool and brittle in texture, break it into roughly 1 inch (2·5 cm) chunks and process in the food processor until like coarse sand. (Alternatively, put it in a plastic bag and crush with a rolling pin.) Store in an airtight container.

1. Preheat the oven to Gas 4 (350°F, 180°C), and line a Swiss roll or roulade tin measuring 12 × 8 inches (30 × 20 cm) with silicone paper.
2. Melt the chocolate gently in the roulade tin in the oven and spread out with a palette knife. Refrigerate until set.
3. Melt the butter, and cool until it stops steaming. Put the coconut, sugar and glacé fruit into a bowl, then add the melted butter together with the beaten eggs, mixing well. Spread over the set chocolate using a flexible knife.
4. Bake for 25 minutes or until set. Leave for 15 minutes, then cut in fingers of about 3 × 1 inches (7·5 × 2·5 cm).
5. Chill for 30 minutes (to set the chocolate), then carefully invert on to a board and peel off the silicone paper. Separate the fingers and store in an airtight container.

Praline Crunchies

Makes about 30

The crunchies will freeze for 3 months or keep for 1 week at room temperature in an airtight container

Cinnamon spiced 'fork' biscuits with a crushed praline topping.

4 oz (125 g/$\frac{1}{2}$ cup) mild butter (see page 169), cut in rough 1 inch (2·5 cm) cubes
2 oz (50 g/$\frac{1}{4}$ cup) caster sugar
4 oz (125 g/1 cup) self-raising flour (or 4 oz/125 g/1 cup plain flour plus 1 teasp baking powder)
1 oz (25 g/4 tbsp) cornflour
1 oz (25 g/$\frac{1}{4}$ cup) ground almonds (or hazelnuts)
1 teasp cinnamon

FOR THE TOPPING
2 oz (50 g/$\frac{1}{2}$ cup) almond praline (see left)

1. Preheat the oven to Gas 5 (375°F, 190°C) and line two baking sheets with silicone paper.
2. By hand or machine, rub the butter into the dry ingredients until the mixture resembles breadcrumbs, then gather or work into a ball.
3. Pinch off pieces the size of a small walnut and roll into balls. Arrange 2 inches (5 cm) apart on the baking sheets.
4. Dip a large fork into a bowl of cold water then press down on each ball to form a biscuit $\frac{1}{4}$ inch (6 mm) thick. (Wet the fork again from time to time.)
5. Scatter evenly with the topping, then bake for 15–20 minutes until golden. Allow to rest for 5 minutes then lift on to a cooling tray.

OF ANTLER'S HORNS AND RAISING AGENTS

Salts of hartshorn is an ancient raising agent – distilled from powdered horn – which, though banned from sale in Britain, is still used in Denmark to give a wonderful open texture to some of their traditional butter biscuits.

Learning that its chemical name is 'ammonium carbonate' we decided to experiment with sodium bicarbonate (bicarbonate of soda), and found we achieved a very similar result. Both salts of hartshorn and bicarbonate of soda are very volatile so that when they are heated in the oven, they immediately form a gas which then lightens the biscuits as they bake. Salts of hartshorn has kept its popularity longer than any of the other medieval leavening agents such as salts of potash, as it does not leave any unpleasant-tasting residue.

RIGHT: *Individual Kataifi (page 166), Brandied Mincemeat and Almond Braid (page 172) and La Pignola (page 164)*

Danish Nut Crisps

Makes 40

The crisps will freeze for 6 months or keep for 1 week at room temperature in an airtight container

Everybody's favourite biscuit – make a batch and you'll taste the reason.

*7 oz (200 g/¾ cup + 2 tbsp) butter
6 oz (175 g/¾ cup) caster sugar
1 packet vanilla sugar (20 g approx.) (or 1 teasp vanilla essence)
8 oz (225 g/2 cups) self-raising flour (or 8 oz/225 g/2 cups plain flour and 1 teasp baking powder)
1 level teasp bicarbonate of soda
2 oz (50 g/½ cup) nibbed or flaked almonds*

1. Work the butter into the sugar using a wooden spoon, mixer or food processor.
2. When the sugar has been absorbed, add the vanilla flavouring and the flour sifted with the bicarbonate of soda. Mix to a dough – don't overwork.
3. Roll into balls the size of a walnut and arrange on ungreased trays, leaving room for the biscuits to flatten and spread.
4. Top with a split almond. Alternatively, dip the balls in a bowl of nibbed almonds before arranging on trays.
5. Bake in a moderate oven, Gas 4 (350°F, 180°C), for 15 minutes or until golden brown.

Mamoules

(Syrian date pastries)

Makes 24

The pastries will freeze for 3 months or keep for 1 week at room temperature in an airtight container

A perfect example of 'harem' (i.e. labour-intensive) food preparation. The casing for each little pastry is shaped by hand – easy when you know how and well worth the effort.

FOR THE PASTRY
*10 oz (275 g/1¼ cups) butter, cut in 1 inch (2·5 cm) chunks
1 lb (450 g/4 cups) plain flour
2–3 tbsp cold water
1 tbsp citrus-blossom water*

TURKISH COFFEE FOR TWO

The richness of Middle Eastern pastries is most effectively tempered by a cup of coffee made Turkish style with pulverised rather than ground beans – in Israel it's called 'bots' (mud in Hebrew!), the reference being to the texture of the coffee at the bottom of each cup. The flavour is superb.

The coffee is made by tradition in a small long-handled metal pot or 'ibrik' although a small saucepan can be used with a less romantic effect. Bring 2 coffee cups of water to the boil with 2 heaped teasp sugar and 1 pod of cardamom (optional), then add 2 heaped teasp of pulverised coffee (ground as fine as flour), stir well and return to the heat. Remove from the heat as soon as the froth reaches the rim of the pot, then repeat this frothing up process twice. Allow to settle for a minute or two before serving.

LEFT: *Roast Shoulder of Lamb stuffed with a Pinwheel of Fresh Herbs (page 192), Champignons à la Grecque (page 191), Ratatouille Niçoise (page 193) and Corbeille de Citron (page 194)*

FOR THE FILLING
1 lb (450 g) stoneless dates
2 tbsp apricot conserve
grated rind 1 lemon
4 tbsp cold water
½ teasp ground cinnamon
4 oz (125 g/1 cup) walnuts, finely chopped

TO COAT THE MAMOULES
4 oz (125 g/⅔ cup) icing sugar, sifted

1. To make the pastry, rub the fat into the flour until the mixture resembles coarse crumbs.
2. Mix the water and citrus-blossom water, scatter on the dry mixture and work to a dough using a fork. Chill.
3. To make the filling, separate the dates and put in a thick-bottomed pan with all the other ingredients, except the walnuts.
4. Cook, stirring, until a smooth paste is formed, then stir in the nuts and allow to cool.
5. To shape the mamoules, divide the dough in half and roll each piece into a rope 12 inches (30 cm) long, then cut into 1 inch (2.5 cm) lengths – twenty-four pieces altogether.
6. Take each piece in turn and place in the palm of the hand then with the fingers of the other hand shape into a little cup.
7. Spoon in a teasp of the filling and pinch the pastry together to enclose it completely. Turn over and place on an ungreased baking sheet. Repeat with the remaining dough and filling.
8. Roughen the surface of each mamoule with little pastry tweezers or with a fork (this makes it easier for the icing sugar to cling to the surface after the biscuits have been baked).
9. Bake in a quick-moderate oven, Gas 5 (375°F, 190°C), for 25 minutes until set but uncoloured.
10. Remove to a cooling tray and leave for 15 minutes, then dredge thickly with the icing sugar. When quite cold, store in an airtight tin.

THE MASTER CLASS WAY TO MESS-FREE PIPING BAGS

First choose your piping bag – a 14 inch (35 cm) size is convenient both from the point of view of its capacity and ease in handling.

Put in the nozzle, if required, then grasp the piping bag in your left hand (right hand if you're left-handed). Fold the top third of the bag over your hand forming a cuff. Release your grip a little so that you can spoon the mixture in with your right hand, then open up the cuff and close the bag by grasping it with the thumb and forefinger of your right hand leaving the three remaining fingers free to press on to the bag to force the mixture down towards the nozzle.

SHELLING PECANS WITHOUT TEARS

The brittle shell of the pecan is extremely difficult to remove even with the most efficient nutcrackers. The solution: steep the nuts for 30 minutes in boiling water to cover. The nuts can then be cracked and shells removed with no problems.

Lemon Pecan Spritz Biscuits

Makes 48

The biscuits will freeze for 3 months or keep for 1 week in an airtight container at room temperature

A biscuit perfumed and flavoured with freshly-squeezed lemon juice.

3½–4 oz (100–125 g/1 cup) pecans, shelled (or walnuts)
4 oz (125 g/⅓ cup) icing sugar, sifted
8 oz (225 g/1 cup) soft mild butter (see page 169), cut in 1 inch (2·5 cm) chunks
1 egg yolk
1 tbsp fresh lemon juice
1 teasp grated lemon rind
1 teasp vanilla essence
8 oz (225 g/2 cups) plain flour
½ teasp salt

TO SPRINKLE ON THE BISCUITS
sifted icing sugar

1. Preheat the oven to Gas 4 (350°F, 180°C) and line two baking trays with silicone paper.
2. Put the nuts in the food processor with 2 oz (50 g/⅓ cup) of the icing sugar and process until finely ground.
3. Add the remaining sugar, the butter, egg yolk, juice, rind and essence and process until smooth.
4. Add the flour and salt and pulse in until evenly mixed and creamy in texture.
5. Fill a 14 inch (35 cm) piping bag fitted with a ½ inch (1·25 cm) rose nozzle with the mixture and pipe in 2 inch (5 cm) crescents or sticks, leaving 1 inch (2·5 cm) between the biscuits.
6. Bake for 12 minutes or until the biscuits are beginning to colour.
7. Lift on to a cooling tray and after 10 minutes coat thickly with icing sugar. Allow to cool completely, then store in an airtight container.

Schneeballen

(Snowballs)

Makes 36–40

The snowballs will keep for 1 week at room temperature in an airtight container or freeze for 3 months

Moist and 'moreish' biscuits with a delicious cinnamon coating.

8 oz (225 g/1 cup) soft butter or margarine, cut in roughly 1
inch (2.5 cm) cubes
4 oz (125 g/$\frac{1}{2}$ cup) caster sugar
2 eggs yolks
1 teasp vanilla essence
5 oz (150 g/1$\frac{2}{3}$ cups) desiccated coconut
8 oz (225 g/2 cups) plain flour
1 teasp ground cinnamon
$\frac{1}{2}$ teasp each baking powder and salt

TO COAT THE BISCUITS
1 teasp ground cinnamon
2 oz (50 g/$\frac{1}{3}$ cup) icing sugar

1. Whether by hand or machine, process or cream the butter until it is like mayonnaise, then add the sugar, egg yolks and vanilla essence and mix until just absorbed.
2. Add the coconut, flour, cinnamon, baking powder and salt, and mix until a rough dough is formed.
3. Turn this dough on to a floured board and divide in two, then knead each portion gently until smooth and pliable. Add a little flour as you go if the dough is sticky.
4. Wrap the dough in film and chill in the refrigerator for 20 minutes, then pinch off pieces the size of a walnut and roll into balls.
5. Arrange these 2 inches (5 cm) apart on trays which have been greased or lined with silicone paper.
6. Bake in a slow moderate oven, Gas 3 (325°F, 160°C) until firm to a gentle touch but only lightly coloured (about 15 minutes).
7. Leave for 5 minutes on the trays then gently dip each biscuit into the mixed cinnamon and icing sugar.
8. When the biscuits are quite cold, dip again in the cinnamon sugar, then arrange in layers in a container and sprinkle with any remaining sugar.

VANILLA, TRUE OR FALSE

As with other rich and rare materials such as gold and chocolate, vanilla was put to especially good use by the Aztecs of Peru: they used it to flavour the native chocolate.

So little has changed over the last 300 years except that the vanilla pod has become even more rare and expensive than it was in those days. A true vanilla pod is black with a white 'frosting' of aromatic vanillin crystals. It can be used to flavour sugar (bury it in the jar) or simmered with milk (for a custard), after which it can be dried off and re-used.

Genuine vanilla *extract* is extremely expensive – you use it literally by the drop. It is made by extracting the vanilla flavouring from the pods, using alcohol. Vanilla flavouring *essence*, which you can buy at any supermarket, is a purely synthetic product. Though pleasant in its own way it has none of the intense flavour of true vanilla and to have any noticeable effect it has to be used by the teaspoonful.

Vanilla Kipferl

(Almond crescents)

Makes 36

The kipferl will freeze for 3 months or keep for 1 week at room temperature in an airtight container
The original melt-in-your-mouth Viennese petit-four. The perfect kipferl should be barely coloured under its dusting of icing sugar – browning coarsens the flavour.

3 oz (75 g/$\frac{3}{4}$ cup) whole almonds, blanched
caster sugar
6 oz (175 g/$\frac{3}{4}$ cup) butter, cut in 1 inch (2·5 cm) chunks
6 oz (175 g/$1\frac{1}{2}$ cups) plain flour
pinch salt
1 teasp vanilla essence (or a 20 g/$\frac{2}{3}$ oz packet vanilla sugar)

FOR DUSTING THE BAKED BISCUITS
sifted icing sugar

1. Preheat the oven to Gas 3 (325°F, 160°C), and have ready two ungreased or silicone-paper lined baking sheets.
2. Process or grind the nuts with a tbsp caster sugar until like fine sand.
3. Add all the remaining ingredients, including 3 oz (75 g/$\frac{1}{3}$ cup) caster sugar, and mix until the dough starts to cling together. Do *not* overmix.
4. Turn on to a board and gather into a dough. Pinch off pieces the size of a walnut and roll into 'pencils' 2 inches (5 cm) long and $\frac{3}{4}$ inch (2 cm) in diameter.
5. Bend into crescents, then arrange 1 inch (2·5 cm) apart on the baking sheets and bake for 18 minutes or just beginning to colour.
6. Leave to cool for 10 minutes, then carefully transfer to a cooling tray. Take care, as they are very fragile.
7. Dust with icing sugar, allow to go quite cold, then dust again just before storing.

Caramelised Stuffed Walnuts

These will keep for 1 week at room temperature in an airtight container

A helpful mother-in-law (with Egyptian connections) taught us how to make these delicious Middle-Eastern sweetmeats. They're very practical for the home cook because unlike the glazed fresh fruits offered 'comme dessert' at some Michelin-starred restaurants, they do not 'weep' and will stay crisp and clear for up to a week.

1 lb (450 g) unbroken walnut halves

FOR THE MARZIPAN
6 oz (175 g/1½ cups) ground almonds
6 oz (175g/1 cup) caster sugar
3 tbsp citrus-blossom water

FOR THE CARAMEL
6 oz (175 g/¾ cup) granulated sugar
2 tbsp cold water

1. To make the marzipan, mix the almonds and caster sugar together then sprinkle with the citrus-blossom water and knead to a firm paste. Do not overwork or the marzipan will become oily.
2. Form into balls the same diameter and thickness as the nut halves, then use to sandwich two nuts together.
3. Arrange side by side, ¼ inch (6 mm) apart on baking sheets lined with silicone paper.
4. To make the caramel, in a small heavy-based pan stir the sugar and water together with a wooden spoon over gentle heat until the grains of sugar have dissolved.
5. Turn up the heat and continue to cook, but more rapidly and without stirring, shaking the pan occasionally to ensure even cooking, until the sugar solution has changed colour from grey to a light caramel.
6. Immediately immerse the base of the pan in some cold water in the sink – be sure to avoid allowing any drops of water to fall into the caramel or it will splutter dangerously.
7. While the caramel is still liquid, carefully spoon a little over each walnut and allow to set. When quite firm place in tiny paper cases.

Crunchy Fruited Macaroons

Makes 15–20

The macaroons will keep for 1 week at room temperature in an airtight container

Moist little biscuits with a delicious citrus flavour.

*4 oz (125 g/1 cup) ground almonds
4 oz (125 g/$\frac{2}{3}$ cup) icing sugar
grated rind $\frac{1}{2}$ large lemon
grated rind $\frac{1}{2}$ large orange
2 egg whites
2 tbsp blanched almonds, chopped, mixed with 2 tbsp caster sugar*

1. Preheat oven to Gas 6 (400°F, 200°C), and line two baking sheets with silicone paper.
2. By hand or machine, mix the ground almonds and icing sugar together with the grated fruit rinds.
3. Add the egg whites, reserving 1 tablespoonful for coating, and beat or process until a plasticine-like soft dough is formed.
4. Pinch off pieces the size of a small walnut, then roll in the hands forming small balls.
5. In a basin mix the reserved egg white with a teaspoonful of cold water and whisk with a fork until frothy.
6. Dip the shaped pieces in the egg white, then in the almond and sugar mixture. Arrange on the trays about 2 inches (5 cm) apart.
7. Bake for 12 minutes until light gold on top and firm to the touch – inside they will be the texture of macaroons. Remove from the trays and allow to cool.

Almond Batons

Makes about 36

The batons will keep for 2 weeks at room temperature in an airtight container

Little sticks of home-made marzipan studded with chopped pistachio nuts.

*6 oz (175 g/1$\frac{1}{2}$ cups) ground almonds
2 oz (50 g/$\frac{1}{2}$ cup) pistachios, blanched and finely chopped
6 oz (175 g/1 cup) icing sugar, sifted
3 tbsp orange-blossom water*

FOR DREDGING THE BATONS
sifted icing sugar

1. Mix the ground almonds, chopped pistachios, icing sugar and enough orange-blossom water to make a stiff paste. Knead by hand until smooth.
2. Sprinkle some extra icing sugar in a thin layer on a pastry board.
3. Divide the paste in four and roll with the hands into four long sausages, each about 12 inches (30 cm) long and $\frac{3}{4}$ inch (2 cm) in diameter.
4. Cut each sausage into $1\frac{1}{2}$ inch (3·75 cm) lengths.
5. Dredge thickly with icing sugar, then arrange in little paper cases.

COMPOSING THE CHEESEBOARD

We are divided as to whether the cheese should come before or after the dessert. The French rarely serve rich and creamy puddings and pies so it makes sense to serve the cheese first and follow with a selection of choice fruits 'comme dessert'. If, however, the dessert is fairly rich, it makes sense to *follow* it with cheese, or indeed omit the cheese course altogether.

Wherever the cheeseboard appears on the menu, we think its contents should be few in number but superb in quality. And the only way to guarantee the quality is by choosing a cheesemonger who is in love with his craft – for fine cheeses need as much expertise in their management as fine wines.

We always buy the cheese on the day as there is then little chance of the cut surfaces drying out.

For a dinner party, you have a choice. Either serve one superb cheese – perhaps a 'Camembert du Ferme' or a princely piece of Roquefort – *or* you can hedge your bets by choosing three different varieties that combine between them the mild and the 'tasty', the soft and the firm – a blue cheese, a creamy cheese and a pressed farmhouse cheese.

Two selections
1. Brie, Blue Stilton, Farmhouse Cheddar
2. Vacherin, Bleu de Bresse, Mature Gouda

Dill and Sesame Butter Puffs

Makes 20

The puffs will freeze for 1 month. Serve the same day

The yoghurt in these little savoury biscuits has a softening effect on the gluten in the flour. The result – a melt-in-your-mouth biscuit ideal to serve with creamy cheeses such as goat's, Campo Sola and Camembert du Ferme.

4 oz (125 g/1 cup) self-raising flour (or 4 oz/125 g/1 cup plain flour and 1 teasp baking powder)
$\frac{1}{4}$ teasp each bicarbonate of soda and salt
1 teasp dried dill
3 level tbsp sesame seeds, lightly toasted
1 oz (25 g/2 tbsp) butter, cut into tiny cubes
3 rounded tbsp plain yoghurt

FOR THE TOPPING
coarsely ground sea salt

1. Preheat the oven to Gas 8 (450°F, 230°C) and line a baking sheet with silicone paper.
2. Put the flour, bicarbonate and salt into a bowl, stir in the dill and the sesame seeds, and rub in the butter until the mixture resembles coarse crumbs.
3. Make a well in the centre, add the yoghurt and mix to a soft dough with a fork.
4. Turn out on to a floured board and knead lightly for 30 seconds.
5. Roll out $\frac{1}{4}$ inch (6 mm) thick and cut into 2 inch (5 cm) circles.
6. Arrange the puffs on the baking sheet 1 inch (2·5 cm) apart, sprinkle lightly with the sea salt then bake for 8–10 minutes or until puffed and golden brown.
7. Serve at once or reheat under a moderately hot grill until warm to the touch.

Home-Made Digestive Biscuits

Makes about 30

Freeze for 3 months. Keep for 1 week in an airtight container at room temperature

A recipe garnered (amongst others) from our frequent visits to White Moss House Hotel in the English Lakes. Jean Butterworth serves these with a sunburst of Cox's apple slices and a selection of superb English farmhouse cheeses.

4 oz (125 g/1 cup) plain wheatmeal flour
4 oz (125 g/1⅓ cups) porridge oats
2 level tbsp soft brown sugar
½ level teasp sea salt
2 oz (50 g/¼ cup) each butter (or sunflower margarine) and white vegetable fat
2–3 tbsp milk
½ level teasp bicarbonate of soda

TO SPRINKLE ON THE BISCUITS
coarsely ground sea salt

1. Preheat the oven to Gas 6 (400°F, 200°C), and line two baking sheets with silicone paper.
2. Mix the flour, oats, sugar and salt together then rub in the fats until the mixture resembles coarse pastry crumbs.
3. Mix to a firm but rollable dough with the milk mixed with the bicarbonate of soda.
4. Roll out ¼ inch (6 mm) thick on a floured board, and cut into 2½ inch (6 cm) circles, then arrange 1 inch (2·5 cm) apart on the trays.
5. Prick all over with a fork then bake for 12–15 minutes or until a rich golden brown.
6. Immediately sprinkle with the sea salt. Remove from the trays and when cool store in a tin.

EFFORTLESS ENTERTAINING WITH THE MICROWAVE

The microwave has an important role to play, particularly when it comes to entertaining. We have devised three different menus which will show you just how effortless entertaining can be.

<table>
<tr><td>

MENU 1

Viennese Tomato Soup with Knödel

*Poulet Sauté Basquaise
An Oriental Pilaff*

or

*Roast Boned Rib of Beef
A Bouquet of Market
Vegetables*

*Whole Stuffed Pears with Two
Sauces*

</td></tr>
</table>

INSTANT SEASONINGS

It makes good sense when time is of the essence to use time-saving flavourings as well – onion salt (instead of sautéed onions), garlic granules (instead of fresh cloves), powdered herbs (instead of the fresh whole ones). However, you do need to discipline yourself to have a 'smelling session' every few weeks and discard any of those seasonings that have either lost their scent or developed even a vaguely unpleasant one.

Viennese Tomato Soup with Knödel

Serves 4–5

The dish will freeze for 3 months or keep for 3 days under refrigeration

A rich red soup with a hint of orange. Extra interest is provided by fluffy little almond dumplings. The flavour deepens if the soup is allowed to mature for several hours before reheating.

FOR THE SOUP
$\frac{1}{2} \times 5$ oz (150 g) can (or 3 tbsp from a tube) tomato purée
5 fl. oz (150 ml/$\frac{2}{3}$ cup) each hot water and tomato juice
$\frac{1}{2}$ teasp each onion salt and garlic granules
2 teasp dark brown sugar
2 strips orange peel
1 bayleaf
10 grinds black pepper
1 teasp dried Herbes de Provence
1 pint (575 ml/$2\frac{1}{2}$ cups) strong hot meat stock

FOR THE KNÖDEL
$1\frac{1}{2}$ oz (40 g/3 tbsp) butter or margarine
1 egg
2 oz (50 g/$\frac{1}{2}$ cup) plain flour
1 oz (25 g/$\frac{1}{4}$ cup) self-raising flour
2 tbsp ground almonds
good pinch salt
pinch white pepper

FOR THE GARNISH
2 teasp chopped parsley

1. To make the knödel, soften the fat in a mixing bowl for 10–15 seconds on 80% power, then beat in the rest of the ingredients in the order given.
2. Freeze whilst the soup is prepared and cooked.
3. To make the soup, put all the ingredients into a large bowl or casserole, cover and cook on 100% power for 8 minutes. Stir and leave whilst knödel are formed.
4. Roll the knödel mixture into marble-sized balls and put into the soup. Cover and cook for 5 minutes.
5. To reheat, cover the soup dish and cook on 100% power for 8 minutes ($2\frac{1}{2}$ minutes for an individual bowl).

TO SERVE
Stir in the parsley just before serving.

A DISH FIT FOR A CHICKEN CASSEROLE

Our favourite is round and 10 inches (25 cm) in diameter, with a base made of translucent ceramic and a lid of heatproof glass. It is large enough to arrange the joints in a circle – the preferred method for microwave cooking, and elegant enough to go straight to the table.

Poulet Sauté Basquaise

(Chicken joints braised in a wine and herb sauce)

Serves 4–6

The dish will freeze for 3 months or keep for 3 days under refrigeration

Chicken breasts are braised in a dark wine sauce, with peppers, mushrooms and olives adding a touch of the southern sun.

4–6 chicken breasts on the bone, trimmed, 2 lb (1 kg) total weight
2 tbsp oil
1 medium (5 oz/150 g) onion, finely chopped
1 medium green pepper, halved, seeded, then cut in thin strips
1 large clove garlic, finely chopped
10 fl. oz (275 ml/1¼ cups) Passata (sieved tomatoes)
5 fl. oz (150 ml/⅔ cup) medium dry red or white wine
2 tbsp each tomato purée and brown sugar
½ teasp each dried basil, tarragon and oregano (or 1½ teasp dried Herbes de Provence)
4–6 oz (125–175 g/1¼–2 cups) button mushrooms, stalks trimmed
15 grinds black pepper
1–1½ teasp salt

FOR THE GARNISH
4 oz (125 g/1 cup) black olives

1. In a casserole large enough to hold the chicken breasts in one layer, put the oil, onion, green pepper and garlic.
2. Cover and cook on 100% power for 6 minutes.
3. Add the chicken joints, spoon over the onion and oil mixture, re-cover and cook for 3 minutes.
4. Meanwhile, in a large jug or bowl, stir all the remaining ingredients together (except the salt and the black olives).
5. Pour this mixture over the chicken breasts, cover and cook for 15 minutes.
6. Remove from the microwave, sprinkle with the salt, then spoon the sauce over the breasts to coat them evenly.

TO SERVE
Garnish with the black olives. This dish will taste even better if allowed to stand for several hours or overnight and then reheated for about 6 minutes or until bubbly.

An Oriental Pilaff

Serves 6

The pilaff will freeze for 1 month or will keep for 2 days under refrigeration

There's no saving of time here from conventional cooking, but the rice won't catch and it cooks to perfection every time without watching. This is a delicious pilaff by any standards, with an interesting blend of flavours and textures.

1½ oz (40 g/3 tbsp) butter or margarine
1 medium onion, finely chopped
10 oz (275 g/1⅔ cups) Basmati rice, soaked in cold water for
15 minutes, then drained in a sieve
1 pint (575 ml/2½ cups) chicken stock
¼ teasp ground turmeric
½ teasp each salt and mixed sweet spice
2 oz (50 g/6 tbsp) sultanas
2 oz (50 g/½ cup) pistachios, blanched and halved (or
2 oz/50 g/½ cup toasted cashews)

1. Melt the fat in a soufflé dish for 1 minute on 80% power.
2. Stir in the onion, cover and cook for 4 minutes.
3. Uncover and add the drained rice and all the remaining ingredients except the nuts.
4. Cover and cook on 100% power for 5 minutes, then reduce to 80% power and cook for a further 10 minutes.
5. Leave to stand, covered, for 5 minutes, then stir in the nuts with a fork.

Roast Boned Rib of Beef

Serves 6–8

The beef will freeze for 3 months or will keep for 3 days under refrigeration

If the beef is well hung by the butcher – for a minimum of fourteen days – microwave cooking will produce a tender joint that is as pink as you please within a crusty brown outside.

It is essential to lift the meat above the base of the dish to prevent it soaking up the fat as it melts. For this purpose use either a special microwave-safe trivet, or an upturned saucer sitting in a quiche dish.

1 × 3 lb (1·5 kg) rolled rib of beef (weight when boned), not
more than 5 inches (12·5 cm) high
freshly ground black pepper
microwave beef browning and seasoning powder
salt

1. Sprinkle the meat on all sides with black pepper and leave at room temperature for 2 hours.
2. Sprinkle evenly with the microwave browning, seasoning powder, then arrange on the trivet or saucer.
3. The meat can be cooked either by time or temperature, but in either case it will take about 35 minutes.

   To cook by temperature, insert the microwave probe into the centre of the meat and cook on 75–80% power according to the manufacturer's instructions.

   To cook by time, allow 11 minutes to the pound (450 g) for medium rare, or 13 minutes to the pound (450 g) for well-done. It is important to turn the meat over half way through – we cooked this piece $16\frac{1}{2}$ minutes each side.
4. When the cooking time is up, sprinkle with salt and leave for 10–15 minutes to rest.

TO SERVE

Serve warm or cold. Delicious juices will have collected at the bottom of the dish and can be used as the foundation of the gravy.

A SAVOURY HERB BUTTER

This is delicious as a garnish for grills, green vegetables and baked potatoes. It freezes for 3 months and can be refrigerated for 1 month:

Cream 8 oz (225 g/1¼ cups) soft butter or best margarine with 4 level tbsp chopped fresh herbs, 2 teasp lemon juice, 1 teasp lemon rind and 15 grinds black pepper. Divide the mixture between two strips of silicone paper, then form each into a sausage about 1 inch (2·5 cm) in diameter. Roll in film and chill. Slice as required.

A Bouquet of Market Vegetables

Serves 6

It would be quite possible to cook each vegetable separately in the microwave; but we think it makes better kitchen sense to blanch them one by one in a pan of boiling water on top of the stove, earlier on in the day. It's at dinner time that the microwave comes into its own when this beautiful platter can be reheated in 5 minutes with no loss whatsoever of colour or texture – which is really impossible to achieve so simply in any other way.

6 oz (175 g) each broccoli florets, mangetout, courgettes,
whole green beans, baby sweetcorn
2 teasp salt
2 oz (50 g/¼ cup) herb butter, bought or home-made

1. Separate the broccoli florets and discard any woody stalk.
2. Remove any strings from the mangetout.
3. Top and tail the courgettes and cut into $2\frac{1}{2} \times \frac{1}{2}$ inch (6 × 1·25 cm) matchsticks.
4. Top and tail the beans.
5. In a large pan of boiling water, with the salt, blanch each vegetable in turn until barely tender – 2–4 minutes according to type – then immediately remove from the water with a slotted spoon, place in a colander or salad spinner and drench with cold water.
6. Drain thoroughly then arrange all the vegetables decoratively on a platter that will fit in the microwave.
7. Scatter with slivers of the herb butter, cover and just before serving reheat on 100% power for 5 minutes.

THE PERFECT PEAR CORER

To core a pear yet leave it whole, simply insert a melon baller into the stem end and 'screw' it into the pear until it has extracted all the core.

Whole Stuffed Pears with Two Sauces

Serves 6

This dish will keep for 1 day under refrigeration

Here, the microwave transforms the humble pear into this exotic dessert, with the Master Class marzipan adding a special flavour dimension.

6 even-sized medium ripe Conference pears, stalks left intact
$\frac{1}{2}$ *lemon*
10 fl. oz (275 ml/1$\frac{1}{4}$ cups) medium dry white wine
2 oz (50 g/$\frac{1}{4}$ cup) caster sugar
2 teasp finely grated orange rind
2 teasp arrowroot
2 tbsp pear liqueur (e.g. Eau de Vie de Poire William) (or 2 tbsp orange liqueur (e.g. Grand Marnier, Cointreau))

FOR THE MARZIPAN FILLING
2 oz (50 g/$\frac{1}{2}$ cup) ground almonds
1 oz (25 g/$\frac{1}{4}$ cup) blanched pistachios, chopped
2 oz (50 g/$\frac{1}{3}$ cup) icing sugar
1 tbsp citrus-blossom water

FOR THE CHOCOLATE SAUCE
4 oz (125 g) plain chocolate, broken into pieces
2 fl. oz (50 ml/$\frac{1}{4}$ cup) boiling water mixed with 1 teasp dark roast instant coffee
1 rounded teasp butter or margarine

1. Make the marzipan by mixing together the ground almonds, pistachios and icing sugar, then moistening with the citrus-blossom water to mix to a paste. Divide into six lozenges and leave to one side.
2. Peel the pears but leave them whole. Scoop out the core using a melon baller. Brush with the cut lemon and arrange in a quiche or other shallow dish.
3. To cook the pears, heat the wine, caster sugar and orange rind in a jug for 1 minute on 100% power, stir well, then pour this syrup over the pears, cover and cook for a further 5 minutes.
4. Turn the pears over and round, re-cover and cook for a further 5 minutes or until tender but not mushy when pierced with a small sharp knife.
5. Lift out with a draining spoon and lay on kitchen paper. Stuff each pear with a lozenge of marzipan. Arrange upright on a serving dish.
6. Slake the arrowroot with the liqueur then add to the liquid in the dish, stir well and cook uncovered for 5 minutes on 100% power until thickened and clear. Spoon over the pears and chill.

7. To make the chocolate sauce, put the chocolate in a basin, pour over the boiling coffee and fat and cook uncovered for 1 minute on 100% power. Allow to stand at room temperature until thickened.

TO SERVE

Arrange the pears on individual serving plates and coat with the wine sauce. Pass the chocolate sauce at table.

MENU 2

Champignons à la Grecque

Roast Shoulder of Lamb Stuffed with a Pinwheel of Fresh Herbs

Ratatouille Niçoise

Corbeille de Citron aux Fruits

Champignons à la Grecque

(Mushrooms in a spicy sauce)

Serves 6

This dish will keep for 3 days under refrigeration

We now prefer this microwave method to the conventional one – it seems to marry all the wonderful flavours of the poaching liquid in a particularly successful way. And it's hard to believe that such a sophisticated dish could be so simple to prepare.

$1\frac{1}{2}$ *lb* (675 g) *tiny button mushrooms*
4 tbsp each olive oil and water
$1\frac{1}{2}$ *tbsp each lemon juice and wine vinegar*
1 teasp tomato purée (or bottled sun-dried tomatoes)
10 grinds black pepper
$\frac{1}{2}$ *teasp ground coriander*
$\frac{1}{4}$ *teasp Italian seasoning*
1 bayleaf (or $\frac{1}{4}$ teasp ground bayleaf)
1 teasp salt
good pinch caster sugar
$\frac{1}{4}$ *teasp garlic granules*
1 tbsp coarsely chopped parsley

1. Trim the mushroom stalks level with the cap.
2. In a large basin put all the other ingredients (except the parsley), cover with a plate and cook on 100% power for $3\frac{1}{2}$ minutes.
3. Add mushrooms and toss to coat with the juices, cover and cook on 100% power for a further 3 minutes. Baste well and continue to cook for a further 3 minutes.
4. Remove the mushrooms to a serving dish (or individual cocottes) with a slotted spoon, draining well.
5. Cook the sauce uncovered on 100% power for 8 minutes, then pour over the mushrooms and stir in the parsley. Leave for at least 12 hours before serving.

OUR BUTCHER, OUR FRIEND

Our butcher rolls up a boned shoulder of lamb with the skill of a master craftsman, and when he has got the time he will even use our own stuffing to do the job for us. This service is now becoming more general among family butchers, many of whom also sell an oven-ready joint stuffed with their own mincemeat. Calculate the microwave cooking time on the weight of the ready-stuffed joint.

Roast Shoulder of Lamb stuffed with a Pinwheel of Fresh Herbs

Serves 6–8

The lamb will freeze for 3 months or keep for 3 days under refrigeration

Being a tender meat by nature, lamb cooks to perfection in the microwave – with the added bonus, in this particular recipe, that the meat is also perfumed with a mixture of aromatic Provençal herbs.

1 × 3 lb (1·5 kg) boned shoulder of lamb, unrolled
$\frac{1}{2}$ teasp salt
10 grinds black pepper
1 teasp microwave browner and seasoning for lamb

FOR THE HERB MIXTURE
4 tbsp finely snipped chives
1 tbsp chopped parsley
1 tbsp fresh basil, torn (or 1 teasp dried basil)
$\frac{1}{2}$ teasp finely chopped rosemary spikes
1 tbsp olive oil
1 teasp grated lemon rind

FOR THE GLAZE
2 tbsp mint jelly (or redcurrant jelly)

1. Combine all the ingredients for the herb mixture to form a paste.
2. Lay the meat, skin side down, on a board. Cut out any lumps of fat, cover with greaseproof paper and pound with a meat mallet or end of a rolling pin, until a fairly even thickness.
3. Sprinkle the meat with the salt and pepper and cover evenly with the herb mixture, then roll up, securing with string in two or three places.
4. Sprinkle with the microwave browner, arrange on a rack in a roasting dish (or on two upturned saucers in a quiche dish). Cover lightly with paper towels.
5. Cook on 80% power for 15 minutes. Turn over carefully and cook for 5 minutes, then turn and spread with the jelly and cook for a further 10 minutes.

TO SERVE
Leave to stand for 30 minutes. This is particularly delicious when served cold in thin slices.

TO SALT OR NOT TO SALT

Salting of aubergines before sautéeing them used to be advised 'to remove the bitter juices'. Rarely have we found this bitterness present in modern varieties of the vegetable, but we continue to salt aubergines before sautéeing them because the amount of oil needed is effectively reduced by half.

A SUITABLE CASE FOR TREATMENT

Small slices of sautéed veal fillet or chicken breast meat are quite delicious served on a bed of ratatouille. While the vegetables cook in the microwave, pound the meat or chicken until paper thin, then dip in seasoned flour and fry in a little sunflower oil until golden brown on both sides, 2–3 minutes in total. Remove to a plate and in the same pan put a cup of rich leftover gravy or 5 oz (150 g) dry white wine and beef stock, a heaped teasp tomato purée, a finely chopped clove of garlic, and a little salt and black pepper. Bring to the boil stirring well, then bubble until syrupy. Arrange the ratatouille around the edge of a hot dish, put the veal or chicken in the centre and spoon over the sauce. Serve at once or reheat later in the microwave.

Ratatouille Niçoise

Serves 6

The ratatouille keeps under refrigeration for 3 days

This dish cooks particularly well in the microwave as each vegetable in the mélange keeps its own character and texture. Delicious, either hot or cold.

1 large red pepper cut in $\frac{1}{2}$ inch (1·25 cm) wide strips
1 medium (5 oz/150 g) onion, finely chopped
1 fat clove garlic, chopped (or 1 teasp garlic granules)
3 tbsp olive oil
1 lb (450 g) aubergines, cut in 1 inch (2·5 cm) cubes and salted for 30 minutes
1 × 15 oz (425 g) can chopped tomatoes
2 teasp caster sugar
15 grinds black pepper
1 teasp salt
8 oz (225 g) courgettes, sliced $\frac{1}{2}$ inch (1·25 cm) thick
1 tbsp wine vinegar

1. Put the pepper strips, onion and garlic into a mixing bowl and pour on the olive oil, stirring well.
2. Cover and cook on 100% power for 2 minutes, then add the rinsed and dried aubergine cubes. Stir to mix, cover and cook for a further 8 minutes.
3. Add the tomatoes, seasonings and sliced courgettes, cover and cook for 8 minutes. Stir and continue to cook for a further 8 minutes.
4. Stir in the wine vinegar.

MERINGUES RECTANGULAR

The pavlova was originally devised in honour of the world-famous prima ballerina Anna Pavlova, with the round and airy shape of the meringue a tribute to her gossamer tutu. But the same meringue – crisp on the outside, marshmallow within – that makes the pavlova so beguiling lends itself to the other shapes, such as the little cups we have suggested here or a rectangular slice which is easier to shape than a cup and easier to cut than a round.

For a 3 egg white pavlova, draw 2 rectangles which measure 5 × 10 inches (12.5 × 25 cm) on a sheet of silicone paper, then reverse it on to a lightly oiled baking sheet to avoid the pen or pencil marks. Pipe the meringue on to the rectangles, or shape it with a spoon, then bake in a slow oven, Gas 1 (275°F, 140°C) for 45 minutes or until the surface feels very crisp to the touch and each one lifts easily from the paper. To serve, arrange on a long platter and sandwich with the lemon filling.

Corbeille de Citron aux Fruits

(Baskets filled with a lemon mousse and garnished with fresh berries)

Serves 6

The baskets will freeze for 1 week

This is a brilliant recipe with a glorious lemon flavour. And what a joy it is to be able to cook a rich custard, yet have to stir it only twice during the cooking time. For a change, garnish with sugared kumquats (see page 144).

6 individual meringue baskets (or make your own using a 3 egg white pavlova mixture)

FOR THE FILLING
3 egg yolks
3 oz (75 g/⅓ cup) caster sugar
2½ tbsp lemon juice
grated rind 1 lemon
5 fl. oz (150 ml/⅔ cup) double (or non dairy) cream

FOR THE GARNISH
4 oz (125 g/¾ cup) each strawberries, raspberries and blackberries

1. For the filling, whisk the egg yolks and sugar in a basin until creamy then whisk in the lemon juice and rind.
2. Microwave on 80% power for 1 minute, stir and cook on 30% power (defrost) for 2 minutes, then whisk and cook a further 30 seconds until as thick as mayonnaise. (If not thickened, cook for a further 30 seconds.) Chill in the freezer for 20 minutes.
3. Whip the cream (a balloon whisk is excellent) until it holds firm peaks, then fold in the custard a tablespoonful at a time.
4. Divide the filling between the meringue baskets, then freeze.

TO SERVE
Transfer to the refrigerator just before the meal and arrange the berry garnish on individual plates in the kitchen. Just before serving place one basket on each plate.

Oeufs en Cocotte, Cheese of the Seven Herbs

Serves 6

Delicately set eggs in a rich cheese and herb cream make a delicious starter for this meal.

6 large eggs
3 teasp soft butter
5 fl. oz (150 ml/$\frac{2}{3}$ cup) double cream
1 oz (25 g/$\frac{1}{4}$ cup) Parmesan cheese, grated
6 oz (175 g/1$\frac{1}{2}$ cups) mature Cheddar cheese, grated
4 tbsp Amontillado sherry
1 teasp Moutarde de Meaux (whole-grain mustard)
good pinch garlic granules (or $\frac{1}{2}$ crushed clove garlic)
6 tbsp mixed fresh herbs, chopped (whatever is available –
parsley, chives, tarragon, dill, marjoram, basil, coriander)

1. Put all the ingredients (except the eggs and butter) into a microwave-safe basin, stir well then cook on 100% power for 4 minutes.
2. Have ready six individual 6 fl. oz (175 ml) soufflé dishes, and put $\frac{1}{2}$ teasp butter on the base of each. Break an egg on top.
3. Spoon 3 tbsp of the herb cream over each egg.
4. Arrange the dishes in a circle in the microwave then cook on 80% power for 5$\frac{1}{2}$ minutes until the yolk is set but the white is still a little wobbly.

TO SERVE
Stand for 2 minutes then serve at once with buttered French bread or Honey and Walnut Knots (see page 21).

Plaited Sole with a Sauce Dugléré

Serves 6

The fish will keep for 2 days under refrigeration

All right, so it is a bit of a 'fantaisie du chef' – but you have to admit that the plaits of sole do look rather splendid, and the sauce is superb.

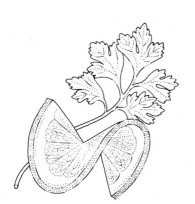

6 × 5 oz (150 g) block fillets of lemon sole, skinned
4 fl. oz (125 ml/½ cup) dry white wine
½ teasp fish seasoning salt

FOR THE SAUCE
white part of 4 spring onions, finely chopped
1 oz (25 g/2 tbsp) butter
4 oz (125 g/1¼ cups) button mushrooms, finely sliced
8 oz (225 g) can chopped tomatoes (or 8 fl. oz/225 ml Passata, sieved tomatoes)
1 rounded tbsp tomato purée (or tomato ketchup)
1 teasp sugar
pinch each dried oregano and tarragon
10 grinds black pepper
½ teasp salt
1 tbsp finely chopped parsley

1. Cut each fillet lengthwise into three strips then plait and arrange side by side in a quiche or gratin dish.
2. Mix the wine and fish seasoning salt, pour over the fish, cover with a lid of pierced clingfilm and cook on 100% power for 5 minutes.
3. Lift out the fish and drain on crumpled kitchen paper.
4. Cook the remaining liquid on 100% power for 4 minutes until reduced by half. Set to one side.
5. To make the sauce, put the spring onions and butter in a bowl, cover and cook on 100% power for 3 minutes.
6. Add all the remaining sauce ingredients (except the parsley) then stir in the reduced stock. Cover and cook for 5 minutes.
7. Meanwhile wash out the fish dish then spoon the sauce over the base.
8. Arrange the plaits of fish on top and scatter with the parsley.

TO SERVE
If freshly made, reheat 2 minutes on 80% power. If made earlier in the day, reheat from room temperature for 5 minutes on 80% power.

TO POACH SALMON STEAKS IN THE MICROWAVE

Arrange 4 × 6 oz (175 g) steaks of salmon round the edge of a round dish about 1½ inches (4 cm) deep, with the thin part of each steak to the centre. Pour on 5 fl. oz (150 ml/⅔ cup) fish stock and a squeeze of lemon juice, cover with a lid or pierced clingfilm and cook on 100% power for 6 minutes, turning the fish over after 3 minutes. Leave to stand for 5 minutes, then sprinkle lightly with salt. Serve warm or cold.

A Whole Poached Salmon with Dill Hollandaise

Serves 6–8

The cooked fish will keep for 2 days under refrigeration

This is pure magic – a whole salmon 'poached' to moist perfection in 11 minutes, and a Hollandaise cooked by a method so simple that a ten-year-old could do it for you.

1 × 3½ lb (1·75 kg) salmon (weight with head on)
1 teasp fish seasoning salt

FOR THE HOLLANDAISE SAUCE
4½ oz (140 g/½ cup + 1 tbsp) unsalted butter or margarine
2 egg yolks
1 tbsp lemon juice
3 teasp wine vinegar
½ teasp caster sugar
pinch salt
speck white pepper
½ teasp grated lemon rind
1 tbsp fresh snipped dill (or 1 teasp dried dill)

1. Remove the head of the salmon or leave on as preferred. Wash the inside and dry well, then sprinkle with the fish seasoning salt. Wrap a little foil around the tail end.
2. Line a quiche dish with clingfilm and arrange the salmon on top, curving in to the shape of the dish, then cover with pierced clingfilm.
3. Cook on 100% power for 11 minutes, then leave to stand (still covered) for 5 minutes.
4. Remove the clingfilm and leave to cool, or skin and serve warm within 20 minutes.
5. To make the sauce (not more than 1 hour before serving), melt the butter in a small basin, uncovered, for 2 minutes on 50% power.
6. Meanwhile, whisk the yolks in a medium (1 pint/575 ml) basin with the lemon juice, wine vinegar, sugar and seasonings.
7. Slowly whisk in the hot melted butter, then cook on 30% power for a further 2 minutes, stirring after 1 minute.
8. Remove, and stir in the lemon rind and dill. The sauce should resemble a thick coating custard. It will thicken further on standing.

CHICORY, FRISÉE AND BLACK GRAPE SALAD WITH TOASTED ALMONDS

Nuts will 'toast' in their own oil in the microwave – which is very useful when you want them really crisp and dry to add to a salad. See page 126.

To toast whole or split almonds in the microwave, arrange in one layer on a plate or shallow dish. Cook on 100% power for 3–4 minutes, stirring twice.

MIX NOW, BAKE LATER

We have found that you can mix a cake like the Swiss Chocolate Ring and leave it in the cooking container (under refrigeration) for a maximum of 6 hours without any loss of 'rise'. Just before the meal, microwave it, unmould it and leave until required. It will still be slightly warm, and the texture light and moist.

Minted New Potatoes, Beurre Noisette

Serves 6

Whole potatoes seem to cook better in a roasting bag as they are then completely enveloped in the tenderising steam.

1½ lb (675 g) small, even-sized new potatoes, scrubbed or scraped
2 tbsp water
3 small sprigs of mint
coarsely ground sea salt
8 grinds black pepper

FOR THE BEURRE NOISETTE
2 oz (50 g/¼ cup) unsalted butter

FOR THE GARNISH
2 teasp chopped fresh mint

1. Put the potatoes in a roasting bag with the water.
2. Add the sprigs of mint, close the bag loosely with an elastic band, then cook on 100% power for 12 minutes. Set to one side.
3. Put the butter in a medium-sized bowl and cook on 80% power for 3 minutes or until a pale fawn.

TO SERVE
Open the roasting bag carefully (it will be full of steam), arrange the potatoes in a shallow serving dish, sprinkle with the salt and pepper, spoon over the butter and garnish with the chopped mint.

Swiss Chocolate Ring with Cinnamon Cream and a Spiced Morello Cherry Sauce

Serves 6–8

This pudding (or it could be a cake) is nicest served newly 'baked' – very easy to arrange when you can mix it, chill it, then bring it to spongy perfection in 4½ minutes flat!

FOR THE CHOCOLATE RING
4 oz (125 g/½ cup) each soft margarine and caster sugar
4 oz (125 g/1 cup) self-raising flour + ½ teasp baking powder
(or 4 oz/125 g/1 cup plain flour + 1½ teasp baking powder)
2 eggs
1 teasp vanilla essence
2 tbsp each drinking chocolate, cocoa powder and milk (or water)

2 oz (50 g/½ cup) nibbed or finely chopped almonds, toasted

FOR THE CINNAMON CREAM
5 fl. oz (150 ml/⅔ cup) whipping cream (or 8 fl. oz/225 ml/1 cup strained Greek-style cow's yoghurt)
2 teasp caster sugar
ground cinnamon

FOR THE SPICED MORELLO CHERRY SAUCE
1 × 15 oz (425 g) can stoned Morello cherries (or black cherries)
1 tbsp each cornflour and soft light brown sugar
2 tbsp lemon juice (only if sweet black cherries are used)
2 strips orange peel, about 1 inch (2·5 cm) wide
1 stick cinnamon
2 tbsp cherry brandy or Kirsch (optional)

1. To make the chocolate ring, put all the ingredients except the almonds into a bowl and beat by hand or machine until the mixture looks smooth and fluffy. Fold in the toasted almonds.
2. Lightly oil a 1½ pint (850 ml) microwave-safe ring mould, and spoon in the cake mixture. Smooth level with a spatula. (The unbaked cake can be refrigerated all day.)
3. To make the cinnamon cream, whisk the cream, sugar and ½ teasp ground cinnamon together until the cream holds soft peaks, then spoon into a small bowl and dust lightly with more cinnamon. Chill.
4. To make the Morello cherry sauce, drain the cherries and reserve the juice.
5. In a medium basin, put the cornflour and sugar, then stir in the fruit syrup, lemon juice (if used), orange peel and cinnamon, then cook for 3 minutes at 100% power. Stir and cook for a further 1 minute until thick and glossy.
6. Stir in the cherries and the cherry brandy or Kirsch (if used). Remove the cinnamon stick and orange peel and spoon the sauce into a basin. Chill.
7. To bake and serve the chocolate ring, take from the refrigerator and cook at once on 100% power for 4½ minutes. Allow to stand for 5 minutes then gently ease out of the container on to a serving dish.
8. Arrange one slice of the ring on each plate and arrange the sauce and the cream decoratively at the side.

INDEX

CREDITS

Evelyn Rose and Sula Leon's clothes by:
Rosy and Co, Altrincham, Cheshire

Dishes by:
Casa Fina, Wilmslow, Cheshire (soup tureen and ladle, opp. p. 16;
greenleaf dish, opp. p. 64; huge white platter, opp. p. 96).

David Mellor, Manchester (black Le Creuset, overleaf opp. p. 17).

Allweis China & Gifts, Manchester (Rosenthal glasses, opp. p. 145;
two Poppy pedestals, opp. p. 144).